MY SECRETS FOR BETTER COOKING

Madame Benoit

My Secrets for Better Cooking

Les éditions Héritage inc.

PRODUCTION
Director: Bernard Benoit
Assistant: Ginette Guétat
Editorial consultant: Michelle Robertson

ART AND DESIGN
Director: Dufour et Fille, Design
Illustrations: Christine Dufour

PHOTOGRAPHY
Director: Paul Casavant

Canadian Cataloguing in Publication Data

Benoit, Jehane, 1904-1987

    My secrets for better cooking

    Issued also in French under title:
    Mes secrets de la bonne cuisine

    ISBN 2-7625-6059-4 (v. 3)

    1. Cookery. I. Benoit, Bernard II. Guétat, Ginette.
    III. Robertson, Michelle. IV. Title.

    TX651.B4613   1992   641.5   C90-096619-X

Copyright© 1993 Les Éditions Héritage Inc.
All rights reserved

Legal deposit: 4th quarter 1993
National Library of Canada

ISBN: 2-7625-6059-4   Printed in Canada

LES ÉDITIONS HÉRITAGE INC.
300, Arran, Saint-Lambert (Québec) J4R 1K5
(514) 875-0327

Contents

Chapter 16
The Versality of Eggs						379

Chapter 17
The Magic of Pies and Ice Cream			417

Chapter 18
Cheese and Nuts						453

Chapter 19
Wine, the Cup that Cheers				465

Chapter 20
Entertaining at Home					483

Table of Contents						545

Index									547

CHAPTER 16

The versatility of eggs

THE EGG has long been regarded as a symbol of life itself. It was revered by the ancients and, to the Orientals and first philosophers, it represented the world as well as the elements.

THE SHELL	=	EARTH
THE WHITE	=	WATER
THE YOLK	=	FIRE
UNDER THE SHELL	=	AIR

We find references to the egg throughout history. The Roman epicure Apicius, the renowned gourmet of his day, for instance, is credited with having invented the omelet with his famous ovamelleta, which was an omelet flavoured with honey and pepper. And the great theologian Thomas Aquinas used the egg as a symbol for the winter of life.

There is no doubt that the egg is one of the most useful and most used foods. It can be served around the clock, as a nutritious and basic part of a healthy breakfast or as a decorative flourish to a midnight snack; it has no season or special time of day. One of its main joys is that it can be prepared quickly in a variety of ways. For this reason, it can be classified as one of the most ancient of instant foods, used from soup to dessert in one form or another and eaten by infants as well as the aged.

To add to their versatility, eggs are handsome to look at, and they make a most attractive centrepiece. They can suggest a genuine country atmosphere when their whiteness gleams in a nest of real straw placed in a wicker basket on the breakfast or luncheon table, or they can enhance a dinner table in a more sophisticated manner when arranged on a pewter dish with avocados and large leaves.

If you find you often don't have a lot of time for cooking, learn to cook a variety of egg dishes. They are quick and easy to prepare and provide nutritionally sound meals as well.

In the first part of this chapter you will find information about dishes in which eggs are served as eggs, but of course this remarkable food package is used in many other preparations in which it is no longer identifiable, but has been beaten or cooked or mixed with other ingredients to form some other kind of dish. In some of these, the egg is the significant part — for instance, hollandaise sauce and mayonnaise, or in desserts such as custards and soufflés. For the use of the egg in emulsified sauces and the egg-thickened dessert sauces, see Chapter 7, Vol. I.

Soufflés and meringue recipes can be found in this Chapter, page 397.

Information on storage of fresh eggs is on page 380. To store eggs, cooked or uncooked, by freezing, see page 160 in Chapter 8, Vol. I.

GRADING

Eggs in the shell are sold by grade throughout Canada. The grade and size are marked on egg cartons. The grade is an indication of freshness and quality and has nothing to do with size. Within any one grade there can be several sizes page 380.

Top-quality eggs are very fresh, with firm well-centred yolks, thick whites and very little air inside the shell.

As to the sizes of eggs, you may not think this makes any difference. But if 4 whole large eggs fill a cup, and 6 whole small eggs fill a cup, you can see that a baking recipe will not have enough liquid if you use 4 small eggs instead of 4 large eggs. Unless otherwise specified, baking recipes in cookbooks are based on large eggs.

If you need part of an egg, break the egg into a cup and mix the yolk and white with a fork. Then measure what you need with a teaspoon or tablespoon. An ounce equals 2 tablespoons (30 ml).

The composition of an egg

To cook an egg properly, it is important to understand its composition. Eggs generally are 13 per cent protein, 9 per cent fat, 60 per cent water, and 18 per cent blood, ash and mineral matter. Vitamins A, B, and D are found in eggs.

The white is mostly albumen, which in turn is mostly protein, a very important factor in cooking.

The yolk is mostly fat in the form of an emulsion and is therefore easily digested. The yolk also contains less water than the white.

The shell consists of lime. It is porous and allows moisture to escape from inside the egg and strong odours to penetrate it.

The colour of an egg yolk depends on the hen's breed and the nature of its feeding. Green forage produces deeply coloured yolks, while grain feed produces light coloured yolks. Whatever the colour, however, the food value and the flavour are exactly the same.

An egg is a protein, as are meat, fish and cheese. Egg protein contains a fairly large amount of combined sulphur, which is what gives a boiled egg its characteristic odour when it has been overcooked.

How to store eggs properly

Eggs are perishable and quickly lose their prime quality unless kept in a cool place, preferably the refrigerator. Never place them uncovered in the refrigerator, as they absorb surrounding odours very easily and lose moisture. Keep them in their container, or in the special egg trays found in some refrigerators. It is best to store them with the narrow end down to keep the egg yolk centred.

Leftover egg yolks should be stored in a clean glass jar. Pour a thin layer of cold water over the eggs in the jar and cover. Leftover egg whites should also be covered and stored in a clean glass jar. Do not keep separated unshelled parts for more than 3 or 4 days.

Effects of cooking heat on eggs

The cooking process solidifies the white and the yolk of an egg. How solid the egg gets varies with the degree of heat and the length of cooking time.

☛ The tough leathery or rubbery texture in a cooked egg is always caused by the use of too high a heat.

BASIC METHODS OF COOKING EGGS

There are hundreds of ways of serving eggs, but all are derived from a few basic methods. Learn each method so you can do it perfectly, then apply the classic variations, or create your own. No other food offers more scope for the creative ability of a good cook.

Eggs in the shell, soft-cooked

Cold-water method

Place the eggs in cold water and slowly bring the water to a boil, uncovered.

For coddled eggs, with creamy whites, remove the eggs from the water as soon as it comes to a full rolling boil.

For 3- to 5-minute eggs, remove the pan from the heat as soon as the water comes to a boil. Cover it and let the eggs stand for 3 to 5 minutes.

Hot-water method

Put enough water in a saucepan to cover the eggs completely. Bring the water to a full rolling boil. Then place the eggs on a spoon one by one and gently slip them into the water. Lower the heat and cook for 3 to 4 minutes, according to taste. In 3½ minutes the white will be almost set, the yolk still runny. From this you can calculate the time needed to suit your taste best.

Another method is to remove the pan from the heat, cover, and let the eggs stand for 6 to 8 minutes.

As soon as cooking time has elapsed, remove the eggs from the water and serve. ⚬⟶ To make the eggs easier to handle and also to stop the cooking, run cold water over them for several seconds.

If cooked eggs in the shell must be kept for a few minutes before serving, place them in a bowl of tepid water.

French method

In classic French cuisine, oeufs mollets are soft-cooked eggs that are shelled, left whole, and used in the same manner as poached eggs, although the final taste and appearance are totally different from poached eggs.

Follow the hot-water method, above. Cook the egg for exactly 6 minutes. Remove the egg, reserving the hot water, and place it in a bowl of ice-cold water. Gently crack the shell with the back of a spoon, then put the egg back in the hot water for a few seconds. Remove from the water, then start peeling by holding the egg in the middle of your hand and gently pulling the shell away.

A perfect oeuf mollet consists of a cooked wall of egg white with a semi-runny yolk inside. Keep the shelled egg in tepid water until ready to use.

Eggs in the shell, hard-cooked

An egg is hard-cooked when the temperature at its core is the same as that of the surrounding water. If it is overcooked, a dark green line will form between the white and the yolk; this is caused by a combination of sulphide from the white with iron from the yolk. This is harmless, but not very attractive.

⚬⟶ If eggs are taken cold from the refrigerator, prick a small hole in the blunt end of the shell with a pin to minimize the risk of the shell cracking. Should the egg crack, immediately add a pinch of salt or a few drops of vinegar to the boiling water to prevent the escape of the white from the crack in the shell.

To hard-cook more than 4 eggs at once, follow the cold-water method p. 380. When the water boils, cover the saucepan, lower the heat, and let it stand for 20 minutes; the heat should be low enough so that the water barely moves.

To hard-cook 1 to 4 eggs, when the water boils, remove the saucepan from the heat entirely and let the egg or eggs stand in it for 20 minutes.

When the eggs are ready, pour the contents of the saucepan — eggs and water — into the sink. This will crack the shells. Then place the eggs in a bowl of cold water and allow them to stand for 5 to 6 minutes so that the cold water will seep through the cracked shells and make them easy to peel.

When peeled, hard-cooked eggs are best kept refrigerated. It is important to cover them or they will dry out.

⚬⟶ To store unshelled hard-cooked eggs, crack the cooked eggshell all over by tapping the egg gently on the kitchen counter; then place, unpeeled, in a bowl and completely cover with water. They are easy to peel even after 3 or 4 days when stored in the refrigerator in this manner.

Poached eggs

A poached egg is an egg cooked without its shell. Eggs must be absolutely fresh to ensure success.

Use a saucepan at least 2 inches (5 cm) deep. Fill it with salted water, and ½ teaspoon (2 ml) vinegar, and bring to a simmer. Break the egg into a cup and then, placing the cup at the edge of the saucepan, slip the egg gently into the simmering water. Cover the saucepan and let cook over very low heat for 3 to 5 minutes. Lift the egg out of the water with a slotted spoon.

For a softer poached egg, grease the frying pan with butter or margarine. Bring the water to the simmering point, as above. Break egg into a saucer and lower the saucer almost into the water in the frying pan, then quickly slip the egg into the simmering water. Cover the frying pan and turn off the heat, but do not remove the pan from the burner. Let the pan stand for 3 to 7 minutes, depending on how well cooked you desire the egg. Lift the egg from the water with a slotted spoon. Drain well, then serve.

Any number of eggs can be cooked in this manner, but when learning it is better to cook only 1 egg at a time.

Eggs in cocottes

An egg in cocotte, or a molded egg, is also called a poached egg à la française. Cocottes are small individual dishes of earthenware, glass or china, with or without covers. They have to be deep enough to hold 1 egg; some English china egg cups with silver covers can take two.

Eggs in cocottes can be served for breakfast or as an entrée. Basically, a piece of butter or a small amount of cream is placed in the bottom of the cocotte, then 1 egg is broken on top. Salt and pepper to taste is sprinkled on the egg. The cocotte can be covered during cooking or left uncovered. The advantage of the cover is that it keeps the egg hot longer once it is cooked.

To cook, place the cocotte in a saucepan with enough hot water, not boiling, to reach within ½ inch (1.25 cm) of the brim. Cover the saucepan and simmer over low heat until the white is set and the yolk is to your taste. This will take from 6 to 9 minutes.

The cocotte can also be cooked in a preheated 400°F (200°C) oven. Place it in an oven pan with hot water, as for top-of-the-stove cooking. This is a more practical method to follow when 6 or more eggs are being cooked, and it is an elegant way to serve eggs for a brunch.

Shirred eggs

Shirred eggs are cooked in flameproof dishes, usually of pottery of some kind, especially designed for oeufs sur le plat, as the French call them. Shirred-egg dishes are different from cocottes, for they are flat and shallow. The shirred egg is always served in the dish it was cooked in, while the molded egg is often turned out of the cocotte for serving.

Put 1 teaspoon (5 ml) melted butter in the dish and tip the dish back and forth to distribute the butter all over the bottom. Sprinkle salt and pepper on the butter and break an egg into the dish. Cook over low heat on top of the stove until the white begins to solidify. Then spoon another teaspoon (5 ml) of butter over the top and finish cooking in a preheated 350°F (180°C) oven for 5 minutes, or until the whites are milky and the yolks shiny and glazed. Be careful not to overcook, for the eggs can become hard and tough. These eggs are never covered during cooking.

Shirred-egg dishes come in more than one size. One large enough to hold 2 eggs and a garnish of tomatoes, ham, cheese or any other flavourful ingredient makes a fine luncheon dish. Put part of the garnish in the bottom of the dish before breaking the egg on top; then arrange the rest of the garnish around the edge of the dish when the egg has been cooked and is ready to serve.

Scrambled eggs

Lots of practice is required to learn how to make perfect scrambled eggs that are both soft and creamy.

Break the eggs, usuallly 2 per person, into a bowl. Season to taste and ⚬━ beat with a fork or with a wire whisk until the white and the yolk are well mixed. If you use a rotary beater, you will overbeat the eggs and affect the creaminess of the finished product.

Use 1 tablespoon (15 ml) butter for each 2 or 3 eggs. This is twice as much butter as the amount used for an omelet. Why so much? Because here the butter is not used to prevent the eggs from sticking to the pan but as the necessary liquid that must become incorporated into the eggs to give them a rich texture and flavour.

Always cook over gentle heat. When the heat is too high, a wheylike liquid is released from the eggs, the heat having forced the coagulated mass to yield up a liquor it should naturally have retained.

Place the frying pan over medium heat, melt the butter, then pour in the whisked eggs. Let them set for a few seconds, then stir with a fork, without stopping, making no attempt to retain any kind of shape. ⚬━ The constant moving of the eggs is the secret in making creamy scrambled eggs. The easiest way is to stir them by lifting the cooked eggs underneath so that the uncooked eggs on top can flow to the bottom of the frying pan. Give one stir all around, then repeat the first operation and keep repeating these two operations until the eggs are almost set but still appear shiny and a bit underdone. At this point, without delay, remove from the heat.

⚬━ Add 1 teaspoon (5 ml) cold light cream or milk for each 4 eggs, and stir fast for a second. This is to stop the cooking, which would otherwise continue for a few minutes because of the internal heat retained by the eggs. Without this last step, the eggs would be overcooked and dry. Turn out on a warm plate and serve.

Double-boiler method to scramble eggs

The advantages of the double-boiler method over the frying-pan method are that the eggs require less care, for they can be cooked practically unattended, and that they can be kept waiting for a few minutes before being served. ⚬━ To succeed, however, you must observe one important precaution: At no point should the water boil in the bottom of the double-boiler. Start the cooking over hot water and finish over simmering water. This is easily controlled if the water is checked 3 or 4 times during the cooking period by lifting the top part of the double boiler. Or use a heatproof glass double boiler so you can see what is happening in the bottom pan without lifting.

Melt the required amount of butter in the top part of the double boiler over hot water. Tilt the top part until the butter coats the sides and bottom. Pour in the eggs and let them set for a few seconds, then stir in the same way as in the frying-pan method.

Serve the eggs as soon as they are ready, if possible, but if you have to keep the eggs waiting for a few minutes, remove the double boiler from the heat while the eggs are still slightly uncooked, but keep them over the hot water. Stir them once when ready to serve.

Fried eggs

To obtain the best results in frying eggs, use a heavy metal 8-inch (20 cm) frying pan; the best is the enameled cast-iron type.

Over high heat, melt the fat you prefer — butter, bacon fat, olive or salad oil, about 1 tablespoon (15 ml) to 2 eggs. When the fat has reached the smoking point, but is not too brown, add the eggs and reduce the heat to low.

The easiest way to add the eggs is to break them, one at a time, into a saucer and lower the saucer almost onto the hot fat. Tip the saucer sideways, with the edge touching the bottom of the pan, allowing the uncooked egg to slip in slowly. When all the eggs are added, cook gently over low heat, basting the eggs with some of the hot fat.

For a leaner egg, cover the frying pan for 2 to 4 minutes after the heat has been lowered and do not baste with the fat.

For a completely fat-free fried egg, break the egg into a cold frying pan with a non-stick coating, cover, and cook over low heat for 3 to 5 minutes.

For crisp lacy edges on the white, pour each egg from a saucer into very hot oil or butter, then quickly tip the frying pan, which will cause the egg to slide where the oil is the deepest; then, also quickly, spoon the white over and on top of the yolk with a wooden paddle or a silver knife. Fry only 1 egg at a time to get these results.

If you like your eggs "over easy" or "sunny side down", proceed the same as for pan fried eggs, but just before they are done to your taste, turn each egg over swiftly with a well-oiled wide spatula; then cook the egg for ½ minute or so, to your taste.

OMELETS ARE SOMETHING SPECIAL

What are omelets?

Omelets are lightly beaten eggs that become a soft blanket of coagulated eggs as they are cooked. A perfect omelet should be plump, fluffy and light, with a glossy top. Overcooking will make it flat, leathery and dull-looking.

There are three fundamental points to master in omelet making. Only practice, while applying these points, will teach you how to make a perfect one.

1. Most omelets should be cooked over brisk heat. If the omelet seems to be cooking too quickly, simply lift the pan off the heat for a few seconds.

2. Use the proper amount of butter or other fat.

3. Beat the eggs briskly for 30 to 40 seconds. If they are beaten with a wire whisk or a fork, count 30 to 40 beatings. Eggs that are not sufficiently beaten will not mix properly. When beaten too much, the eggs get thin and watery, and this changes the texture of the omelet. ⊶ Beat eggs just before you pour them into hot butter, otherwise they lose their liveliness.

Omelet pan

Once you have mastered the basic techniques of a simple omelet, it will be easy for you to proceed through the endless world of omelets. Making a perfect omelet is not easy; you must practice to reach perfection. It is a fallacy to believe a particular unwashed frying pan or a special omelet pan is an absolute necessity for making the perfect omelet. ⊶ What is important is that the pan should be of thick cast aluminum or iron, but not too heavy for you to handle easily with either hand. A good omelet pan should have a perfectly flat bottom and curving sides, which help in sliding the omelet onto a platter.

For low-fat or fat-free diets, a pan with a non-stick coating can be used, but the heat must be lowered.

A new pan, of whatever metal, must be seasoned — unless it is already a non-stick pan. Wash and dry the pan, then fill it with vegetable oil and heat very slowly until the oil seems to move at the bottom; this may take from 20 to 30 minutes, as the heat must be kept very low. Turn off the heat then and let the oil cool in the pan. Drain from the pan when cool. (Do not throw the oil away; use it for cooking.) Wipe the pan thoroughly with absorbent paper. By then the inside of the pan should be perfectly smooth, with a slightly greasy feeling.

Never use scouring powder on an omelet pan. After you have made an omelet, simply wipe the pan with a paper towel. If anything sticks, throw in

a spoonful of coarse salt and rub with a paper towel. Or, if you prefer, rinse it under running hot water and wipe dry.

The size of an omelet pan is important. An omelet made with 2 or 3 eggs requires a pan 7 to 8 inches (17.5 to 20 cm) in diameter. A 6-egg omelet requires a 10-inch (25 cm) pan. Any omelet made with more than 6 eggs is rarely perfect; it is better to make two omelets in that case.

A 2-egg omelet can serve 1 or 2 portions, depending on appetites. A single egg yolk added to 2 whole eggs will make quite a bit more.

Another piece of equipment needed for omelets is either a wire whisk, the very best, or a plain table fork. For some types of omelets a rotary beater can be used.

Classic or French omelet

Practice the following steps one by one and you will soon be an omelet expert:

1. Warm the prepared frying pan over low heat just until you can touch the bottom of the pan quickly with the tips of your fingers without getting burned.

2. Place in the hot pan a well-rounded tablespoon (15 ml) of butter. (Unsalted butter gives a perfect creamy flavour, but salted butter can be used.) Let the butter melt.

3. While the butter is melting over low heat, break 3 eggs into a bowl; add salt and pepper to taste and 1 tablespoon (15 ml) cold water. Now beat the eggs briskly as previously explained, for no more than 40 seconds. For 6 eggs, add 2 tablespoons (30 ml) water.

4. Turn the heat high under the frying pan. When the butter has a deep gold colour, after a few seconds, pour the eggs into it. Wait 10 seconds.

5. Take the handle of the pan in your left hand and a fork in your right hand. With the fork, gently push the eggs from the side to the middle, going around and around the pan. Do this as quickly as possible, shaking the pan gently to keep the eggs from sticking to the bottom of the pan. Continue to push the eggs from the outside edge to the middle, lifting with your fork the part that has set and allowing the liquid to run under it. This operation should not take more than 1 to 1½ minutes.

6. Now quickly transfer the omelet to a warm plate or dish. (Never allow an omelet to wait in the pan after being cooked.) Transfer the omelet by lifting the edge of the omelet that is nearer to you and folding the omelet in half, tilting the pan as the folding proceeds. Tilt the pan still further and let the omelet slide onto the plate. Use a large spatula at the beginning. With experience, this folding and slipping will take only 10 seconds to accomplish. If the omelet does not slide freely onto the plate, you can free it with the spatula and also slip a little piece of butter underneath to act as lubrication.

How to fill an omelet

To fill an omelet, some recommend placing the filling on the omelet before folding, others, that the filling should be placed around the folded omelet.

My own favourite way, for perfect results and ease of work, is the technique I learned from my teacher, Dr. de Pomiane. He referred to it as the paysan method. Begin by warming butter in the pan then add the filling, warm it for a few seconds, pour on the eggs, and cook. When the omelet is folded, the filling will be evenly distributed and the whole omelet beautifully flavoured.

Leftovers in omelets

Any small amount of leftovers can be used to fill an omelet.

Any little bits of cheese, even dry or hard, can be diced and rolled in parsley or chives or dried basil or curry powder, or simply left as is. Little pieces of cooked fish or seafood, can be used as is or blended with herbs or curry. Diced or chopped leftover roast can be flavoured with chutney or chili sauce, or combined with a bit of sour cream or gravy.

A few classic variations
The following variations are based on a 3-egg omelet, made according to the steps for Classic or French omelet.

Tomato omelet

3 eggs

1 unpeeled tomato, diced

Salt and pepper to taste

¼ tsp (1 ml) sugar

Pinch of dried basil or curry powder or 1 tbsp (15 ml) chopped fresh parsley

1 tbsp (15 ml) butter

⊙━┱ Remove the seeds from the tomato as you cut it into small dice, as the seeds have a tendency to give an acid taste to an omelet. Add salt and pepper to taste, sprinkle sugar, and add dried basil or curry powder, or chopped fresh parsley.

Melt the butter. Add the tomato to the melted butter. Cook over a brisk flame for 1 minute. Pour the 3-egg mixture over the top. Cook and serve.

Fresh chives omelet

This is a spring delight.

3 eggs

1 tbsp (15 ml) fine-cut chives

1 tbsp (15 ml) butter

Add fine-cut chives — use a kitchen shears to cut them — to the beaten 3-egg omelet mixture. Cook and serve.

Fines-herbes omelet

The herb combination in this recipe can be changed to suit your own taste. Dried herbs can be used, but always try to have either fresh parsley, chives or dill with the dried herbs.

3 to 6 eggs

2 tbsp (30 ml) minced parsley

1 tsp (5 ml) minced chives

Pinch of basil or 1 tsp (5 ml) minced fresh chervil

½ inch (1.25 cm) white of leek, minced (optional)

1 tbsp (15 ml) butter

Mix together the minced parsley, chives, basil and fresh chervil. If you are using minced leek, you can omit the chives.

The amounts given are for 3 to 6 eggs, depending on the amount of herbs you prefer in an omelet.

Melt the butter, remove the pan from the heat, add the herbs, and stir once. Pour the 3-egg omelet mixture on top. Herbs are added to the butter first to bring out their full flavour. Put the pan containing the mixture back on the heat. Cook and serve.

A very nice variation of the classic fines herbes is first to proceed as above, but add 2 to 3 tablespoons (30 to 50 ml) grated Swiss cheese to the eggs before cooking. Then cook and serve.

THE VERSATILITY OF EGGS

Bercy omelet

1 sausage

1 tbsp (15 ml) butter

1 tbsp (15 ml) minced parsley

or ¼ tsp (1 ml) minced marjoram

3 eggs

2 tbsp (30 ml) tomato sauce

Cut the sausage into 5 or 6 pieces. Brown over low heat in the omelet frying pan. Pour off the fat. Add the butter and minced parsley or minced marjoram. Pour the 3-egg omelet mixture on top. Cook and serve with tomato sauce poured over the top.

Omelette bonne femme

A delicious country omelet; it must be made with cubes of salt pork, as the flavour is not the same.

1 slice of fat and lean salt pork, cubed

¼ cup (60 ml) small bread cubes

1 thick slice onion, chopped fine

3 eggs

Cut the salt pork into small cubes. Slowly melt in the frying pan over medium heat until the dice are golden brown. Add bread cubes and stir them in the fat over low heat until crisp and brown. Add chopped onion. Stir for a few seconds. Pour on top a 3-egg omelet mixture without salt. Cook and serve.

Potato omelets
There are 2 methods to make a potato omelet. They are quite different from one another. One is quick and one takes somewhat longer to prepare.

Potato omelet moissonneur

1 raw potato

2 tbsp (30 ml) butter

1 tsp (5 ml) salad oil

1 thick slice of onion

3 eggs

1 tbsp (15 ml) grated cheese

Peel a raw potato and slice it as thinly as possible. Melt the butter and add salad oil. Add the potato. Cook over medium heat, turning a few times, until the potato slices are cooked and slightly browned. This takes 10 to 15 minutes. Break the slice of onion into rings and add. Cook for a few minutes with the potato.

Beat the 3 eggs with grated cheese. Pour over the potato, cook, and serve.

Cooked-potato omelet

1 hot boiled potato, sliced thinly

1 tbsp (15 ml) butter

1 tbsp (15 ml) minced parsley or 1 tsp (5 ml) minced chives

3 eggs

When using a leftover potato, pour boiling water on top and let it stand for 2 minutes, then drain and slice. This is done because hot potatoes make a better omelet.

Melt the butter, add the potato slices, and brown on both sides over low heat. Sprinkle with minced parsley or minced chives. Pour a 3-egg omelet mixture on top. Cook and serve.

Fresh mushroom omelet

2 or 3 medium-sized fresh mushrooms, thinly sliced

1 green onion or 1 inch (2.5 cm) white of leek, minced

Pepper to taste

1 tbsp (15 ml) butter

3 eggs

Mix together fresh mushrooms and minced green onion or white leek. Pepper generously. Melt butter until it is a light brown colour. Add the mushroom mixture. Stir constantly over high heat for 30 seconds. Pour a 3-egg omelet mixture on top. Cook and serve.

Chicken-liver omelet

1 chicken liver

A few drops vinegar or Madeira wine

1 tsp (5 ml) butter, unsalted

Salt and pepper to taste

Pinch of dried tarragon or basil

1 tbsp (15 ml) butter

3 eggs

Wash the chicken liver with vinegar or Madeira wine — how much difference just a few drops can make! Cut into small pieces.

Melt 1 teaspoon (5 ml) butter, preferably unsalted, in a small frying pan. When the butter is light brown, add the cut-up pieces of liver and stir quickly over high heat for a few seconds. Remove from heat, sprinkle with salt and pepper, and add a pinch of dried tarragon or basil.

Melt 1 tablespoon (15 ml) butter in the omelet pan and add the liver and the 3-egg omelet mixture. Cook, fold and serve.

I sometimes pour 2 tablespoons (30 ml) Madeira sauce or a sprinkling of chives on top, or garnish with crisp bacon.

Walnut omelet

This omelet may come as a surprise, a pleasant one when you first taste it, especially when served with a salad of endives or a bowl of black olives.

2 tbsp (30 ml) walnuts, chopped fine

½ tsp (2 ml) curry powder

1 tbsp (15 ml) butter

3 eggs

Mix walnuts with curry powder.

Melt butter in your omelet pan and add the walnuts and curry. Stir for a few seconds. Add a 3-egg omelet mixture. Cook and fold. Serve with chutney.

Now you have learned how to make a basic omelet and several variations, but there are many other types. If you have mastered the technique of the basic omelet, you will quickly master the others.

Mousseline omelet

Do not confuse this basic omelette mousseline with the puffy dessert omelet. Although they have similarities, the end product is quite different. The plain omelet requires a quick short beating of the eggs, but the mousseline takes its name from the lightness of texture of "muslin" that results from a more involved beating. Follow this recipe for a perfect omelette mousseline.

3 eggs, separated

Salt to taste

Drop of hot-pepper sauce

2 tbsp (30 ml) butter, salted

Separate the eggs at least 1 hour before making the omelet. Keep the yolks covered. ⊶ This is done because the fat in the yolk will be softer at room temperature, resulting in a perfect omelet.

Beat the yolks with salt and a drop of hot-pepper sauce until thick and pale. Use a wire whisk if possible, or a hand beater. Beat the whites stiff but not dry. Gently blend the whites into the yolks, using a rubber spatula.

Heat the pan. Add butter; for a mousseline salted butter gives more flavour. When the butter is light brown, gently pour in the egg mixture. Cook and fold, just as for a plain omelet, with one exception — do not use high heat. After the butter is brown, lower the heat to medium-low. The beating of both whites and yolks gives dryness to the mixture. Too high a heat will give the omelet a burnt taste. Be careful not to overcook. Fill and fold in the same manner as a plain omelet.

German omelet

This type of omelet is a cross between a very light pancake and a French omelet. It can be used as a dessert omelet as well as a main course. Well made, it is light and pleasant.

2 tbsp (30 ml) all-purpose flour

3 eggs

½ cup (125 ml) light cream or milk

Salt and pepper to taste

Pinch of grated nutmeg

Measure flour into a bowl. Add eggs, one at a time, beating well at each addition, preferably with a wire whisk. Add light cream or milk, a few pinches of salt, a dash of pepper and a pinch of grated nutmeg. Mix thoroughly. Refrigerate the mixture for about 30 minutes.

This mixture can be cooked as 2 thin omelets, the classic way, or as 1 thicker omelet.

To cook 2 omelets, heat the omelet pan and add 1 teaspoon (5 ml) butter. When hot, pour in half the egg mixture and quickly spread it out by moving the pan back and forth to make a very thin omelet. Cook over medium-low heat and, when brown on one side, turn and brown the other side. This is very quick to do, in all about 1 minute.

For a single thick omelet, cook all the mixture at once, allowing a longer cooking time.

When the omelet is cooked, turn onto a hot plate and roll up tightly in the shape of a cigar. When all the omelets are cooked, serve.

To stuff a German omelet, simply fill with hot ingredients before rolling. This type of omelet is sometimes cut into strips after being rolled, whether stuffed or plain.

VARIATIONS FOR THE GERMAN OMELET: Any of the omelet variations can be used, but everything must be chopped fine and warmed before being rolled into the omelet just after it is cooked.

Italian omelet-frittata

The difference between a frittata and a basic type of omelet is that the filling is mixed with the eggs before they are poured into the pan. It is always served flat instead of rolled. Often it is broiled under direct heat for 1 or 2 seconds, especially when the top has been sprinkled with grated cheese.

This is the perfect omelet to make use of leftovers, whether they are fish, meat, vegetables or fruits.

3 eggs

1 tbsp (15 ml) butter

½ to 1 cup (125 to 250 ml) leftovers

Follow the steps for making a plain or French omelet. However, when the eggs are beaten, add ½ to 1 cup (125 to 250 ml) of whatever ingredients you choose. Then proceed to cook, but do not fold; simply slip onto the plate flat.

Spanish omelet-tortilla

The true Spanish omelets are the tortillas redondas, or flat omelets. They are made with 1 to 6 eggs and are always cooked very quickly in olive oil or lard, the way most omelets are cooked in Spain.

They are nice for a party, as each can be cooked into a little omelet in 40 to 60 seconds and can be served piping hot with different garnishes. No liquid is added to a tortilla. A 1-egg omelet must be cooked in a 4- or 5-inch (10 or 13 cm) frying pan.

3 eggs

Pinch of salt

1 tsp (5 ml) olive oil or lard

Beat eggs with a pinch of salt, just long enough to mix the yolks and whites. Heat olive oil or lard in the frying pan; when it is very hot, lower the heat and pour in the eggs. Let the bottom set for 1 second, then lift the pan from the heat for 1 second. Then start moving the eggs around the edges for another second, keeping the pan on low heat. Turn the omelet in a flip movement, or turn onto a plate and slip the uncooked side back into the pan by touching the bottom of the pan with the edge of the plate and turning the plate upside down with one quick movement. Cook for 1 second and serve.

The pipérade Basque and family

Many years ago a very elegant, charming, witty young Frenchman, invited me to a lunch at an authentic Basque restaurant in Paris for the sole purpose of having me enjoy a pipérade.

I remember how great my disappointment was when, with much fanfare, the chef came in bearing a large, shining, copper frying pan filled with a steaming hot pipérade. It seemed to be nothing more than a Spanish omelet, the sort I had been eating at home for years. But what a delight! I learned that one must not always trust appearances. As a matter of fact, this Spanish omelet has little relation to Spain's tortilla.

The pipérade, as well as the omelettes niçoise and Matignon, are scrumptious variations on what we think of as the Spanish omelet. They are all part of the pipérade family.

La pipérade

1 small green pepper

1 small onion

1 small garlic clove

2 tomatoes

1 tbsp (15 ml) salad oil

1 tbsp (15 ml) butter

¼ tsp (1 ml) sugar

Few drops hot-pepper sauce or pinch of cayenne

4 to 6 eggs

Salt and pepper to taste

Cut green pepper into long thin shreds. Chop onion and garlic clove. Peel, seed and chop tomatoes. Set all these aside.

Heat salad oil and butter. When quite hot, add the green pepper, onion and garlic. Stir over high heat for 30 to 40 seconds. Add the tomatoes; stir. Remove the pan and mixture from the heat. Sprinkle with sugar, a few drops of hot-pepper sauce or a pinch of cayenne, and salt to taste. Stir and put back over low heat while you beat 4 to 6 eggs with salt and pepper to taste, just as you beat eggs for an omelet. No water is added to the eggs, as the cooked tomato replaces it. Pour the eggs over the simmering vegetables. Over high heat, stir the eggs vigorously into the vegetables, cooking them as quickly as possible. The secret of a perfect pipérade is speed, which is easily achieved if everything is ready when the omelet starts to cook. Serve directly from the pan, when possible.

The following omelets are cousins of the pipérade, yet each is different. Make these variations, then invent your own, using other vegetables.

THE VERSATILITY OF EGGS

Omelette niçoise

1 tbsp (15 ml) salad oil
1 tbsp (15 ml) butter
1 tomato, sliced thinly
3 thin slices of peeled eggplant
1 garlic clove, crushed
Pinch dried thyme
½ tsp (2 ml) sugar
2 or 3 chopped olives
3 to 6 eggs

Heat salad oil with butter. Add tomato, eggplant cut into long sticks, garlic, dried thyme and sugar. Cook over medium heat for 1 minute, stirring most of the time. Then sprinkle chopped olives on top and pour a 3- to 6-egg omelet over all. Cook, fold in two and serve.

Omelette Matignon

Make this omelet when you have cooked rice on hand. Because of the rice, 3 eggs will serve 3 persons.

1 small tomato, diced
1 tsp (5 ml) diced green pepper
3 tbsp (50 ml) cooked rice
1 small garlic clove, chopped or crushed
3 to 5 olives, chopped fine
Salt and pepper to taste
2 tbsp (30 ml) butter
3 eggs

Mix together the diced tomato, peeled or unpeeled, green pepper, cooked rice, garlic and chopped olives, black when possible. Add salt and pepper to taste. Mix well.

Heat butter until light brown and add the vegetable and rice mixture. Stir over high heat until hot. Pour on a 3-egg omelet mixture. Cook, fold and serve.

DESSERT OR SWEET OMELETS

These great continental favourites are spectacular, yet easy to make. They can be cooked in the kitchen or at the table. Guests enjoy watching them being made and the cook doesn't have to leave the party.

The sweet omelet is always fluffier than the basic omelet. It is a close relative to the omelette mousseline and it can be served plain or filled. Whichever way, it is always sprinkled with icing sugar just before serving.

The French chef usually marks or glazes the sugar with a red hot poker, which gives the omelet a professional finish with little effort. However, that step can be performed only in the kitchen.

Dessert omelet — basic technique

Count on 1 egg per person.

2 eggs, separated

2 tsp (10 ml) sugar

½ tsp (2 ml) vanilla

Pinch of salt

1 tsp (5 ml) water

1 tsp (5 ml) butter

3 tbsp (50 ml) icing sugar

Separate eggs at room temperature for 1 hour.

To the yolks, add sugar and vanilla extract. Beat with a wire whisk or rotary beater until very light and fluffy. This beating is very important, as it dissolves the sugar, which then will be less apt to burn; it also introduces air into the eggs, which will give lightness to the cooked omelet.

To the egg whites, add a pinch of salt and the water. Beat until stiff. Carefully fold the beaten whites into the yolks. Up to this point the work can be done in the kitchen; the bowl of egg mixture can be brought to the table when you are ready to cook.

Get the frying pan somewhat hotter than for an entrée omelet, add butter. Make sure it is spread all over the pan and becomes light brown. Then carefully add the egg mixture. Tilt the pan back and forth, so the eggs will be evenly distributed. Smooth the top with a spatula if necessary.

A sweet omelet is never stirred during the cooking period, so that the lightness may be preserved. Because of this, the cooking is done over low heat from beginning to end. If you are using an electric stove, move the pan from the burner on which you heated the butter to another burner set at low the instant you are ready to pour in the egg mixture. It takes too long for the hotter element to cool down, and the eggs would be overcooked on the bottom. The omelet is cooked when the edges are lightly brown and the top, in the middle, still a bit uncooked. The inner heat of the omelet will finish cooking the middle while it is being folded.

Run a spatula all around the edges to loosen the omelet. Tilt the pan, holding it with your left hand. With the help of the spatula fold the omelet in half. Tilt the pan further over a warm plate or platter, and turn the omelet onto it in a sort of slip movement.

Sprinkle the top with icing sugar. Serve plain, or glaze the top.

If you add filling, do so just before folding the omelet.

How to glaze the top of a sweet omelet

Use an old sharpening steel, a long skewer or, as in the old days, a fireplace poker.

Place the steel or the skewer directly over a hot stove-top burner. Heat it until it is red hot, then draw it lightly across the top of the sugared omelet in lines or in a crisscross pattern. It takes but a second to do this and the perfume of the caramelized sugar is wonderful.

How to flame a dessert omelet

When the omelet is ready to be served, sprinkle with a mixture of 3 tablespoons (50 ml) icing sugar and 2 tablespoons (30 ml) fine fruit sugar. Warm 3 to 5 tablespoons (50 to 75 ml) brandy. Pour over the omelet and flame.

Sour-cream omelet

This type of sweet omelet is completely different from the preceding one but also is delicious. It cooks first on direct heat, then is finished in the oven. This type of omelet is never folded; it is cut into wedges like a pie and served with fruit and sour cream.

5 eggs, separated

½ cup (125 ml) commercial sour cream

½ tsp (2 ml) salt

2 tbsp (30 ml) butter

Beat egg yolks until thick and lemon-coloured. With a hand beater this will take about 5 minutes, or 3 minutes with an electric beater. Add sour cream and salt. Beat until well mixed. Beat egg whites until stiff. Fold into yolks.

Melt butter in a 10-inch (25 cm) frying pan; use one with a heatproof handle that can go into the oven. Pour in the omelet mixture, leveling it gently with a spatula. Cook the omelet over very low heat until the bottom is lightly browned. Lift here and there to check. It usually takes 8 to 10 minutes.

Set the omelet in a preheated 325°F (160°C) oven. Bake it until it is puffed and dry on the top, 15 to 20 minutes. (After you have made this omelet once, you can adjust the baking time to suit your taste; if it is baked longer it will be dryer; if it is baked for a shorter time, it will still be a little moist in the middle.)

Serve the omelet as soon as it is baked, for it will not stay puffed up if it has to wait. Pull it into wedges with 2 forks, as a knife would mash it down. Garnish each wedge to taste with sliced or whole sugared fresh fruits, whipped cream, or sour cream. Or serve fruit and cream separately, allowing people to help themselves to taste.

Variations for sweet omelets

Fresh berry omelet

1 cup (250 ml) sliced fresh strawberries or whole fresh raspberries

3 tbsp (50 ml) fine fruit sugar

Juice of ½ lemon

or 1 tsp (5 ml) vanilla extract

or 1 tbsp (15 ml) orange liqueur

3-egg sweet omelet mixture

Mix strawberry slices or raspberries with fine fruit sugar and lemon juice or vanilla extract or orange liqueur. Let stand for 30 to 40 minutes.

Make the 3-egg sweet omelet. Surround with the berries, or place them in the middle before folding. Glaze or flame, or serve with whipped cream.

Marmalade omelet

3-egg sweet omelet mixture

¼ cup (60 ml) marmalade, heated

Juice of 1 orange, heated

2 tbsp (30 ml) icing sugar

Rum, for flaming (optional)

Make a 3-egg sweet omelet. Fill with hot marmalade; warm it over low heat before cooking the omelet. Fold and serve with hot orange juice mixed with icing sugar, or sprinkle the omelet with sugar and flame with rum.

Macaroon omelet

2 large dry almond macaroons, crushed

1 tbsp (15 ml) butter

3-egg sweet omelet mixture

2 tbsp (30 ml) currant or apricot jam

Icing sugar

Melt the butter and add the crushed macaroons. Stir with a fork over medium heat for 2 or 3 seconds. Pour the 3-egg sweet omelet on top. Cook. Fill with currant or apricot jam before folding. Sprinkle with icing sugar. Glaze and serve.

Now you know the secrets of a perfect omelet: Beat the eggs slightly; cook quickly, so the omelet will be soft in the middle and always delicate and tender; serve at once, on a hot plate.

Sauces for omelets

The best sauces to serve with entrée omelets are Madeira sauce, tomato sauce, white-wine sauce, sauce fines herbes, sauce suprême and sauce velouté.

You will find them all in the sauce chapter Vol. I; see index. Dessert omelets usually need no sauces.

SOUFFLÉS

No egg dish is more spectacular than a perfect soufflé. And soufflés can be served to begin a meal, as a main course or as a true grande finale.

They would be served more often if they did not have the reputation of being so difficult to make. Actually, soufflé is as simple to make as cream sauce plus eggs.

A soufflé is composed of 3 parts — the thick sauce base, the egg yolks and added ingredients and the egg whites. The first and second parts can be prepared ahead of time, covered carefully and kept on the kitchen counter. The third part, the beaten egg whites, is added when you are ready to bake the soufflé. Keep the egg whites in a bowl next to the sauce, with a wire whisk or hand beater handy, ready to beat the whites and fold them in. It is only a 3- to 4-minute operation when time comes to add the egg whites.

Soufflé base

The base of a soufflé is the sauce, which is composed of butter, flour and liquid. Unsalted butter is used for sweet soufflés, salted butter for the others. The sauce must be perfectly smooth, as lumps will affect the texture and interfere with the uniform rising of the soufflé as it bakes. Constant stirring of the sauce while it cooks prevents lumps from forming. ⛉ If you beat the sauce with a wire whisk rather than a spoon, it will never form lumps.

The various ingredients added to a soufflé sauce, such as onions, chicken, cheese and fish, should be grated or chopped very finely, then incorporated into the sauce.

⛉ When the cooked sauce is cooling for 10 minutes before the egg yolks are added, cover it with a piece of waxed paper or plastic wrap, pushing the paper onto the sauce. This will prevent a skin from forming that could cause unpleasant lumps when the sauce is stirred.

The egg

The main ingredient — and the most important to understand in a soufflé — is the egg, which rules the play and makes or breaks the rising of the soufflé.

The eggs should be fresh, of good quality, and Grade A Large. They should be at room temperature when you are ready to start the soufflé. ⛉ Eggs can be more easily separated when cold, but the whites will beat up to more volume when at room temperature. So separate the eggs when they are cold, then cover them and keep them on a kitchen counter.

Egg yolks

Egg yolks, slightly beaten, are always added to the hot base after it has cooled for 10 minutes; then the mixture is thoroughly stirred together. Do not put the base back on the heat to cook further. There is a preliminary cooking of the eggs by their contact with the hot sauce; the cooking is finished when the soufflé is baked. The sauce with the incorporated egg yolks serves to stabilize the airy mixture that results when the beaten egg whites are added. Egg yolks also add lightness and thickening power.

Cover the sauce again if you are not going to finish the soufflé at once.

Egg whites

In all soufflés, an added egg white — for example, with 2 yolks, use 3 whites — gives extra lightness.

To obtain fluffy, air-filled whites, beat with a wire whisk; failing this, use a hand beater. Do not use an electric beater, for it beats too quickly and not enough air is incorporated into the whites. The amount of air beaten into the egg whites determines the high rise of the soufflé during the baking. For more details on the changes in egg whites as they are beaten, and for information on the technique of beating, see the section on meringues.

Egg whites should be beaten stiff but not dry. This point is reached when the whip or beaters are lifted and the egg whites stand high, but bend a little. If the shiny look disappears and the peaks stand straight up, or if the beaten whites slide out of the bowl, then the whites have been overbeaten.

Folding

Beaten egg whites must be folded by hand into the soufflé base, not beaten in. This is how to fold them in: Move a rubber spatula clockwise around the side of the bowl. Then go underneath the mixture in the bowl and back over the top. The whole movement must be done slowly and without lifting the spatula. When one movement is complete, start again. Repeat until all the egg whites are blended. Fold in half of the beaten egg whites thoroughly, then gently fold in the remaining half, even leaving an occasional white spot of egg.

The soufflé dish

The classic soufflé dish is round, with perfectly straight sides and the bottom slightly raised in the middle. It is made of ovenproof glass or pottery and usually is highly glazed. The straight-sided dish permits the soufflé to rise to its maximum height. A dish with sloping sides may be used, but the soufflé will rise higher in the middle, with a sort of round shape or mound in the centre. To obtain the highest soufflé, the dish is not greased; that is why these dishes are highly glazed. However, there is an exception. For some soufflés the dish is buttered, bottom and sides, then sprinkled generously with sugar for dessert soufflés or with fine dry crumbs and/or grated cheese for savory soufflés. This gives the finished dish a delicate crust.

A 4-egg soufflé requires a 4-cup (1 L) soufflé dish with a 2- to 3-inch (5 to 8 cm) collar tied around it; without a collar, use a 6-cup (1.5 L) dish.

A 6-egg soufflé needs an 8-cup (2 L) dish.

How to make a collar on a soufflé dish

If a soufflé dish is filled only three quarters full, a collar is not necessary, as the soufflé will rise above the dish without a collar. When a soufflé dish is filled to the top, a collar is needed to guide the high rise of the soufflé.

To make a collar, cut a wide strip of foil or waxed paper long enough to go around the dish, usually 22 to 24 inches (55 to 60 cm) long. Fold it in 2 or 3 times lengthwise (this gives it greater stiffness to make a piece large enough to overlap the top edge of the dish about 2 inches (5 cm) from the rim and to extend 1½ to 2 inches (3.75 to 5 cm) above the rim all around. Butter or oil the side of the folded foil or paper that will touch the food. Place it around the rim of the dish and tie it on securely with string, or fasten it with paper clips. When the soufflé is baked, remove the collar carefully, so as not to break the surface of the soufflé.

Always prepare the baking dish before starting the sauce.

How to make a hat on a soufflé

A hat is the chef's touch to a soufflé. After the soufflé has been poured into the baking dish, run the smooth handle of a table knife around the mixture about 1½ inches (3.75 cm) from the outside edge and about 1 to 2 inches (2.5 to

5 cm) deep. Hold the knife straight up and run it around in a complete circle. When the soufflé is baked, it will rise more in the centre than on the sides, creating the hat or crown effect.

Baking the soufflé

A French-type soufflé is baked in a preheated 400°F (200°C) oven, which makes it brown and rise quickly, leaving the centre very moist.

Most soufflés are cooked in a preheated 375°F (190°C) oven for a longer period. The soufflé is cooked throughout, does not rise quite so high, but does not collapse as quickly as the French type. Those are the basic temperatures, depending on the soufflé made. There can be slight variations.

○━ Do not open the oven door until 5 minutes before the end of the specified baking time. This is important: Opening the door admits cool air and disturbs the expansion of the soufflé. If cold air touches the soufflé before it is sufficiently firm, the cells will contract and the soufflé will fall. Open the door slowly and do not let it slam shut. The soufflé is done when the top is golden brown, with a very light crust.

To bake a moist soufflé with a liquid centre, set the soufflé dish directly on the centre shelf of a preheated oven. To bake a soufflé evenly cooked throughout, set the dish in a shallow pan of hot water, and put that on the bottom shelf of a preheated oven.

○━ When necessary, a soufflé can be prepared in its dish, all ready to be baked, 1 hour before baking. Keep the dish covered until ready to place it in a preheated oven. Uncovered, the soufflé will fall or form water in the bottom.

○━ Another way to deal with a soufflé if the guests are not ready is to reduce the heat of the oven to 250°F (120°C). The soufflé will then bake for an extra 20 minutes without spoiling or falling. If it is not ready when you wish to serve it, increase the heat to 450°F (230°C). It will then take 10 to 15 minutes less to bake. But, of course, the ideal situation is to have the guests ready for the soufflé the minute it is perfectly done.

Freezing a soufflé

An unbaked 4-egg soufflé, in a dish with the top covered with foil, can be frozen and will keep for 2 months. Larger ones are not recommended; as the outside gets overcooked before the inside is thawed. A 4-egg soufflé bakes perfectly in a 350°F (180°C) oven, in 35 to 40 minutes.

Serving the soufflé

A hot soufflé must be served at the peak of its perfection and that is as soon as it is out of the oven.

A soufflé is cut into portions with a fork, or with 2 forks if you find it easier, (although 1 fork does less damage to the structure of the soufflé). As each portion is cut, spoon it onto a warm plate.

Common errors in making soufflés

Any one of these errors can result in a less than perfect soufflé:

— Egg whites are beaten in a plastic bowl, or a bowl with even a small trace of fat (see more about this under Meringues).

— Egg whites are too cold to beat to high volume.

— Egg whites are beaten dry, breaking into flecks.

— Egg whites are beaten with an electric beater, which does not incorporate enough air into the mixture.

— Egg whites are overstirred when added to the sauce, instead of being gently folded in; this results in a heavy loss of trapped air.

— Sauce is lumpy, or the added ingredients are not cut into small enough pieces.

— Egg yolks are added to a sauce that is too hot, or are added too quickly, resulting in cooked hard particles.

— Baking for the wrong length of time or setting the oven temperature too high or too low will result in underbaking or overbaking.

Cheese soufflé

A cheese soufflé can be served as an hors d'oeuvre, a luncheon dish or a main course at a light supper. It can be baked in individual dishes or in a single large dish. Many types of cheese can be used; 2 or 3 different types can even be mixed.

2 tbsp (30 ml) butter

2 tbsp (30 ml) flour

¾ cup (190 ml) cold milk

½ tsp (2 ml) salt

¼ tsp (1 ml) dry mustard

Pinch of cayenne or a few drops hot-pepper sauce

1½ cups (375 ml) shredded sharp Cheddar

4 egg yolks

5 egg whites

Have ready a 4-cup (1 L) soufflé dish, ungreased.

FIRST PART: Make the sauce: Melt butter then add flour. Remove from heat and stir until flour and butter are thoroughly mixed. Put back over low heat; stir and cook for 1 minute. Remove from heat and add cold milk all at once. Stir until the milk, butter and flour are well mixed. It will appear lumpy, but all will be right once it starts to heat. Put back over medium heat and beat with a wire whisk or spoon constantly, until the sauce is smooth and creamy.

SECOND PART: Add to the sauce the salt, the dry mustard, cayenne or hot-pepper sauce, and shredded sharp Cheddar, or any other cheese or combination you prefer. Stir until thoroughly mixed. Remove from heat. Cover the sauce with paper and let it cool 10 minutes.

Beat 4 eggs yolks slightly and gradually beat them into the cooled sauce, stirring briskly.

THIRD PART: Beat 4 to 5 egg whites until stiff but not dry. Fold gently into the cheese sauce.

Pour the mixture into the soufflé dish. Bake in a preheated 450°F (230°C) oven for 25 to 30 minutes (the French way), or in a preheated 375°F (190°C) oven for 50 to 60 minutes.

This soufflé makes 4 servings.

For a 6-serving cheese soufflé

Have ready a 2-quart (2 L) soufflé dish. Use ¼ cup (60 ml) butter, ¼ cup (60 ml) flour, 1½ cups (375 ml) cold milk, 1 tsp (5 ml) salt, ½ tsp (2 ml) dry mustard, hot-pepper sauce to taste, 2 cups (500 ml) cheese, 6 egg yolks, 6 egg whites. Bake in a 375°F (190°C) oven for 1¼ hours, or in a 400°F (200°C) oven for 40 to 50 minutes.

Chicken soufflé

A cup of leftover chicken or turkey can be used. Part of the liquid can be concentrated chicken stock or sherry.

- 3 tbsp (50 ml) butter
- 3 tbsp (50 ml) flour
- ¾ cup (190 ml) milk
- ½ cup (125 ml) concentrated chicken stock or sherry
- ¼ tsp (1 ml) dry mustard
- 1 tsp (5 ml) salt (or less)
- ¼ tsp (1 ml) pepper
- ½ tsp (2 ml) ground tarragon
- 1 cup (250 ml) cooked chicken or turkey
- 4 eggs yolks
- 6 egg whites

FIRST PART: Make the sauce with butter, flour, milk and chicken stock or sherry as in the recipe for Cheese soufflé.

SECOND PART: Add to the sauce the dry mustard, salt (use less if the chicken stock is very salty), pepper and ground tarragon. Pass the cooked chicken or turkey through a meat grinder and add. Mix thoroughly and cool, covered, for 10 minutes. Slightly beat 4 egg yolks, then add.

THIRD PART: Beat 6 egg whites. Fold gently into the sauce mixture.

Make a collar on a 4-cup (1 L) soufflé dish. Pour in the mixture. Bake in a preheated 375°F (190°C) oven for 40 to 45 minutes.

Fresh mushroom soufflé

In this variation, only ¾ cup (190 ml) of liquid is used for the sauce, which obtains its proper texture from the natural water the mushrooms release during baking.

- 3 tbsp (50 ml) chicken fat or butter
- 3 tbsp (50 ml) flour
- ¾ cup (190 ml) milk
- ½ tsp (2 ml) salt
- ¼ tsp (1 ml) curry powder
- ½ lb (250 gr) mushrooms, thinly sliced
- 1 tbsp (15 ml) melted butter
- 2 tbsp (30 ml) grated Parmesan cheese
- 4 egg yolks
- 5 egg whites

FIRST PART: Make a sauce with chicken fat or butter, flour and milk.

SECOND PART: Add salt and curry powder. Quickly sear the mushrooms in the melted butter over high heat. Add to the sauce, with grated Parmesan. Cover and cool for 10 minutes. Slightly beat 4 egg yolks and add gradually, stirring briskly.

THIRD PART: Beat 5 egg whites. Fold into the sauce.

Pour into a 6-cup (1.5 L) soufflé dish. Bake in a preheated 375°F (190°C) oven for 30 to 40 minutes.

Chicken-liver soufflé

For this recipe you need to butter the dish and coat it with fine bread crumbs. 🔑 *In this type of meat soufflé, 2 extra egg whites are used to give the necessary lightness.*

2 tbsp (30 ml) butter

6 chicken livers

1 or 2 cloves garlic, crushed

1 tsp (5 ml) curry powder

3 tbsp (50 ml) butter

3 tbsp (50 ml) flour

1 cup (250 ml) milk

½ tsp (2 ml) salt

¼ tsp (1 ml) pepper

½ tsp (2 ml) ground tarragon

4 egg yolks

6 egg whites

PREPARING THE SOUFFLÉ DISH: Butter a 4-cup (1 L) soufflé dish, then coat it well with very fine bread crumbs. Refrigerate the prepared dish to set the butter and crumbs, until you are ready to pour in the soufflé.

FIRST PART: Melt the 2 tablespoons (30 ml) butter in a frying pan until light brown, then add chicken livers, garlic and curry powder. Sauté together over medium heat, stirring most of the time, for 3 or 4 minutes. Chop the livers into very fine pieces with a sharp knife.

Make a sauce with the 3 tablespoons (50 ml) butter, flour and milk.

SECOND PART: Add to the cooked sauce the salt, pepper, ground tarragon and the chopped, cooked livers. Cool the covered sauce for 10 minutes. Slightly beat 4 egg yolks and add.

THIRD PART: Beat 6 egg whites stiff but not dry. Fold into the soufflé sauce. Pour into the prepared dish. Bake in a preheated 375°F (190°C) oven for 30 to 35 minutes.

Seafood soufflé

This basic seafood soufflé can be made with cooked shrimp, chopped lobster, crabmeat or a mixture of two, such as shrimp and crabmeat.

🔑 *To give the necessary lightness to a seafood soufflé, 1 tablespoon (15 ml) flour is used. The rest of the needed starch is replaced by ½ cup (125 ml) cooked rice. If you prefer, the rice can be omitted and the flour can be replaced with 2 tablespoons (30 ml) cornstarch. However, the rice gives a lighter and more attractive texture to the soufflé.*

2 tbsp (30 ml) butter

2 green onions, finely chopped

1 or 2 tsp (5-10 ml) curry powder

1 tbsp (15 ml) flour

1 cup (250 ml) milk

½ tsp (2 ml) salt

¼ tsp (1 ml) pepper

½ cup (125 ml) cooked rice

1 cup (250 ml) cooked seafood, finely chopped

4 egg yolks

5 egg whites

FIRST PART: Melt butter in a saucepan without browning. Add green onions. Stir over low heat for about 2 minutes, then add curry powder and flour. Stir until thoroughly blended and add milk. Cook over medium heat until creamy, stirring constantly.

THE VERSATILITY OF EGGS

SECOND PART: Add to the sauce the salt, pepper, cooked rice and cooked seafood of your choice. Stir until well mixed. Cover the sauce and let cool for 10 minutes. Slightly beat 4 egg yolks and add, stirring briskly.

THIRD PART: Beat 5 egg whites stiff but not dry and fold gently into the sauce. Pour into a 6-cup (1.5 L) soufflé dish. Bake in a preheated 350°F (180°C) oven for 45 to 50 minutes.

Coffee soufflé

In this dessert soufflé, 2 tablespoons (30 ml) butter are used instead of 3, because it is made with cream, which gives the necessary amount of fat. The original French recipe calls for very strong black coffee, made with French roasted beans. But there is hardly any difference in replacing the black coffee with instant coffee powder. This soufflé also uses a prepared soufflé dish so that the baked soufflé will have a crust.

In many dessert soufflés, the egg whites are beaten with sugar to form a meringue, and no sugar is used in the sauce itself; this makes a light, sweet soufflé.

2 tbsp (30 ml) butter

3 tbsp (50 ml) flour

1 cup (250 ml) light cream

2 tbsp (30 ml) instant coffee powder

1 tbsp (15 ml) fine-ground black coffee (optional)

1 tbsp (15 ml) brandy

4 egg yolks

5 egg whites

½ cup (125 ml) granulated sugar

PREPARING THE SOUFFLÉ DISH: Butter a 4-cup (1 L) soufflé dish. Sprinkle with granulated sugar until the dish is well coated. Refrigerate until ready to use.

FIRST PART: Make a white sauce with butter, flour and light cream.

SECOND PART: Remove the sauce from the heat and add instant coffee powder, fine-ground black coffee (optional) and brandy. Stir until well mixed. Cover, and cool for 10 minutes. Beat 4 egg yolks lightly and add to the sauce, stirring briskly.

THIRD PART: Beat 5 egg whites until stiff but not dry, then beat gradually into the egg whites, 1 tablespoon (15 ml) at a time, the granulated sugar. Keep beating until you have a thick, smooth meringue. Fold this into the sauce. Pour into the prepared dish. Bake in a preheated 375°F (190°C) oven for 25 to 30 minutes.

Liqueur soufflé

This dessert soufflé is an example of a custard-base type; it can be made with any type of sweet liqueur, or a mixture of liqueur and brandy. The sauce is actually a stirred custard quite different from the usual soufflé.

¼ cup (60 ml) sugar

¼ cup (60 ml) flour

Pinch of salt

3 egg yolks

1 cup (250 ml) light cream, heated

2 to 4 tbsp (30 to 60 ml) liqueur

4 egg whites

PREPARING THE SOUFFLÉ DISH: Butter a 3-cup (750 ml) soufflé dish and dust with sugar. Refrigerate until ready to use.

FIRST PART: Blend in the top part of a double boiler the sugar, flour and pinch of salt. Beat egg yolks well and add. Mix thoroughly with the first ingredients. Add slowly the hot light cream, stirring constantly. Cook this mixture over hot water, stirring constantly, until the sauce is smooth and thickened like a custard. Remove from heat.

SECOND PART: Add liqueur of your choice. Stir until well mixed. Cover and cool for 15 minutes.

THIRD PART: Beat egg whites until stiff but not dry. Fold into the cooled custard, gently but thoroughly. Pour into the prepared dish. Bake in a preheated 350°F (180°C) oven for 20 to 25 minutes.

Chocolate soufflé

In this soufflé, chocolate provides most of the sweetening. Two 4-ounce (113 gr) fancy European chocolate blocks can be used. No butter is used in a rich chocolate soufflé because of the fat contained in the chocolate.

4 tbsp (60 ml) sugar

4 tbsp (60 ml) flour

¼ tsp (1 ml) salt

1 cup (250 ml) milk

4 egg yolks

4 oz (113 gr/4 squares) semisweet or sweet chocolate, melted

6 egg whites

PREPARING THE SOUFFLÉ DISH: Butter a 4-cup (1 L) soufflé dish and sprinkle it with sugar. Refrigerate until ready to use.

FIRST PART: Place in a saucepan the sugar, flour and salt. Stir until well mixed, then add milk; stir well. Cook over low heat, stirring constantly, until the sauce is thick and creamy.

SECOND PART: Remove the sauce from heat, cover and cool for 10 minutes. Slightly beat egg yolks and add, stirring briskly. Stir in melted chocolate until thoroughly mixed.

THIRD PART: Beat egg whites until stiff but not dry. Fold gently into the sauce. Pour into the prepared soufflé dish. Bake in a preheated 375°F (190°C) oven for 25 minutes if you want a moist soufflé, or for 35 minutes if you prefer a well-cooked soufflé.

Maple-syrup soufflé

This soufflé is made with egg whites only. It is cooked for a much longer period than the usual soufflé and is very airy and light. The maple syrup can be replaced by an equal amount of sweet, thick fruit purée, or thick jam such as apricot.

Egg-white soufflés are also different in that they require baking powder. And because of their high sugar content, they must bake slowly to prevent the tops from overcooking. That's why the soufflé dish is set in a pan of hot water. They also are twice the size of an ordinary soufflé.

1 cup (250 ml) maple syrup

½ cup (125 ml) icing sugar

2 tsp (10 ml) baking powder

4 egg whites

FIRST PART: Boil maple syrup until it is reduced to ¾ cup (190 ml). Cool. When using fruit purée or jam, measure ¾ cup (190 ml) and heat over low heat.

SECOND PART: Sift together the icing sugar and baking powder.

THIRD PART: Beat egg whites until stiff but not dry. Add the icing-sugar mixture and fold gently into the cooled syrup. Pour into 6-cup (1.5 L) soufflé dish. Set the dish in a shallow pan with 1 inch (2.5 cm) of hot water. Set on the bottom shelf of a preheated 300°F (150°C) oven, and bake for 1 hour.

Brandy or liquor in a soufflé

Liquor, especially brandy, can be added to a soufflé, and it actually helps it to rise. Up to 2 tablespoons (30 ml) can be added to any soufflé recipe. It will not change the basic taste, as the alcohol evaporates during the baking.

Sauces with soufflés

An appropriate sauce can enhance the taste of many a soufflé. A mushroom or curry sauce is wonderful with seafood or fish soufflés. A mustard, caper or Madeira sauce should be the choice for meat soufflés. Any mustard and cream sauce is ideal with a cheese soufflé.

For dessert soufflés, a rich custard sauce, flavoured in the same way as the soufflé, is always nice. To make a quick sauce, soften good-quality ice cream, then beat it until light and serve it with a sweet soufflé. It can also be flavoured. For instance, beat vanilla ice cream with instant coffee powder, to serve with a coffee or chocolate soufflé. Cool a custard sauce and flavour it with rum or brandy, then make it light and fluffy by folding in ½ cup (125 ml) cream, whipped until stiff, just before serving. This is excellent with chocolate or fruit soufflés; serve it cold with a hot soufflé.

MERINGUES

Here is another preparation based on eggs, but this one uses only the whites.

Over the years, I have been asked why meringues weep, more than any other question. The problem is not difficult to solve. If you study the mechanics of meringues and follow these instructions, I guarantee you will be able to make meringues that will not shrink, will never fail and will not weep; as a result, neither will you.

Basically, the only ingredients in meringues are egg whites, sugar, and air. A meringue can be a soft spreading cream, a spongy white topping or a crunchy shell of hard-baked foam. Meringue can be folded into other preparations to give them height and pride. And, of course, it is the finishing touch for pies.

For any kind of meringue you must learn to beat air into egg whites and add sugar or any other ingredient at just the right moment. To get this timing just right, learn to recognize the stages the egg whites go through. As they are beaten, they undergo a transformation, increasing in bulk because of the air you are beating into them.

THE FIRST STAGE: Beat the egg white into a soft foam. At this point only, add 1 teaspoon (5 ml) of sugar.

THE SECOND STAGE: Continue to beat the egg white, adding 1 tablespoon (15 ml) of sugar at a time, until a thick foam is formed.

THE THIRD STAGE: While the last of the sugar is being added and the beating continues, the meringue in this third stage will be glossy and soft, and rounded peaks will form when the whisk or beater is lifted gently from the mixture.

THE FOURTH STAGE: Finally, the whites become stiff, the mass is moist and smooth, and pointed peaks stand up when the whisk is withdrawn.

What are the keys to arriving at this peak of perfection?

⚬─🔑 Be sure to separate the whites from the yolks while the yolks are still firm, just as you take them from the refrigerator. Cover the yolks and return them to the refrigerator. ⚬─🔑 Leave the whites out to reach room temperature; egg whites beat to a greater volume when at room temperature than when cold.

⚬─🔑 The best beater to use for meringue is the French wire whisk. Nothing is better than the whisk, because it incorporates a great deal more air in the egg whites than any other type of beater. If you do not have a wire whisk, use a hand beater. Do not use an electric beater or mixer, unless you are making a specific type of meringue that requires this kind of beating.

Next in importance is the type of bowl in which to beat the meringue. French chefs insist that only large copper bowls give satisfactory results. They are very good, but expensive and not always readily available. A large metal bowl proportioned to the number of egg whites being beaten is the kind to use. The bowl must be nonporous, which excludes certain plastics, and you must make absolutely certain there is no hidden grease on it. Even minute particles, invisible to the naked eye, will cut the volume of the egg whites being beaten. ⚬─🔑 To make sure the bowl is clean, fill it with cold salted water. If you use a wire whisk, wash it in the salted water too. Then rinse both whisk and bowl under running cold water and use without drying. Another method is to rub both whisk and bowl with absorbent paper dipped in vinegar.

⚬─🔑 Use fine fruit sugar for meringue, when available. A sugar that is too coarse will make the meringue weep. Too much sugar of any kind will also make it weep.

Salt in meringue helps to increase the volume, but too much will decrease it. Use ¼ teaspoon (1 ml) salt for each 1 cup (250 ml) of egg whites.

THE VERSATILITY OF EGGS

Cream of tartar is often added to meringue. It is a stabilizing agent that keeps the whites firm so they do not reach that dry, overbeaten stage. Folding is easier when cream of tartar has been added, because it keeps the beaten whites in a soft, well-beaten mass. Use ⅛ teaspoon (0.5 ml) cream of tartar for each egg white; never use more than this.

To help you in measuring, 7 to 8 egg whites of large eggs or 8 to 9 egg whites of medium-sized eggs will fill a 1-cup (250 ml) measure. You will need 4 or 5 to fill ½ cup (125 ml).

The basic meringues

There are many variations and uses of meringues, but only three basic types — hard meringue, soft meringue and cold-water meringue.

Hard meringue

For the best results, choose a cool dry day to make this type. To be perfect, it must be crisp but tender and of the palest shade of beige. This kind can be made for small individual meringues, or for a large shell filled with sweetened fruits, whipped cream, ice cream or any other filling you prefer. It will keep in a metal box in a cool dry place for three weeks, but do not refrigerate.

2 egg whites

Pinch of salt

¼ tsp (1 ml) cream of tartar

½ cup (125 ml) fine fruit sugar

¼ tsp (1 ml) extract of your choice

Beat the egg whites with salt and cream of tartar to a soft foam. Sprinkle 1 teaspoon (5 ml) of the sugar over the surface and beat until completely incorporated. Continue adding sugar, 1 tablespoon (15 ml) at a time, until all the sugar is added. Beat in the flavouring and continue to beat until the mass holds its shape.

Prepare a baking sheet; sprinkle with flour, or cover with freezer paper or parchment paper (this can be found in department stores at kitchen and freezer counters).

To shape small to medium meringues, use a spoon or a pastry bag and drop the meringues onto the prepared baking sheet, allowing ½-inch (1.25 cm) space between them.

To make a shell, shape meringue into a round of 8 to 10 inches (20 to 25 cm) in diameter right on the baking sheet, or in an 8-, 9-or 10-inch (20, 23 or 25 cm) pie plate; flatten the middle gently with the back of a spoon.

Bake in a preheated 300°F (150°C) oven until the meringues reach a delicate shade of pale brown, 20 to 60 minutes, depending on their size and shape.

Soft meringue

Soft meringue is fine-grained, easier to cut than the hard variety and has no tendency to shrink or weep. This is the type used for baked Alaska; the air beaten into the egg whites acts as an insulating agent that prevents the ice cream from melting. The differences between hard and soft meringues result from differences in baking time and oven temperatures.

A 1-egg meringue covers a surface of 3 inches (8 cm). Increase proportions as required.

2 egg whites

¼ tsp (1 ml) cream of tartar

Pinch of salt

4 tbsp (60 ml) fine fruit sugar

¼ tsp (1 ml) extract of your choice

Beat just as for hard meringue.

Spread the meringue over pies, puddings, etc., while they are still warm, but not hot. Make sure the filling is completely covered. Meringue acts as an insulating agent so the filling underneath will not be overcooked. Bake immediately in a preheated 425°F (220°C) oven for 5 to 6 minutes.

If you are used to baking a soft meringue topping on a pie in a slow oven, you will be pleased with this hot-oven technique. For best results, pile the meringue on the pie or pudding shortly before serving. This is easy to do, since soft meringue will hold up for 1 hour, refrigerated, before baking. This is the only type that can be refrigerated in this fashion. But never refrigerate it after baking.

○━┱ A soft meringue on a pie is easier to cut if you first dip the knife into hot water, or rub it with butter.

THE VERSATILITY OF EGGS

Cold-water meringue

This meringue belongs to French classic cuisine. It never shrinks, weeps or falls and is used on pies, tarts and fancy cakes. It is slow cooking and can be successfully beaten with a hand rotary beater or with a hand electric beater at slow speed.

The beating method and sugar content are quite different from the other types of basic meringues.

2 egg whites

1¾ tbsp (25 ml) cold water

Pinch of salt

⅛ tsp (0.5 ml) cream of tartar

¼ tsp (1 ml) extract of your choice

2 tbsp (30 ml) fine fruit sugar

Add the water to the egg whites and beat until a soft foam is formed. Add the salt, cream of tartar and extract. Continue to beat until stiff. Add the sugar and go on beating until the meringue is stiff enough to form peaks.

Pile on pies, tarts or cakes and bake in a 325°F (160°C) oven for 12 to 20 minutes, or until pale brown.

Electric-mixer meringue

To make this, an electric mixer is essential, contrary to the usual rule that prohibits an electric mixer with meringue. This meringue is similar to Swiss broyage and is sometimes referred to as Swiss meringue.

½ cup (125 ml) egg whites (from about 4 large eggs)

1 cup (250 ml) granulated sugar

½ tsp (2 ml) salt

Place the egg whites in the top part of a double boiler. Beat with an electric hand beater set at medium speed until bubbly, or to the soft-foam stage — the first stage. Then place over lukewarm water and stir with the electric hand beater until the egg whites are lukewarm. Do not let the water boil in the bottom of the double boiler. Remove from heat. Add, all at once, the sugar and salt. Beat again with the electric hand beater for 10 minutes, or until stiff enough for the meringue to hold its shape. (The meringue can be poured into the bowl of an electric mixer for the 10-minute beating if you do not wish to hold the beater by hand for that length of time.)

This meringue can be used as a topping without being baked; it is an uncooked meringue. Or, if you prefer to have a browned meringue, place it in a preheated 425°F (220°C) oven for 5 minutes.

These ingredients make enough meringue to fill and top two 8-inch (20 cm) layer cakes, or to top two 9-inch (23 cm) pies. Any unused portion can be refrigerated for use within 24 hours.

Swiss broyage

This is a fancy meringue used by bakers for fancy cakes and French pastry, or by itself topped with buttercream or whipped cream and fresh sweetened berries. It is not as sweet as the basic meringues and the texture differs slightly because it contains grated almonds. It is crisp when it comes from the oven, but it will mellow if you keep it refrigerated for 12 to 24 hours. Broyage can be prepared with an electric mixer.

3 egg whites

⅛ tsp (0.5 ml) cream of tartar

Pinch of salt

1 tsp (5 ml) vanilla or almond extract

¾ cup (190 ml) fine fruit sugar

¼ cup (60 ml) finely ground blanched almonds

⅓ cup (80 ml) sifted cornstarch

In the large bowl of your electric mixer, place the egg whites, cream of tartar, salt, and vanilla or almond extract. Beat at medium speed until the egg whites form soft peaks when the beater is lifted from the mixture. Add ½ cup (125 ml) sugar, 1 tablespoon (15 ml) at a time, while beating constantly at medium speed.

When the ½ cup (125 ml) sugar has been added, continue to beat until mixture is very stiff and dull.

Combine the remaining sugar, the ground almonds and the cornstarch. Fold gently into the mixture.

Grease a baking sheet, then sprinkle lightly with flour. Shake to remove excess flour. To make a guiding pattern, press the rim of a 9-inch (23 cm) pie plate, or a 2-inch (5 cm) cookie cutter, or any fancy cutter, on the baking sheet. Spread meringue within the outline.

Bakers fill a pastry bag fitted with a No. 3 or No. 5 tube with the broyage in a continuous pencil-thick strip, curling it round and round, until the traced design is completely filled.

Whichever method you use, bake the broyage in a preheated 325°F (160°C) oven, 25 minutes for small pieces, 40 to 45 minutes for 9-to 10-inch (23 to 25 cm) circles. Cool and garnish to taste.

The 3-egg-white broyage will make 2 thin 9-inch (23 cm) layers, or 24 thin 1½- to 2-inch (3.75 to 5 cm) designs.

Italian meringue

This type of cooked meringue is the ancestor of our seven-minute icing. It is much smoother and very thick, with a creamy light texture. Like Swiss meringue, it does not require baking. It is the perfect meringue to top angel food cake, chiffon pie or sweet dessert omelets.

To make individual meringues to be filled with whipped cream or ice cream, Italian meringue must be cooked.

2 cups (500 ml) granulated sugar

1 cup (250 ml) water

5 egg whites

1 tsp (5 ml) extract of your choice

Boil the sugar and water until the mixture forms a firm ball when dropped into cold water. Beat egg whites with a wire whisk until stiff. Gradually add the hot syrup you have just made, while beating constantly with a wire whisk; or place the beaten egg whites in the bowl of an electric mixer and add the syrup while beating at medium speed.

Set the bowl over another bowl of ice water, add the extract, and with a rubber spatula fold over and over for 5 minutes. Cover and let stand for 15 minutes.

When the meringue is used to make individual meringues, shape with a spoon or pastry bag on a buttered baking sheet dusted with cornstarch. Bake at 300°F (150°C) for 30 minutes.

To halve this recipe, use 3 egg whites and half of the other ingredients.

Meringue buttercream

This soft, creamy meringue is used primarily to garnish French pastry, but it is also very nice with sponge cake. It makes a perfect filling to place between two thin layers of cold Swiss broyage.

1 cup (250 ml) granulated sugar

½ cup (125 ml) water

1 tbsp (15 ml) corn syrup

3 egg whites

1 cup (250 ml) unsalted butter

Flavouring

Place in a saucepan ⅔ cup (160 ml) of the sugar, all the water and the corn syrup. Stir over low heat until the sugar is completely dissolved. Raise the heat to medium and boil the syrup without stirring until it forms a soft ball when dropped into cold water.

While the syrup is cooking, beat the egg whites until they form soft peaks. Gradually add the remaining sugar, 1 teaspoon (5 ml) at a time, beating hard after each addition. Beat until you have a firm meringue. Pour the boiling syrup into the egg whites in a fine stream, beating constantly. This can be done with an electric mixer at medium speed. After all the syrup is added, continue to beat until the meringue is very smooth and very stiff. Cool completely. It will take an hour or more.

Cream the butter until soft and fluffy. Then beat the cold meringue mixture into the butter. Flavour to taste with any of these: 1 tablespoon (15 ml) instant coffee powder, 3 tablespoons (50 ml) brandy or rum, 2 tablespoons (30 ml) Dutch cocoa, 1 tablespoon (15 ml) vanilla or almond extract.

American pie meringue

Lemon juice and boiling water added to this meringue make it different from the classic types. It is perfect to use on pies.

2 egg whites

3 tbsp (50 ml) granulated sugar

½ tsp (2 ml) lemon juice

2 tsp (10 ml) boiling water

Beat the egg whites with an electric beater or a wire whisk until stiff. Add the sugar, 1 tablespoon (15 ml) at a time, beating hard with each addition. Add the lemon juice when adding the last tablespoon (15 ml) of sugar. Beat until the meringue is smooth and glossy. Beat in the boiling water. Spread on a pie and brown in a 425°F (220°C) oven for 5 to 8 minutes.

A few elegant dishes with meringues

Swiss strawberry meringue

Any type of small baked meringue can be used to make this beautiful dessert. Use a clear glass bowl so your guests can see the contrast of the ingredients.

1 quart (1 L) fresh strawberries

4 tbsp (60 ml) icing sugar

8 to 10 small meringues

1 cup (250 ml) whipped cream

2 tbsp (30 ml) icing sugar

1 tsp (5 ml) vanilla extract

or ½ tsp (2 ml) rosewater

Set aside 6 to 8 of the best strawberries. Clean the others and slice into halves. Sweeten with 4 tablespoons (60 ml) of icing sugar.

Place the small meringues in the bottom of the bowl. Sprinkle the sweetened sliced berries on top. Whip the cream, sweetening it with 2 tablespoons (30 ml) icing sugar and flavouring it with vanilla extract or rosewater. Cover the berries with whipped cream.

Bury the whole strawberries, points up, in the top of the cream, so just the tops of the berries show. Refrigerate for 1 or 2 hours before serving.

French crêpe meringue

This is a filled French crêpe, topped with frangipane cream, rolled, and garnished with meringue. In summer, use sweetened berries for the filling; in winter, use apricot or other jam. The crêpe can be cooked in the early morning to be served later in the day or at night, with only the meringue topping to be added at the last minute.

Crêpes

1 cup (250 ml) all-purpose flour

½ tsp (2 ml) salt

1 cup (250 ml) milk

2 eggs

Stir together the flour, salt and milk. Beat in eggs until thoroughly mixed. Let this batter rest for 30 minutes.

Grease and heat a 5-inch (13 cm) frying pan. Pour in just enough batter to cover the pan with a very thin layer. Tilt the pan to spread the batter evenly. Cook to a light brown on one side, then set cooked side down on a cloth. If the crêpe batter seems too thick, beat in 1 tablespoon (15 ml) of water or a little more. Continue until all the batter is used, cooking the crêpes only on one side. This will make 18 to 20 crêpes.

Frangipane cream

1 cup (250 ml) sugar

½ cup (125 ml) all-purpose flour

Pinch of salt

3 cups (750 ml) milk

3 egg yolks

2 tbsp (30 ml) butter

1 tsp (5 ml) vanilla extract

or 3 almond macaroons, crushed

Rind of ½ a lemon, finely grated

Mix together the sugar, flour and a pinch of salt. Add milk and stir over medium heat until creamy and smooth. Slightly beat egg yolks and slowly add, beating with a wire whisk or hand beater. Cook for 3 minutes while beating. Add butter and vanilla extract or 3 crushed macaroons and the finely grated lemon rind. Cool.

⚬⊸ Prepare a recipe of Swiss or Italian meringue.

To assemble crêpes

Spread each crêpe with fruit or jam to taste and top with a portion of frangipane cream; roll. Place the rolls in a shallow baking dish, folded side down. Top with meringue. Sprinkle with 2 tablespoons (30 ml) of fine fruit sugar. Bake in a 400°F (200°C) oven for 15 minutes. Serve hot.

Meringue lemon pie

This lemon pie is made with a meringue pie shell instead of a pastry-dough crust. The filling can be topped with sweetened fresh berries or whipped cream. Or try filling with scoops of ice cream or sweetened berries topped with whipped cream or ice cream.

Meringue pie shell

4 egg whites (½ cup/125 ml)

¼ tsp (1 ml) salt

1 tsp (5 ml) lemon juice or vinegar

1 cup (250 ml) sugar

Beat egg whites until fluffy. Add salt and lemon juice or vinegar. Beat until the whites are stiff. Add sugar, 1 tablespoon (15 ml) at a time, beating hard after each addition.

Butter an 8-inch (20 cm) pie plate. Fill with the meringue, pushing it up on the sides and hollowing the centre lightly. Bake in a 275°F (140°C) oven for 1 hour and 15 minutes.

Lemon filling

4 egg yolks

⅔ cup (160 ml) sugar

2 tsp (10 ml) grated lemon rind

⅓ cup (80 ml) lemon juice

Beat egg yolks until thick and lemon-coloured. Continue to beat and gradually add sugar, grated lemon rind and lemon juice. Cook in the top part of a double boiler over simmering water, stirring constantly, for approximately 5 minutes, or until thickened. Pour into the cooled baked meringue shell.

Makes six servings.

CHAPTER 17

The Magic of Pies and Ice Cream

A PIE with a crisp flaky crust and a thick filling never fails to please. But cooks have many problems making them. Why is my piecrust so hard? Why is it always soggy at the bottom? Why does it shrink away from the edges and burn in the middle? Why is it that my hot, thick, lemon filling runs all over the plate when I cut the pie? Why does the dough break everywhere when I roll it? Why does it stick so terribly to my rolling pin, the floured board and my hands? You would not be human if you did not have an occasional failure with a pie.

For some reason, making piecrust has been among the least explained culinary techniques, and the words "line a pie plate with pastry" have been enough to stop many a cook from ever taking out the rolling pin.

There are, of course, many types of pastries, each different in terms of method, flavour and texture. Once the mechanics are understood — mixing, rolling, cooking — the only essential that remains is enthusiasm. It is enthusiasm, more than anything else, that makes good pies.

PASTRY INGREDIENTS

The principal ingredients of all pastry crusts are flour, fat and liquid. Their proportions and the methods of combining them account for the differences in the various types of piecrusts.

Flour
The best flour for pastry, in general, is all-purpose flour, sifted once before measuring. Cake flour is not satisfactory and instantized flour works well only in specially adapted recipes. Pastry flour can be used, but it is not easy to work with and the baked pastry is often brittle. Use it only for recipes that call for it specifically.

⚬━⚘ Whichever flour you choose, remember this: If you have been successful with a flour, use the same brand again, for each brand will produce a slightly different finished product.

Measure the flour accurately. ⚬━⚘ In pastry, it is important to sift the flour before measuring it.

Fat
Lard, butter, margarine or vegetable shortening are the fats used in pastry making. They are what makes the pastry "short" — that is, tender, flaky and crumbly. The fat in pastry dough coats the particles of flour so water cannot reach them. This keeps the gluten strands shorter, since only particles not coated with shortening develop gluten. Gluten, so essential for yeast doughs, makes pastry tough.

Lard is the shortest of all shortenings and makes excellent pastry.

Butter is the best when flavour and flakiness are the prime requirements, as in puff pastry, but it is difficult to make such pastry without lots of practice, and butter pastry does not keep for any length of time. For other types of pastry, do not use all butter, because it does not have the proper shortening power and it provides too much moisture.

Vegetable shortening is used most often in pastry. While the word shortening is sometimes applied to any fat, including butter and margarine and even oil, in baking it usually refers to the vegetable shortenings that are solid at room temperature and have no characteristic taste or odour of their own. They make a short pastry, but not a truly flaky one.

Whatever the fat used, it should be well chilled before it is used.

LIQUIDS

The most-used liquid in piecrusts is water, but milk, cream, lemon juice or eggs (considered a liquid in this case) are used in various recipes. Cold liquid, not necessarily iced, gives the best results. Lukewarm liquid softens the fat and produces pastry that is too hard or brittle. The exception to this is hot-water pastry, which is made with very hot water according to a different set of rules.

MIXING PIECRUST

The first step is to measure the once-sifted flour with whatever other dry ingredients are called for the recipe. Put these dry ingredients in a bowl large enough to blend everything easily.

The next step is to cut in the cold shortening. "Cutting in" means literally to cut the fat into tiny particles as you mix it in the flour. A pastry blender is designed especially for this purpose, but you can use two round-ended knives. Hold a knife in each hand and cut through the fat and flour, moving the knives in opposite directions but parallel to each other. In a few minutes you will have a mixture that looks like rough cornmeal — not smooth but a little lumpy. The finer the fat cut into the flour, the more tender and crumbly the crust will be. Larger pieces of fat make the piecrust more flaky.

Since it is important that the pastry be both tender and flaky, it is best to divide the fat required for the recipe into two lots. ☛ Cut the first lot into the flour as finely as possible, then cut the other half into bits the size of large peas. A good rule is: A little cutting is better than too much with the second half of the fat.

Do not be tempted to mix the fat into the flour with your hands. The fat must be well chilled; if you were to work it with your hands you would warm it, preventing formation of the little pieces of fat and their even distribution throughout the mix. Do not use a fork either, for it will tend to mash the fat and make it too soft.

Then comes the addition of the liquid. This is the step that causes most of the trouble. Since flours vary greatly, some absorb much more liquid than others. It is therefore impossible to give exact measurements for the amount of liquid required to give a perfect texture. To understand the desired texture, you have to learn how to feel it.

Add cold measured liquid one tablespoon (15 ml) at a time, sprinkling it over the dry mixture and mixing lightly, preferably with a fork. Little clumps will form; push them to one side of the bowl and sprinkle in more liquid until all the mixture is lightly moistened. It should be stirred only enough to make a shapeless mass. Do not try to make a ball of dough in the bowl — that would require the addition of too much liquid. The dough should be soft, semi-dry, not sticky but moist enough to hold together when you start working it together with your fingertips.

At this point, do not worry about handling the dough too much. Turn the dough out onto a floured board and form it into a round ball with your fingers. If any of it falls away from the

1. Measure the once-sifted flour and any other dry ingredients.

2. Cut the cold shortening into small pieces and add to the dry ingredients.

3. Cut the shortening into the flour mixture with a pastry blender or two round-ended knives.

4. When the liquid is added, work the dough into a round mass with the tips of the fingers.

THE MAGIC OF PIES AND ICE CREAM

mass, moisten it with a few drops of water until it will cling to the rest in the ball.

Some types of pastry dough, usually those made with lard or vegetable shortening, are ready to be rolled out at this point. But pastry made with butter benefits from chilling for 4 to 12 hours in the refrigerator, which firms the butter and produces flakier crusts.

Rolling piecrust

Many a good pastry recipe has been spoiled at this stage. ⊶ Do not use too much flour on the board or on the rolling pin, as it hardens the best of doughs. A stockinette covering the rolling pin helps greatly, but it is not essential.

First, cut off a piece of dough big enough for a crust, then shape it into a semi-flat round. Now use the rolling pin to stretch it out to a flat round sheet. Roll the pastry from the centre out, all around. Never roll completely across from end to end, as this is sure to harden the finished product.

Lift the pastry when necessary to add more flour on the board, but try not to turn it over. If some corners break, simply stick them together with your fingers. When the rolling is finished, the easiest way to transfer the dough to the plate is the professional way: Place the rolling pin gently on the dough at one edge and roll the dough onto the pin. Then place the rolling pin over one side of the plate and unroll the dough over it.

The next step is to fit the pastry very loosely into the pie plate. ⊶ Do not attempt to smooth it out, for this will cause shrinkage during baking.

How to prevent a soggy bottom crust

⊶ If you are filling an unbaked crust with a wet filling such as custard, first sear the crust. Prick the crust all over. Brush the inside with 1 egg white lightly beaten with 1 teaspoon (5 ml) of cold water. Chill for 30 minutes, then sear in a preheated 450°F (230°C) oven for 5 minutes. This will set the crust and prevent bottom sogginess. Cool the crust, fill and bake according to recipe directions.

⊶ If your pie recipe calls for a single crust that is baked, then filled when cooled, prick the crust, brush it with 1 egg white lightly beaten with 1 teaspoon (5 ml) of cold water and chill for 1 hour. Then bake, cool, and fill.

⊶ Never pour a hot filling into a hot or cold shell; both must be cooled.

⊶ For a pie to be filled with fruit, it helps to coat the bottom crust with a mixture of 1 teaspoon (5 ml) each of flour and sugar. After the pie is filled, sear it in a preheated 425°F (220°C) oven for 15 to 20 minutes, then lower the heat to recipe specifications to finish the cooking.

In general, sear all wet pies in a preheated 425°F (220°C) oven for 15 minutes. Then lower heat to 350°F (180°C) and avoid overcooking.

⊶ Bake an unfilled shell quickly in the middle of an upper shelf of the oven, but bake a double-crust pie on a lower shelf where the bottom crust will set faster.

1. Sprinkle a board with flour and use a rolling pin with a stockinette covering.

2. Shape a piece of dough into a semi-flat round.

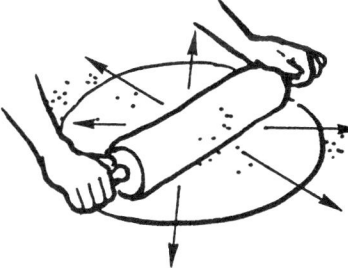

3. Roll the pastry from the centre out, all around.

4. Roll the finished dough onto the rolling pin and transfer to the pie plate.

HOW TO SOLVE SOME PASTRY PROBLEMS

Here are answers to some of the problems you may encounter.

Why is the crust hard? Too little shortening, or too much water, or handling the dough too long when adding the water, or excess flour on the board and rolling pin.

Why does lemon pie filling turns runny when cold? Not only lemon pie does this; chocolate cream pie or butterscotch pie made with brown sugar may also become runny. All these fillings include ingredients that act on the starch used in thickening and prevent its full effectiveness.

In a lemon pie, your recipe may be right one time and runny the next; an extra-sour lemon may cause the trouble. To be sure with lemon pie, add 1 teaspoon (5 ml) more of the starch thickener called for in your recipe.

In cream fillings thickened partly with starch and partly with eggs, incomplete cooking is usually the cause of trouble. Be sure to cook the thickened mixture thoroughly before adding the eggs. The best way to make sure is to taste a bit of the thickened mixture. You will feel the grittiness of the flour or cornstarch on your tongue if the mixture is not thoroughly cooked. When the maximum thickening is obtained, add the eggs called for in the recipe and cook for at least 3 minutes longer.

A runny filling may also be caused by too much sugar. Sugar liquefies during cooking and tends to thin the filling.

Why does the crust shrink in the plate? Too much fat in the pastry, or pastry not fitted loosely enough in the plate. It is better to allow it to crease a bit in the middle than to stretch it and to smooth it neatly.

Why does a single crust puff and get bumpy? Puffiness and bumpiness are caused by failure to get all the air out from under the crust before baking. Tap the crust set in the plate with the tips of the fingers, then prick the pie shell all over with the tines of a fork before it goes into the oven. And be sure the oven is preheated.

How do you stop juices in fruit pies from running all over the stove? The best method is to use what our grandmothers used with their fruit pies — a ceramic bird, head up, mouth open. Called "pie birds," they are still sold. If you don't have one, insert four or five pieces of uncooked macaroni in the upper crust. As in the pie bird, the excess juice boils up into these and not out at the edges of the pie. Another method is to use a funnel or tube made of stiff paper. Remove before serving.

How do you prevent weepy meringue? Common causes include improper beating of the egg whites, the addition of too much sugar or it being added too quickly. Also, meringue must be placed over cooled filling, and spread so that it touches the edges of the pie all around. When the meringue is baked, make sure to cool it away from drafts and never in the refrigerator. For more about meringues, see the section on meringues in the chapter on eggs.

Fluting

To flute is to pinch the edges of pastry together along the rim of a pie, making little folds or pleats at regular intervals. You can do this with your fingertips or with a knife handle, and you can make the fluting as simple or fancy as you wish. Another way to make an edge is with the tines of a fork pressed into the dough along the rim. These finishes not only look good but seal together the upper and lower crusts in a 2-crust pie so the filling will not ooze out, or to give

1. Use your fingertips to make a folded or pleated edge.

2. Make an edge around the pie by pressing with the tines of a fork.

Lattice top

Prepare pie dough for a 2-crust 9-inch (23 cm) pie. Divide the dough. Roll out half and fit it into the pie plate. Roll out the rest and cut it into strips ½ inch (1.25 cm) wide. Spoon the filling into the dough-lined pan and lay half the pastry strips over the filling about 1 inch (2.5 cm) apart. Turn every other strip back. Place a strip of dough across the filling at right angles to the first strips. Return folded strips to first position. Turn back the strips that were flat when the first cross strip was placed. Lay second strip across the filling. Return folded strips to flat position. Continue this process to the opposite edge. This will give a basket-weave lattice, which was typical of old-fashioned pies.

Cut the strips even with the edge of the pie plate. Fold lower crust over these ends and press together tightly. Flute to form a standing edge. Bake the same as for a 2-crust pie.

Professional finish of top crust

When ready to bake, brush the top crust or the lattice top with either 1 egg white lightly beaten or 1 egg yolk beaten with 2 teaspoons (10 ml) cold water and ½ teaspoon (2 ml) sugar, or simply brush with cream or milk. It will add crispness, glaze and a rich colour to the top crust.

1. Placing the second strip across; alternate strips are folded back.

2. Placing the third strip across; when the original strips are returned to place, the over-under lattice will be complete.

BASIC PASTRIES

All-Purpose Shortening Pastry

All-Purpose Shortening Pastry is a basic crust, light and flaky, and a good one for beginners to practice on. The basic ingredients are nothing more than pastry flour and shortening.

Size of pie	Shortening	Pastry flour sifted once	Salt	Cold water
1 crust 7 or 8 in. (17.5 or 20 cm)	⅓ cup (80 ml)	1 cup (250 ml)	½ tsp (2 ml)	1 to 2 tbsp (15-30 ml)
2 crusts 7 or 8 in. (17.5 or 20 cm)	½ cup (125 ml)	1½ cups (375 ml)	1 tsp (5 ml)	2 to 3 tbsp (30-50 ml)
1 crust 9 in. (23 cm)	½ cup (125 ml)	1½ cups (375 ml)	1 tsp (5 ml)	2 to 3 tbsp (30-50 ml)
2 crusts 9 in. (23 cm)	⅔ cup (160 ml)	2 cups (500 ml)	1¼ tsp (6 ml)	3 to 4 tbsp (50-60 ml)

1. Sift some flour. Measure what you need and sift it with the salt into a bowl.

2. Cut in the shortening with a pastry blender or a blending fork or two knives, until the mixture has the general consistency of cornmeal with some of the lumps the size of small peas.

3. Sprinkle cold water, 1 tablespoon (15 ml) at a time, over different parts of the flour mixture. Toss together lightly with a fork. Use just enough water to moisten the dough.

4. Turn dough out on waxed paper. Knead three to six times with the tips of the fingers. Press gently with the waxed paper to form into a ball. Let stand for 15 to 20 minutes.

5. Lightly flour a pastry cloth or board and the rolling pin (or the pin can be covered with a stockinette).

Rolling and fitting dough

These rules for rolling and fitting dough apply to most crusts.

For 1-crust pie

1. Roll the dough into a circle ⅛ inch (3 mm) thick. To measure, invert the pie plate on the dough and mark a circle 1½ inches (3.75 cm) larger than the plate.

2. Fold the rolled dough over the rolling pin and lift onto the plate. Fit the pastry, but remember, do not stretch it. Fold edges of pastry under to fit the rim of the pie plate. Flute the edges.

3. For a baked pastry shell, prick pastry evenly with a fork. Bake in a preheated 450°F (230°C) oven for 10 to 12 minutes.

For unbaked pastry, sear in a preheated 450°F (230°C) oven for 5 minutes, then cool. Add filling and bake according to directions for that particular filling.

For 2-crust pie

1. Divide dough into halves

2. Roll dough for bottom crust as for the 1-crust pie, but trim the pastry at the rim of the pie plate.

3. Roll out a strip of dough 1 inch (2.5 cm) wide and long enough to go around the edge of the plate. It can be in 2 or 3 pieces. Use water to moisten the edge of the dough on the plate. Press the strip to the edge all around, making it even with the outside edge of the plate.

4. Roll out the rest of the dough into a circle ⅛ inch (3 mm) thick and large enough to extend ½ inch (1.25 cm) beyond the edge of the pie plate. Cut a few slits in it, to allow steam to escape.

5. Pour the filling into the pastry.

6. Place top crust over the filling. Fold the edge of the top pastry under the edge of the bottom pastry and seal by pressing the two crusts together. Flute the edge of the crust. Bake according to directions for the particular filling.

The 45-second electric-mixer pastry

Size of pie	Shortening (soft)	Pastry flour sifted once	Salt	Cold water
1 crust 8 or 9 in. (20 or 23 cm)	¼ cup (60 ml)	¾ cup (190 ml)	½ tsp (2 ml)	2 tbsp (30 ml)
2 crusts 8 in. (20 cm)	½ cup (125 ml)	1½ cups (375 ml)	1 tsp (5 ml)	¼ cup (60 ml)
2 crusts 9 in. (23 cm)	⅔ cup (160 ml)	1¾ cups (440 ml)	1 tsp (5 ml)	¼ cup (60 ml)

1. Place shortening, pastry flour and salt in the bowl of an electric mixer. Blend at low speed for about 30 seconds, or until the mixture has the consistency of coarse cornmeal.

2. Add the cold water all at once and mix at low speed for about 15 seconds, or until dough clings together.

3. Shape dough into a ball with floured hands. The dough should feel wet.

4. Turn onto a floured board and roll according to directions for All-Purpose Shortening Pastry p. 421.

Vegetable-oil pastry

For a 2-crust 8- or 9-inch pie

2 cups (500 ml) sifted pastry flour

or 2 cups (500 ml) all-purpose flour

1 tsp (5 ml) salt

1 tsp (5 ml) sugar

½ cup (125 ml) vegetable oil

½ cup plus 1 tbsp (140 ml) ice water

1. Stir salt and sugar into flour.
2. Combine vegetable oil and ice water in a small bowl and beat with a fork until creamy.
3. Pour the oil and water mixture all at once over the flour and salt, and mix with a fork. The dough will be moist. Flour your hands and shape the dough into a ball. Divide into halves.
4. With floured hands shape each half into a flat round and place between two 12-inch (30 cm) squares of waxed paper. Pass a damp cloth over the counter under the waxed paper before rolling, to keep the paper from slipping. This method avoids the possibility of extra flour getting into the pastry and makes rolling easy; the wet-textured dough does not stick to the waxed paper. Roll out the dough between the sheets of paper to make a circle.
5. Remove the top sheet of paper and invert the pastry over the pie plate. Peel off the other sheet and fit the pastry loosely into the plate. Trim edges. Fill pie. Roll the second piece in the same manner as the bottom crust and set it over the filling. Fold edges, seal, flute. Bake the pie according to the directions for the filling you are using.

For two 1-crust pie shells

Divide dough into halves, roll, and set in 2 pie plates. Prick all over with a fork. Bake in a 425°F (220°C) oven for 14 minutes.

1. Roll out the dough between two 12-inch (30 cm) squares of waxed paper; then peel off the top sheet.

2. Lift the round of dough onto the pie plate with the bottom sheet of waxed paper on top.

3. Peel off the remaining sheet of paper.

4. Pour the filling into the dough-lined pie plate.

No-roll pastry

This pastry has merit when you are in a rush or when you want a pie with a special texture. The bottom crust is not rolled, but pressed into the plate; the top crust is made by crumbling bits of the dough mix over the filling.

For a 2-crust 8- or 9-inch (20 to 23 cm) pie

2 cups (500 ml) all-purpose flour

2 tsp (10 ml) sugar

1 tsp (5 ml) salt

⅔ cup (160 ml) salad oil

4 tbsp (60 ml) cold milk

1. Sift together directly into a pie plate the flour, sugar and salt.
2. Combine the salad oil and cold milk in a measuring cup. Beat with a fork until creamy. Pour all at once into the centre of the flour mixture.
3. Mix with a fork until the flour is completely dampened. Set aside one third of the mixture for the topping.
4. Push and press the remaining mixture with the fingers to line the bottom and sides of the pie plate with a layer of uniform thickness. Shape and press to even the edges, and pinch lightly to flute the crust.
5. Fill with the desired filling. Crumble the reserved mixture into small bits with the fingers. Sprinkle over the filling.
6. Bake this type of pie in a preheated 400°F (200°C) oven for 15 minutes, then reduce heat to 350°F (180°C) and bake for 30 to 40 minutes longer, or until filling is done.

For a 1-crust 8- or 9-inch pie

1½ cups (375 ml) all-purpose flour

1½ tsp (7 ml) sugar

¾ tsp (3 ml) salt

½ cup (125 ml) vegetable oil

3 tbsp (50 ml) cold milk

Proceed just as for the 2-crust pie, but use the entire amount without reserving any for the topping. Prick the entire surface of the dough with a fork. Bake in a preheated 425°F (220°C) oven for 12 to 15 minutes.

IMPORTANT: Prepare this type of pastry just before baking; never store or refrigerate it unbaked.

Cornflake crust

4 cups (1 L) cornflakes

⅓ cup (80 ml) melted butter

¼ cup (60 ml) sugar

Pinch of grated nutmeg or ground cinammon

Crush cornflakes and measure again; there should be 1 cup (250 ml). Add melted butter, sugar and a pinch of grated nutmeg or ground cinnamon. Press firmly into a pie plate. Chill for 1 hour.

THE MAGIC OF PIES AND ICE CREAM

Lard pastry

This is the very best pastry to use for fruit or meat pies, as well as for deep-dish pies. It can be rolled as soon as it is ready. Also, it keeps in excellent condition, refrigerated, for 10 to 12 days. Lard is the old-fashioned type of fat used for piecrust and is still the very best.

For two 2-crust pies or four 1-crust pies

3 cups (750 ml) all-purpose flour

½ tsp (2 ml) salt

¾ tbsp (12 ml) sugar

⅛ tsp (0.5 ml) baking soda

1 cup (250 ml) pure lard

1 egg

2 tbsp (30 ml) lemon juice

4 tbsp (60 ml) ice water

1. Sift flour (do not use pastry flour) with salt, sugar and baking soda.
2. Cut in lard until the mixture has the consistency of small peas.
3. Beat together egg, lemon juice and ice water. Add this, a little at a time, to the flour mixture, until the pastry holds together. Turn out on board and knead into a ball. Use immediately, or refrigerate wrapped until ready to use.

Baking-powder pastry

Many find the following method failure-proof.

2¼ cups (560 ml) all-purpose flour

1 tsp (5 ml) baking powder

¾ tsp (3 ml) salt

¼ cup (60 ml) cold water

½ cup plus 1 tbsp (140 ml) ice water

¾ cup (190 ml) shortening

1. Mix and sift once the flour (do not use pastry flour for this crust), baking powder and salt.
2. Measure cold water in a bowl. Add ⅓ cup (80 ml) of the sifted flour mixture. Blend them together into a smooth paste.
3. Cut cold shortening into the remaining flour mixture until the shortening particles are the size of peas.
4. Drop the moist flour paste here and there over the dry flour and shortening mixture. Mix lightly with a fork until the pastry will just hold together. Do not overmix.
5. Gather into a ball and wrap in waxed paper. Chill for 30 minutes. Sufficient for 2 pie shells or a 2-crust pie.

Graham-cracker crust

1½ cups (375 ml) crushed graham crackers (about 18 crackers)

⅓ cup (80 ml) melted butter

2 tbsp (30 ml) fruit sugar

To crushed graham crackers, add melted butter and fruit sugar; mix. Press firmly into a pie plate, making a layer on bottom and sides. Chill for 30 minutes. Fill and bake.

For a firmer crust, chill the graham-cracker crust for several hours, then bake in a preheated 350°F (180°C) oven for 8 minutes. Cool and fill.

Lemon-juice pastry

This is a perfect pastry for tarts, rich fillings and fancy pies.
For two 2-crust pies or four 1-crust pies

3 cups (750 ml) sifted pastry flour

1 tsp (5 ml) salt

1 cup (250 ml) shortening or lard

1 egg

3 tbsp (50 ml) fresh lemon juice

4 tbsp (60 ml) ice water

1. Sift flour again with salt.
2. Cut in shortening or lard with a fork until the mixture has the consistency of cornmeal and small peas.
3. Beat together egg, fresh lemon juice and ice-cold water.
4. Add the liquid mixture, a little at a time, to the flour mixture; use only what you need to hold the pastry together. Then knead, and roll or store the same as for lard pastry.

Viennese cream-cheese pastry

1 cup (250 ml) unsalted butter

8 oz (227 gr) cream cheese

2 cups (500 ml) all-purpose flour

1. Cream butter until very light. Add cream cheese. Beat the two until very creamy. This is quickly and easily done with an electric mixer.
2. Add flour and stir gradually into the creamy mixture with a large fork, until there are no visible crumbs left.
3. Turn out the mixture onto a sheet of waxed paper. Bring the paper up around the mixture and work the dough until it is in a ball. Refrigerate for 6 to 12 hours.
4. To roll, remove from the refrigerator 30 to 60 minutes before rolling. Roll out on a lightly floured board.
5. When baking for a shell, fit the dough into the pie plate and refrigerate for 1 hour before baking. Prick the dough all over. Bake in a preheated 450°F (230°C) oven until the pastry begins to take on a light colour, 5 to 8 minutes, then lower the heat to 400°F (200°C) to finish the baking for 10 to 15 minutes, or until golden brown.
6. ⊙⇒ When baking this pastry with a juicy fruit filling, line the pie plate with the pastry, then sprinkle crushed ladyfingers or fine bread crumbs over the bottom before putting in the fruit; ⅛ inch (3 mm) of crumbs is sufficient. The crumbs will absorb the berry juice and will prevent the crust from becoming soggy.

Chocolate piecrust

1 cup (250 ml) once-sifted pastry flour

¼ tsp (1 ml) salt

4 tsp (20 ml) powdered cocoa

4 tsp (20 ml) sugar

⅓ cup (80 ml) shortening

1 tsp (5 ml) vanilla extract

4 tbsp (60 ml) cold water

1. Sift together the once-sifted flour, salt, powdered cocoa and sugar.
2. Cut in shortening until the mixture has the consistency of cornmeal and small peas.
3. Stir together vanilla extract and cold water. Gradually sprinkle enough of this over the flour mixture to dampen it. Blend with a fork. Place the dough on waxed paper; lift the paper all around the

dough and knead while holding the paper until the dough shapes into a ball. Then let it stand for 15 minutes.

4. Roll out the dough and fit into a pie plate. Flute the edge. Fill to taste. Or bake as a pie shell in a preheated 425°F (220°C) oven for 8 to 10 minutes. Cool.

European flan pastry

European flan pastry is used for small tarts to be filled with cream and fruits. A flan pastry is something of a cross between pastry and rich biscuit.

½ cup plus 1½ tsp (132 ml) soft unsalted butter

3 tbsp (50 ml) fruit sugar

1 egg

1¼ cups (310 ml) all-purpose flour

1. Place in a bowl the soft butter. Add fruit sugar and stir until creamy and light. Add egg and stir until creamy, soft and fluffy. An electric beater works very well for this.

2. Sift and measure flour. Mix with the creamed mixture until well blended.

3. Remove the dough from the bowl, wrap in foil, and refrigerate for 1 hour.

For baked pastry rounds
Divide the dough into 2 or 3 pieces. Roll each piece into a 7- or 8-inch (17.5 or 20 cm) round. Place the rounds on a baking sheet and bake them in a preheated 400°F (200°C) oven for 20 to 25 minutes, or until golden brown. Cool.

Use them this way: Sandwich the cooled baked rounds with fruit purée and whipped cream, custard or chiffon-pie mixture, or other appropriate fillings. Decorate the top with whipped cream. Or use only 1 circle and top it with fresh berries, cover with melted apricot jam or jelly, and decorate with whipped cream.

For baked pastry shells for small or large tarts. Many a French dessert is prepared from these little pastry shells. The shells are always removed from the baking pan for serving.

Roll out the flan pastry and use it to line shallow individual tart pans or an 8- to 9-inch (20 to 23 cm) flan ring or springform pan. Flan rings are metal loops of various heights and diameter that are placed on baking sheets. Flan pastry is loosely fitted into the ring and on the baking sheet. After baking and cooling, the pastry shell is placed on a serving plate and the flan ring is removed.

Pat the dough onto the pan or into the ring so it takes the shape of it. Put a strip of lightly greased foil along the edges, as a support, so the dough does not slide down during baking. Bake in a preheated 400°F (200°C) oven. Cool. Unmold before filling.

1. Fit the pastry into the flan ring or tart pan and cut off the dough even with the top edge.

2. Put a strip of lightly greased foil along the inside edges to keep dough from sliding down during baking. When the pastry is set, remove the foil and finish baking.

3. When using a springform pan with a bottom, set it on a can or jar to cool. When the pastry is cool, release the spring and slide off the ring that made the sides. With a spatula, gently slide the baked shell onto a serving plate.

Scandinavian flan crust

This is a rich biscuit dough, quite different in texture from European flan pastry. Handle it like the No-Roll Pastry. It is perfect for all fruit tarts or rich fillings.

¼ lb (½ cup/125 ml) soft unsalted butter

1 tbsp (15 ml) sugar

1 cup (250 ml) sifted pastry flour

1. Cream butter with sugar until very creamy.
2. Sift and measure pastry flour. Add to the butter mixture, working it in with your hands, until it is shaped into a ball.
3. Pat the dough into a 9-inch (23 cm) pie plate with your hand and flute the edge. Refrigerate for 1 hour.
4. Bake in a preheated 450°F (230°C) oven for 5 minutes. Reduce heat to 400°F (200°C) and bake for 10 to 15 minutes more. Check often, so it will not brown too much. Cool thoroughly before unmolding.

Puff pastry

3 cups (750 ml) sifted pastry flour

1 tbsp (15 ml) soft unsalted butter

¾ cup (190 ml) ice-cold water

Juice of 1 lemon

½ to ¾ lb (125-187.5 ml) unsalted cold butter

1. Place the flour, sifted once before measuring, into a large bowl. Work in the soft butter with a pastry blender.
2. Make a well in the centre and pour in the ice-cold water and lemon juice. Work together with the tips of the fingers, gradually adding the flour to the cold water. Keep blending with the fingers until you have a sort of smooth dough. Then flour your hands and knead for a few minutes. Cover the mixture and refrigerate for 15 to 20 minutes.
3. Roll out the cold dough on a lightly floured board into a square ½ inch (1.25 cm) thick.
4. Cut the cold butter into thin, neat, even slices. Place the butter squares on the dough, one next to the other, in such a way that only half the dough is covered. Fold the other half of the dough over the butter.
5. Check to make sure the edges are even with each other. Then lightly press together the 2 layers of dough and the butter. Form the dough into a rectangle by rolling toward the folded edge. Make sure you roll with light, even strokes, as the butter must not ooze out.
6. When the dough is stretched, fold it into thirds, like an envelope. Place on a sheet of foil and refrigerate for 1 hour.
7. Then place the dough with the open edge farthest away from you and roll again into a rectangle the same as before. Then again fold into thirds and refrigerate, this time for 20 minutes.
8. Repeat the rolling and 20 minutes of cooling in the refrigerator twice, or even three times, if you have the patience. The rolling and folding is what produces the multiple layers in the cooked pastry. After the final rolling, wrap in foil and refrigerate overnight.

1. Make a smooth dough with the first 4 ingredients; blend with the fingers.

2. Flour your hands and knead for a few minutes.

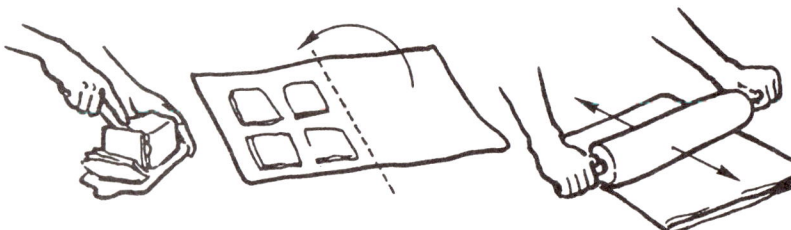

3. Cut the cold butter into thin even slices.

4. Place the butter slices on half of the rolled-out square of dough and fold over the other half.

5. Roll the dough into a rectangle by rolling in the direction of the fold; do not let the butter ooze out.

THE MAGIC OF PIES AND ICE CREAM 429

9. The next day, roll half or all of the cold dough into a sheet ¼ inch (6 mm) thick and cut into rounds or ovals or squares according to needs.

10. Puff pastry is baked in a preheated 475°F (240°C) oven for 25 minutes, or according to the special directions for a particular recipe.

6. Fold the stretched dough into thirds, like an envelope, and refrigerate.

PUFF PASTRY

Puff paste is made of many thin layers — or leaves — of dough, and that's how it gets its name, *pâte feuilletée,* from the French word for leaf. To make the layers, the pastry is folded, rolled, then chilled over and over again. Each folding and rolling is called a "turn". This pastry is never baked filled, because filling would prevent perfect rising. You can use puff pastry for pies or tarts, but it is more often used for fancy French pastry, patty shells, miniature patty shells for hors d'oeuvre, and for vol-au-vent, a large patty shell that, when filled with some delicious mixture of your choice, can serve as an entrée.

Never discard trimmings from puff pastry. They can be used for appetizers or for teatime snacks just as bits and pieces of pie dough are used.

This is a difficult pastry to work out successfully without practice, but what a joy when you have acquired the doigté and you see the high-rise puff, as light as air, full of the perfume of sweet butter.

Puff pastry, like all other pastry, consists of flour, fat and water. It is the way it is worked — the mixing, rolling, folding and cooling — that makes the difference, and the fat must be butter. It is not the type of pastry that is made in a jiffy, but it is very nice to know how to make it when you want something special.

For patty shells

1. Roll the pastry into a sheet ¼ inch (6 mm) thick. Cut out rounds with a buttered 3- or 4-inch (8 or 10 cm) cookie cutter. Use another cutter, slightly smaller, or an inverted glass, to make holes in half the rounds. Do not remove the small rounds of dough after they are cut.

2. Moisten the edges of the solid rounds with cold water. Place the rounds with the holes on top of the solid rounds and press the edges of the two gently together. Brush the tops lightly with cold water.

3. Bake in a preheated 475°F (240°C) oven for 25 minutes, or until well puffed and golden brown. Remove from the oven and cool on a cake rack.

4. When cool, carefully remove the pre-cut piece of dough in the centre of the top. Use a sharp knife. Scrape the inside of the patty to make a hollow. Put back the little lid.

5. These will keep fresh and crisp in a cool place for 2 to 3 days, but do not refrigerate them. If you want to serve them hot, warm them in a 300°F (150°C) oven for 10 minutes.

To freeze, place patty shells between layers of waxed paper in a metal or plastic box. They will keep in your freezer for 3 to 4 months. Thaw out in a 300°F (150°C) oven before using.

1. Cut out rounds with a cookie cutter and then make holes in half of the rounds with a smaller cutter. Do not lift out the small rounds.

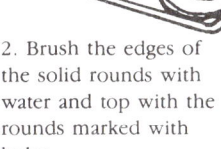

2. Brush the edges of the solid rounds with water and top with the rounds marked with holes.

3. When the patty shells are baked, lift out the small rounds with a sharp knife and scrape out any soft dough to make a little hollow.

4. Fill the shell with the prepared filling and top with the little lid.

VOL-AU-VENT

1. Use a full recipe (3 cups/750 ml flour) of puff pastry to make a 7- to 8-inch (17.5 to 20 cm) (baked size) vol-au-vent. To give such pastry a good appearance, it is important that the dough be rolled and folded very carefully to make sure that the edges are very even.

2. When the dough is well chilled, roll out a little more than half of it into a thin sheet about ⅛ inch (3 mm) thick. Roll the dough on a large piece of waxed paper placed on a dampened board. This eliminates the use of flour for rolling and makes a better, lighter vol-au-vent. Then, with a circle or pie plate, cut a perfect round of 6 to 7 inches (15 to 17.5 cm). Carefully lift this to a lightly moistened baking sheet.

3. Roll out the rest of the dough into a sheet just a little thicker, about ¼ inch (6 mm) thick, and cut out a round of the same size as the bottom piece. Then cut a hole from the centre and remove it, leaving a ring about 1 inch (2.5 cm) wide. Brush the bottom round with lightly beaten egg white, which will effectively act as a seal, and place the ring on top of the round base.

4. To have a professional topping, proceed in this manner: Roll the small round of pastry removed from the centre into a thin sheet and cut it into strips with a crimper or knife. On greased waxed paper form a lattice of three bands one way, three bands the other. Then cover the edges with a strip of dough going all around. Place the lattice on a baking sheet.

5. When all this is ready, refrigerate for 30 to 40 minutes. Then brush the tops with 1 egg beaten with 1 teaspoon (5 ml) cold water. ⚿ *Be careful to brush only the top,* for if any of this mixture falls on the sides, it could prevent even rising.

6. Stick 4 to 5 wooden food picks through the ring of pastry into the base. Bake in a preheated 475°F (240°C) oven for 10 minutes. Remove the wooden picks. Lower the heat to 400°F (200°C) and continue to bake for another 20 to 25 minutes.

7. When the bottom part is cooked, place the lattice top, also brushed with the egg, in a 400°F (200°C) oven and bake for 20 to 25 minutes, or until well puffed and golden brown. In either case, if the pastry is browning too fast, cover it lightly with foil.

8. Cool the vol-au-vent and the top, or use hot. Fill to taste and use the beautiful lattice top as a cover.

Make-your-own pastry mix

	SMALL RECIPE YIELD: About 9 cups (2.25 L)	LARGE RECIPE YIELD: About 18 cups (4.5 L)
Pastry flour	6½ cups, sifted (1.625 L)	13 cups, sifted (3.25 L)
Salt	1 tbsp (15 ml)	2 tbsp (30 ml)
Shortening	2 cups (500 ml)	4 tcups (1 L)

Sift flour with salt into a bowl. Cut in the shortening, using a pastry blender or two knives, until the mixture has the consistency of cornmeal and small peas. Store in a covered container in a cool place. Use as needed to make pie dough.

SIZE OF PIE	PASTRY MIX	WATER
1 crust 7 or 8 inches (17.5 or 20 cm)	1¼ cups (310 ml)	1 to 2 tbsp (15 to 30 ml)
2 crusts 7 or 8 inches (17.5 or 20 cm)	2 cups (500 ml)	2 to 3 tbsp (30 to 50 ml)
1 crust 9 inches (23 cm)	1½ cups (375 ml)	2 to 3 tbsp (30 to 50 ml)
2 crusts 9 inches (23 cm)	2½ cups (625 ml)	(50 à 60 ml)
8 tart shells 3½ inches (9.25 cm)	4½ cups (1 L 125 l)	5 to 7 tbsp (75 to 105 ml)

Place pastry mix in a bowl. Sprinkle cold water, a little at a time, over different parts of the mix. Toss together lightly with a fork. Use as little water as possible, just enough to moisten the dough. Place the dough on waxed paper and knead three times.

Press gently with the paper into a ball. Let stand at room temperature for 15 to 20 minutes. Shape the dough for 1- and 2-crust pies according to the basic directions.

A FEW FAVOURITE PIES

What is North America's favourite dessert? Most people probably would put pie at the top of the list. Here are a few of my favourite pie recipes.

Scandinavian apple pie

- 1 cup (250 ml) brown sugar
- ½ tsp (2 ml) ground coriander
- 1 tsp (5 ml) ground cardamom
- ⅛ tsp (0.5 ml) salt
- ¼ cup (60 ml) all-purpose flour
- Pie pastry for a 1-crust 9-inch (23 cm) pie
- 1 cup (250 ml) commercial sour cream
- 6 cups (1.5 L) thinly sliced peeled apples

Mix brown sugar, ground coriander, ground cardamom, salt and flour. Line a 9-inch (23 cm) pie plate with a pastry of your choice and flute the edge. Sprinkle ¼ cup (60 ml) of the sugar and flour mixture on the bottom of the crust.

Add the remaining mixture to the sour cream. Mix well and fold in the apples. Turn into the pastry-lined pie plate. Bake in a preheated 450°F (230°C) oven for 10 minutes. Reduce the heat to 350°F (180°C) and continue baking for 40 minutes longer. Cool before serving.

Makes 6 to 8 servings.

Balcom apple upside-down pie

- 4 to 6 apples
- 1½ cups (375 ml) sugar
- 1 tsp (5 ml) ground cinnamon
- 1 tbsp (15 ml) water
- ½ cup (125 g) butter
- 2 eggs, separated
- 1½ cups (375 ml) all-purpose flour
- 2 tsp (10 ml) baking powder
- ¼ tsp (1 ml) salt
- 1 tsp (5 ml) vanilla extract
- 1 cup (250 ml) milk
- Grated nutmeg

Peel, core, and slice enough apples to cover the bottom of a deep 9-inch (23 cm) pie plate with a thick layer. Put a pie bird or a piece of stiff paper rolled into a tube in the middle of the apples. Mix ¼ cup (60 ml) of the sugar with the ground cinnamon. Sprinkle this over the apples, along with the water. Cover the pie dish with its own cover or a piece of foil and bake in a preheated 350°F (180°C) oven for 15 minutes.

Cream butter and gradually add 1 cup (250 ml) of the sugar, creaming both together. The sugar granules must be almost dissolved in the butter and the mixture should be light and fluffy and not gritty. This can be done with an electric mixer; 5 to 10 minutes usually is required.

When well mixed, add the egg yolks (save the whites) and beat by hand until smooth and light.

Sift together flour, baking powder and salt. Add vanilla to the milk. Add the dry mixture alternately with the milk to the creamed mixture, beating well after each addition. Spread this cake mixture over the apples, leaving the top of the pie bird or funnel uncovered.

Bake in a preheated 350°F (180°C) oven for 35 to 40 minutes, or until the top is golden brown. Cool on a cake rack.

Invert the pie on a deep, heatproof serving plate. Beat the reserved egg whites until stiff, add the remaining sugar gradually, and continue to beat until stiff. Spread this meringue on top of the inverted pie. Sprinkle with a dash of grated nutmeg. Brown the meringue in a preheated 400°F (200°C) oven. Serve cold.

Makes 8 servings.

Country apple pie

The success of an apple pie depends partly on the apples you use. Juicy summer apples, such as green apples or Duchesse apples, make tasty, soft-textured pies. In the winter, the very best pie apple is Rome Beauty.

Pastry for a 2-crust 9-inch (23 cm) pie

1 tbsp plus ½ tsp (17 ml) granulated sugar

1¼ tsp (6 ml) grated nutmeg

6 cups (1.5 L) sliced peeled apples

1 cup (250 ml) light brown sugar

2 tbsp (30 ml) all-purpose flour

2 tbsp (30 ml) butter

¼ to ½ cup (60 to 125 ml) grated Cheddar cheese

Line a deep 9-inch (23 cm) pie plate with a pastry of your choice. Sprinkle it with 1 tablespoon (15 ml) of the sugar mixed with ¼ teaspoon (1 ml) of the grated nutmeg.

Mix in a bowl the apples, brown sugar, flour and the remainder of the nutmeg. Toss together until apples are well covered with the flour mixture. Fill the piecrust with the apple mixture. Dot with butter.

Roll the second part of the pastry into a round and sprinkle it with the grated cheese. Fold in three and roll again to fit the top of the pie. Press the edges of the pastry together and flute them. Sprinkle the remaining sugar on top of the crust. Bake in a preheated 425°F (220°C) oven for 40 to 45 minutes, or until the apples are tender. Serve hot or cold.

Makes 8 servings.

Glazed strawberry pie

4 cups (1 L) fresh strawberries

½ cup (125 ml) sifted icing sugar

1 cup (250 ml) water

1½ tbsp (22.5 ml) cornstarch

½ cup (125 ml) granulated sugar

8-inch (20 cm) piecrust, baked

Wash fresh strawberries and remove the hulls. Add icing sugar to 3 cups (750 ml) of the berries. Let stand for 1 hour. Crush the remaining berries. Cook these with the water for 2 minutes. Mix the cornstarch and sugar and stir into the cooked berries. Cook gently, stirring constantly, for about 20 minutes, or until clear.

Fill a baked 8-inch (20 cm) piecrust with the whole berries. Cover with the hot sauce. Cool. The sauce will become a beautiful clear glaze when it's cold.

Makes 6 servings.

VARIATIONS: Other fresh berries can be used instead of the strawberries in this recipe. Raspberries, blackberries and blueberries are excellent. Berries heavy with seeds should be passed through a sieve before being thickened.

Classic lemon meringue pie

Pastry for a 1-crust 8-inch (20 cm) pie

Grated rind of 1½ lemons

¼ cup (60 ml) cornstarch

1½ cups (375 ml) milk

¾ cup (190 ml) granulated sugar

¾ tsp (3 ml) salt

2 eggs, separated

1 tbsp (15 ml) butter

5 tbsp (75 ml) lemon juice (about 2 lemons)

4 tbsp (60 ml) fruit sugar

Prepare the pastry of your choice. Add one third of the grated lemon rind to the flour and fat mixture. Bake before filling.

Dissolve the cornstarch in a little of the milk. Add the remaining milk, sugar and ½ teaspoon (2 ml) of the salt. Cook over low heat until thick, stirring constantly. Gradually stir a little of the hot mixture into the well-beaten egg yolks (save the egg whites).

Add the egg mixture to the rest of the hot mixture, stirring as you do. Cook for 2 minutes longer, stirring constantly. Add butter, 1 teaspoon (5 ml) of the grated lemon rind and the lemon juice. Cool the filling while making the meringue. When cooled, pour into the baked 8-inch (20 cm) piecrust.

To make the meringue, sprinkle the remaining salt over the reserved egg whites. Beat the whites until soft peaks form when the beater is lifted. Sprinkle the fruit sugar, a little at a time, over the whites. Continue to beat until the meringue forms definite peaks. Fold in 1 teaspoon grated lemon rind. Spoon the meringue over the pie, making sure the meringue touches the crust all the way around; that anchors the meringue and keeps it from shrinking as it bakes. Bake in a very slow oven, 300°F (150°C), for 15 to 20 minutes.

Makes 6 servings.

Luscious lemon pie

I made this lemon pie for my first beau, who proclaimed it "luscious". It remained my favourite.

1½ cups (375 ml) granulated sugar

¼ cup (60 ml) cornstarch

¼ cup (60 ml) all-purpose flour

2 cups (500 ml) boiling water

4 eggs, separated

Grated rind of 2 lemons

¼ tsp (1 ml) salt

2 tbsp (30 ml) butter

½ cup (125 ml) fresh lemon juice

Pastry for a 1-crust 9-inch (23 cm) pie, baked

½ cup (125 ml) fruit sugar

Thoroughly mix the sugar, cornstarch and flour. Gradually add boiling water, stirring constantly. If you have a wire whisk, use it for this operation. Then cook over medium heat, stirring constantly, until the mixture is creamy and somewhat transparent.

Leave over very low heat while preparing the next step.

Beat the egg yolks slightly (save the whites), stir in a couple of tablespoons (30 ml) of the hot mixture and beat hard. Then add to the egg yolks the grated lemon rind, salt and butter. Pour this mixture into the hot sugar mixture. Place over low heat and cook and stir until the whole is clear yellow and thick. Remove from the heat and add the lemon juice. Stir until well blended. Then set the mixture aside to cool.

Bake a pie shell of your choice; cool. Fill with the cooled mixture. Make the meringue by beating the reserved egg whites stiff and then gradually adding the fruit sugar, 1 tablespoon (15 ml) at a time. Spoon the meringue over the pie, spreading it to the edge all around. Brown the meringue in a preheated 400°F (200°C) oven for 3 to 5 minutes.

Makes 6 to 8 servings.

Citrus chiffon pie

There is something special about a chiffon pie, especially when the crust is prepared from Viennese Cream-Cheese Pastry or Scandinavian Flan Crust. The lime juice and rind in the recipe can be replaced by lemon or orange juice and rind.

Pastry for a 1-crust 9- or 10-inch (23 to 25 cm) pie, baked

1 envelope unflavoured gelatin

¼ cup (60 ml) cold water

½ cup (125 ml) granulated sugar

½ tsp (2 ml) salt

4 eggs, separated

⅓ cup (80 ml) fresh lime juice

Grated rind of 1 lime

Food colouring

½ cup (125 ml) fruit sugar

Soften the gelatin in the cold water. In the top part of a double boiler, beat the granulated sugar, salt and egg yolks (save the whites). Cook over boiling water, stirring often, until the mixture reaches the consistency of custard. Add the gelatin and the grated lime rind. Stir until the gelatin is melted. Add a few drops of green colouring. (Use yellow colouring for lemon, and yellow mixed with a little red for orange.) Then chill the gelatin mixture in the refrigerator until it is slightly thickened, like white of egg.

Beat the reserved egg whites stiff and gradually add the fruit sugar. Beat the thickened gelatin mixture with a wire whisk or a hand beater. Fold in the beaten whites until thoroughly incorporated. Pour this chiffon mixture into a baked and cooled 9- or 10-inch (23 or 25 cm) pie shell. Chill in the refrigerator until firm. Garnish with whipped cream, fresh berries or slices of citrus.

Makes 8 servings.

BITS AND PIECES OF DOUGH

What can you do with the bits and pieces of dough leftover after rolling and cutting pie dough? As a child, I waited eagerly to munch the funny-shaped little bits of dough my mother placed on a buttered baking sheet and sprinkled with pink or white sugar, sometimes with a dash of ground cinnamon or cardamom, then baked.

You can follow my mother's example or, if you prefer to use the leftover dough for appetizers, here are a few ideas. Remember, you can use bits of puff pastry in the same way.

Deviled appetizers

Roll out the pastry and cut it into squares or oblongs. Brush half of them with soft butter and spread the rest with deviled ham or any seasoned spread you prefer, or place an anchovy or a small sardine in the middle of each. Sprinkle with a dash of curry powder or red pepper. Cover with the buttered squares. Press edges together. Brush with a bit of milk. Bake in a preheated 425°F (220°C) oven for about 10 minutes.

Economy cheese straws

Roll pastry into an oblong ¼ inch (6 mm) thick. Sprinkle generously with grated cheese; a perfect combination is 2 parts strong Cheddar to 1 part Parmesan. Press the cheese into the dough and sprinkle with red pepper. Fold the dough into thirds and press down firmly. Roll again into an oblong. With a pastry wheel or a knife, cut strips measuring 1

THE MAGIC OF PIES AND ICE CREAM

by 5 inches (2.5 by 13 cm). Twist each strip gently two or three times. Place on a baking sheet; press the ends down firmly to make them secure. Bake in an oven preheated to 425°F (220°C) for about 10 minutes.

Cinnamon rolls

These rolls make a delicious teatime snack, but they taste good any time.

Gently pat leftover pieces of dough into a ball. Roll into a thin oblong. Sprinkle with a mixture of 1 part ground cinnamon and 3 parts sugar. Roll up tight like a jelly roll and cut the roll into 1-inch (2.5 cm) slices. Place them, cut sides flat, on a baking sheet. Bake in a preheated 425°F (220°C) oven for about 10 minutes, or until browned.

ICE CREAM

Ice cream is one of the most universally popular desserts ever created. We can give three cheers for the ancient Persian chefs who first had the idea of freezing the juices of crushed fruits and dairy products. The first printed recipe for ice cream that we know of appeared in an English book in 1769. However, it was an Italian, Carlo Gatti, who in 1860 first introduced this dessert to the general public. Gatti's recipe used a custard base; his preparation resembled the present-day French ice cream. The mixture was placed in a pewter dish, covered, surrounded with ice and salt, and then frozen in a type of hand freezer.

The commercial ice cream we know today became available little more than half a century ago. Today, most commercial ice creams are made of skim milk, vegetable stabilizer, gelatin, artificial flavouring, water and sometimes titanium and air. As a matter of fact, most ice creams today contain no cream at all; as a result, most of us have forgotten, if indeed we ever knew, what real homemade ice cream tastes like. Ice cream is not difficult to make. Here are a few basic rules.

Equipment for ice-cream making

First, buy a 4-quart (4 L) ice-cream freezer. You will have a choice of a hand type or an electric type; the first, needless to say, is considerably cheaper than the second. You can get either at most hardware or department stores. By all means, read and follow carefully the instructions that come with the machine before you start to use it.

Second, get a 4-pronged ice shaver, available at hardware stores or hotel supply outlets. This is not indispensable, but it does make the work easier.

Third, unless you make your own ice, find a place where you can buy a cake of ice. Or try this trick: Fill three plastic bowls with water and place them in the freezer overnight. The next day it takes only a few minutes to break the ice with the ice shaver.

Chemical reaction of ice and salt

The ice, which is packed with salt around the ice-cream can, does not actually chill the mixture, but it is vitally important. Through a chemical process, salt reduces the ice to water without raising its temperature. In other words, it does not melt the ice in the sense we usually associate with the process of melting — a process that requires energy, which is heat.

The outside of an ice-cream freezer is made of a material that acts as insulation to prevent melting of the ice by external heat. The salt acting on the ice reduces the temperature inside sufficiently to freeze water, so the creamy mixture soon freezes.

Only ice-cream salt, rock salt or coarse kosher salt will work. Rock salt is the best and is not difficult to find, but they all work effectively.

Packing the freezer

Fill the can with the ice-cream mixture. (Recipes for various mixtures follow.) Set it in the ice bucket and then affix the dasher and the cover. When this is tightly set, prepare the ice.

Shave the ice into small pieces with the 4-pronged ice shaver. Place enough chopped ice in the freezer to fill about 4 inches (10 cm) of the space around the can. Add a thin layer of rock salt. The proportions should be 3 parts ice to 1 part salt. Then put in more ice, then more salt, until the freezer is full of layers of ice and salt, ending with a layer of salt. With the handle of a fork or any type of stick, shove or poke the ice down around the container. Make sure to fill the bucket to the very top. Now you are ready to start turning.

Keep turning until the handle becomes difficult to turn, or, if you are using an electric freezer, until the motor starts to labor. Stop turning and open the can, making sure to clean the top of the can so that no ice or salt spills into the ice cream. Taste the ice cream to test whether it is sufficiently frozen; if it is, remove the dasher.

When the dasher is out, put the cover back on the metal can and use either a cork or a paper plug to close the hole into which the dasher fitted. At this point only, pour out most of the salty water in the bucket and add more chipped ice. Just a little more salt is needed at this stage. Pack the top and all around tightly with layers of newspaper. The ice cream will then ripen and keep perfectly for 3 to 4 hours.

Ice-cream mixtures

Homemade ice cream takes about 20 minutes to freeze. Very rich mixtures may take 10 to 15 minutes longer. Fruits such as peaches, strawberries, bananas and raspberries seem to make the ice cream freeze more quickly.

When fruits are used, it is better to crush them, thoroughly and very quickly, in an electric blender or food mill. Or push them through a sieve, which takes the longest but can be done without difficulty with any of the fruits mentioned. Some soft fruits, such as strawberries, can be crushed with a fork in a bowl, or directly in the freezer can itself. Whichever way you choose to crush the fruit is fine, just as long as they are crushed. When fruits are quite acid, sweeten them before adding them to the cream.

Cream, both light and heavy, is usually the base of homemade ice cream. But you can make ice cream better than almost any you can buy with a quart (1 L) of milk, a can of evaporated milk, a cup (250 ml) or so of sugar and 2 tablespoons (30 ml) vanilla extract. It will not be rich, but it will be very tasty.

0→ The point is that the more cream you can afford to put into the mixture, the smoother the ice cream will be. This is because there is more water in milk than there is in cream, so milk naturally freezes with more tiny granules of ice in it. This is why evaporated milk is added to milk when ice cream is being made with milk, for while it is not as rich in butter fat as cream is, evaporated milk has a good deal of the water removed and it freezes more smoothly. However, do not add evaporated milk when you are using all light or heavy cream, or mostly cream. By the way, if you don't like the taste of evaporated milk, you can still use it in your ice-cream mixture. Once it is frozen the taste is completely lost.

Eggs used in ice cream act as a binder, leavener, thickener and stabilizer. They also give texture and flavour.

THE MAGIC OF PIES AND ICE CREAM

Sugar sweetens the ice cream and also prevents crystallization. However, too sweet a mixture delays the freezing.

Gelatin also acts as a stabilizer and holds the ice crystals apart.

When milk is used, it should always be scalded or brought to the boil, to reduce its water content and concentrate its protein. Evaporated milk, however, need not be scalded; its proteins have already been concentrated during the manufacturing process.

Flavouring has no effect on the freezing. It is added only to give the ice cream flavour.

When making ice cream, always make a full can. After serving, pack what is left into plastic containers, leaving 1-inch (2.5 cm) headspace in each container. Fill this space with crumpled waxed paper. Cover and keep in the freezer.

American vanilla ice cream

This is a basic ice cream that can be made with many variations. It requires preliminary cooking.

1 tbsp (15 ml) flour

1 cup (250 ml) sugar

¼ tsp (1 ml) salt

2 egg yolks, slightly beaten

2 cups (500 ml) milk, scalded

2 tsp (10 ml) vanilla extract

4 cups (1 L) light cream or 4 cups (1 L) undiluted evaporated milk

In a saucepan combine the flour, sugar, salt and beaten egg yolks. Then slowly, while stirring briskly, pour the scalded milk over the mixture. Cook over very low heat, stirring constantly, for 6 to 8 minutes, until the custard coats the spoon. Strain and cool. Add the vanilla and the light cream or evaporated milk. Pack in 3 parts ice, 1 part rock salt, and freeze until solid.

Makes about 2 quarts (2 L).

French vanilla ice cream

The difference between American and French ice cream is slight. In one, flour is used; in the other, more egg yolks are used and heavy cream is used instead of light cream. Both are cooked before freezing.

½ cup (125 ml) sugar

¼ tsp (1 ml) salt

4 egg yolks, slightly beaten

2 cups (500 ml) milk, scalded

1 cup (250 ml) heavy cream

2 tsp (10 ml) vanilla extract

In a saucepan combine the sugar, salt and beaten egg yolks. Pour in the scalded milk, slowly stirring all the time. Cook over low heat, stirring constantly, until mixture coats the spoon. Strain through a sieve. Chill. Add heavy cream (do not whip). Add vanilla. Pack in 3 parts ice, 1 part salt. Freeze.

Makes about 1½ quarts (1.5 L).

Philadelphia vanilla ice cream

Philadelphia ice cream, in contrast to American and French ice creams, requires no preliminary cooking and it is richer than either of the other two.

3 cups (750 ml) light cream

1 cup (250 ml) heavy cream

1½ cups (375 ml) fine fruit sugar

¼ tsp (1 ml) salt

2 tsp (10 ml) vanilla extract

Combine all the ingredients in the freezer can. Stir until the sugar is dissolved. Pack in 3 parts ice, 1 part rock salt. Freeze.

Makes about 1½ quarts (1.5 L).

Strawberry ice cream

This recipe can be used year round, as it is made with frozen strawberries.

2 10-oz (284 gr) packages frozen sliced sweetened strawberries

2⅔ cups (660 ml) milk, scalded and chilled

2 cups (500 ml) light cream

1½ cups (375 ml) undiluted evaporated milk

1 cup (250 ml) sugar

2 tsp (10 ml) vanilla extract or 1 tsp (5 ml) rosewater

Thaw the strawberries and crush to a liquid purée either in a blender or by passing through a food mill or sieve. Add the milk, light cream, evaporated milk and sugar. Stir and taste for sweetness, adding some more sugar if you feel it is required. 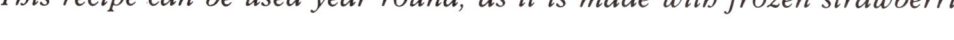 At this stage, all ice cream should taste a little sweeter than you think you will like, because it is slightly less sweet when frozen. Add the vanilla or rosewater. Pack in 3 parts ice, 1 part rock salt. Freeze.

Makes about 3 quarts (3 L).

Banana ice cream

Use only very ripe bananas and the recipe for either French or American vanilla ice cream.

1 recipe vanilla ice cream (1½ to 2 quarts/1.5 to 2 L)

4 bananas, peeled and mashed

Juice of ½ lemon

¼ tsp (1 ml) salt

Prepare the ice cream. Before putting the mixture in the freezer can, mash the bananas with the lemon juice and salt. Add to the ice cream. If you wish, you can add 1 teaspoon (5 ml) vanilla extract and 3 tablespoons (50 ml) rum or 1 teaspoon (5 ml) rum extract to the mixture when adding the bananas. Pack in 3 parts ice, 1 part rock salt. Freeze.

Makes about 2 quarts (2 L).

Chocolate ice cream

1¼ cups (310 ml) granulated sugar

¼ tsp (1 ml) salt

4 to 6 tbsp (60 to 100 ml) powdered cocoa
or 2 oz (50 gr/2 squares) unsweetened chocolate

2 cups (500 ml) milk, scalded

2 whole eggs, beaten

2 cups (500 ml) heavy cream

1 tbsp (15 ml) vanilla extract

Sift together the sugar, salt and cocoa (or omit cocoa if chocolate is used). Add the unsweetened chocolate (if that is your choice) to the scalded milk. Remove the mixture from the heat when chocolate is melted. Add the beaten eggs and mix well. Then pour the scalded milk over the sugar mixture, stirring all the time. Cook over low heat, stirring constantly, until the mixture coats the spoon. Chill. Add heavy cream and the vanilla. Pack in the freezer, using 3 parts ice, 1 part rock salt. Freeze.

Makes about 2 quarts (2 L).

Perfect coffee ice cream

This superb Austrian ice cream is made with whole coffee beans. A large quantity of beans is used because they are not ground.

1 cup (250 ml) coffee beans

4 cups (1 L) light cream

½ to 1 cup (125 to 250 ml) sugar

¼ tsp (1 ml) salt

1 tsp (5 ml) vanilla extract

Place the coffee beans in a cake pan. Set in a 300°F (150°C) oven for 15 to 20 minutes, or until quite hot. Scald the cream and add the coffee beans. Simmer together over low heat for 5 minutes. Remove from heat and add the sugar. Stir until sugar is melted. Cover the saucepan and chill the mixture. Strain through a fine sieve. Add the salt and vanilla. Pack in the freezer, using 3 parts ice to 1 part rock salt. Freeze.

Makes about 1½ quarts (1.5 L).

For a quick coffee ice cream, add 2 tablespoons (30 ml) instant coffee powder to either the French or American ice-cream recipe before freezing.

Maple walnut ice cream

This is an old Vermont classic. Only pure maple syrup should be used, since imitation maple syrup can give an off-taste to the finished ice cream.

1½ cups (375 ml) maple syrup

2 whole eggs, slightly beaten

2 cups (500 ml) heavy cream

⅛ tsp (0.5 ml) salt

½ tsp (2 ml) vanilla extract

½ cup (125 ml) chopped walnuts

Heat syrup, but do not boil. Slowly add the beaten eggs while beating hard. (A wire whisk is perfect for this operation.) Remove from the heat and continue to beat until the mixture is tepid.

Whip the cream until it has reached the consistency of custard. Add to the cool syrup with the salt, vanilla and walnuts. Pack in the freezer, using 3 parts ice and 1 part rock salt. Freeze.

Makes about 1½ quarts (1.5 L).

Variations with vanilla ice cream

If your family loves ice cream, keep vanilla and chocolate in the freezer for everyday use. It's a good idea to have a few ice creams that have something special about them on hand for special occasions or when guests arrive unexpectedly.

To prepare, make vanilla ice cream, using whichever recipe you prefer or use commercial ice cream.

Dutch chocolate ice cream

1 quart (1 L) vanilla ice cream

3 tbsp (50 ml) Dutch cocoa

3 tbsp (50 ml) strong coffee

1 tsp (5 ml) vanilla extract

2 oz (50 gr/2 squares) sweet chocolate

½ cup (125 ml) finely chopped pecans

Soften the ice cream. Heat together in a small saucepan the cocoa, prepared coffee, vanilla extract and chocolate. Stir until the chocolate is melted and the whole is blended. Cool and add to the ice cream with the chopped pecans. Blend. Package and freeze.

THE MAGIC OF PIES AND ICE CREAM

Chocolate-butterscotch ice cream
Soften slightly 1 quart (1 L) vanilla ice cream. Place a layer of ice cream in the bottom of a container. Drizzle 4 tablespoons (60 ml) chocolate sauce on top. Cover with another layer of ice cream and drizzle 4 tablespoons (60 ml) butterscotch sauce on top, and so on until all the ice cream is used. With a long-handled knife, stir the ice cream lightly back and forth three or four times This will make uneven stripes of the sauce. Package and freeze.

You can substitute sieved fruit purées or layers of sherbets for the chocolate and butterscotch sauces.

Double-coffee ice cream
Place 1 quart (1 L) vanilla ice cream in a bowl and let it soften slightly. Add ½ cup (125 ml) instant coffee powder. Grind 3 tablespoons (50 ml) black coffee beans until powdery. Add both to the ice cream and beat in until thoroughly blended. (You can do this with an electric mixer.) Put back in container, cover and freeze.

Double-raspberry ice cream

1 quart (1 L) vanilla ice cream

1 10-oz (284 gr) package frozen raspberries, thawed

1 cup (250 ml) raspberry jelly or jam

3 tbsp (50 ml) brandy
or grated rind of 1 orange

Soften ice cream. Pass thawed raspberries through a fine sieve. Mix with raspberry jelly or jam, and brandy or the grated orange rind. Blend. Package and freeze.

REFRIGERATOR ICE CREAM

Invest in 1 or 2 ice-cube trays with removable partitions and keep them just for making refrigerator ice cream; use plastic containers for storing ice cream.

If you are not making your ice cream in an ice-cream freezer, it is better to freeze it in ice-cube trays with the partitions removed in a freezer or refrigerator-freezer combination rather than in a conventional refrigerator.

Rich chocolate ice cream

This is a rich, tasty ice cream, almost a parfait. The buttered toasted diced almonds can be omitted, but think of them at party time.

1 tbsp (15 ml) maple syrup

¼ cup (60 ml) corn syrup

2 tbsp (30 ml) cold water

3 oz (85 gr/3 squares) semi-sweet chocolate

2 tsp (10 ml) vanilla extract

½ tsp (2 ml) almond extract

2 cups (500 ml) heavy cream

1 tsp (5 ml) butter

¼ or ½ cup (60 to 125 ml) almonds, diced

Place in a small saucepan the maple and corn syrup, the water and chocolate. Stir over low heat until chocolate is melted. Remove from the heat. Add vanilla and almond extracts. Cool.

Place the cooled mixture and the cream in the large bowl of an electric mixer. Refrigerate for 30 to 40 minutes. Then beat at high speed until mixture is thick and soft peaks form when beaters are lifted. Spoon the mixture into an ice-cube tray, cover with foil and freeze until firm.

Melt the butter, add the almonds and stir over low heat until light brown. Spread on absorbent paper. Sprinkle on ice cream when serving.

Makes about 1½ quarts (1.5 L)

Refrigerator vanilla ice cream

Use a vanilla bean to make this ice cream; the flavour it imparts is hard to substitute.

1 piece (4 in/10 cm) vanilla bean

½ cup (125 ml) light cream

½ cup (125 ml) milk

2 egg yolks

Pinch of salt

½ cup (125 ml) fruit sugar

1 cup (250 ml) heavy cream

Place in the top part of a double boiler the vanilla bean, light cream and milk. Simmer over direct low heat until the milk is scalded.

Beat the egg yolks with the salt and sugar until creamy and thickened. Slowly add this to the milk mixture, beating all the time. Cook over hot water, stirring constantly, until the custard coats the spoon, 12 to 15 minutes. Cool, then chill in the refrigerator. This will take about 1 hour.

Remove the vanilla bean. (Wash it, let it dry and store it in a jar of sugar.)

Whip the cream until it has the consistency of custard. Fold into the chilled mixture and pour into an ice-cube tray. Freeze until almost firm, about 1 hour. Turn into the large bowl of your electric mixer and beat at high speed until smooth. Return to the tray and freeze until firm, for 4 or 5 hours or overnight. Cover with foil.

Makes about 1 quart (1 L).

NOTE: The vanilla bean can be replaced with 2 teaspoons (10 ml) vanilla extract added just before the whipped cream.

THE MAGIC OF PIES AND ICE CREAM

Refrigerator fresh strawberry ice cream

The marshmallows in this are used as a stabilizer.

1 pint (500 ml) basket fresh strawberries

12 marshmallows

¾ cup (190 ml) sugar

1 tsp (5 ml) fresh lemon juice

2 cups (500 ml) heavy cream

1 tbsp (15 ml) vanilla extract or 1 tsp (5 ml) rosewater

Wash and hull the strawberries. Place in a saucepan with the marshmallows, sugar and lemon juice. Cook over low heat for 10 to 15 minutes, stirring occasionally, until it forms a thick syrup.

Remove from the heat and pass through a sieve or food mill. Cool in the refrigerator. Whip the cream until stiff. Blend in the cooled strawberry mixture and the vanilla or rosewater. Pour into an ice-cube tray. Freeze until mushy.

Beat thoroughly with a hand beater. Then freeze again until firm. Cover the tray with foil.

Makes about 1½ quarts (1.5 L)

Toffee ice cream

This is a creamy, smooth ice cream with a wonderful flavour. By simply varying the pudding and the garnish, presto, you have a completely new ice cream.

1 4-oz (113 gr) package butterscotch pudding mix

1 to 2 tbsp (15 to 30 ml) instant coffee powder

¼ cup (60 ml) firmly packed brown sugar

2 cups (500 ml) milk

1 cup (250 ml) heavy cream

½ tsp (2 ml) vanilla or caramel extract

½ cup (125 ml) chopped pecans or walnuts

1 tbsp (15 ml) butter

Combine the pudding mix, instant coffee powder, sugar and milk. Cook, stirring constantly, over medium heat until the mixture comes to a full, rolling boil. Pour pudding mixture into a freezing tray and freeze for 30 minutes.

Whip the cream.

Beat the cold pudding mixture with a hand beater, fold in the whipped cream, and add the vanilla or caramel extract. Pour into a freezing tray and freeze for about 1 hour, or until partially firm.

Sauté the pecans or walnuts in the butter until golden; set aside.

Spoon the partially frozen mixture into a bowl and beat with a hand beater until smooth. Fold in the nuts and pour back into the freezing tray. Freeze for 3 to 4 hours, until firm. You must cover the tray with foil if you are not serving the ice cream immediately.

Makes about 1 quart (1 L).

SHERBETS

Many people bypass ice creams because of their rich cream content and, instead, develop a partiality for sherbets, which have fewer calories.

Sherbet can be a water ice, a frozen punch, a milk ice or a frappé.

Water ice consists of fruit juices, water and sugar.

Frozen punch is a water ice that is highly flavoured, sometimes with spices. It is often made with a mixture of fruit juices.

Milk ice is the same as water ice, but with milk replacing all or part of the water.

Frappé is a fruit water ice frozen to a coarse mush.

A sherbet is made by freezing a water ice to a mush, adding gelatin or beaten egg whites, then completing the freezing.

Ice-cube trays with the partitions removed can be used to freeze sherbet and with the proper beating, a very good sherbet or ice can be made this way. Ice-cube trays come in different sizes, of course, so the number of trays needed for these recipes will depend on the size of tray you use. Of course, sherbet can also be frozen in an ice-cream freezer.

The size of the crystals, which give sherbet its texture, can be regulated by the amount of air beaten in before freezing the ice, by the texture of the mixture itself and by the speed of the freezing process. It is important to use recipes especially designed for freezing in the refrigerator. Well made, the following ices and sherbets should have a flaky, crystalline texture that you will find very pleasant.

Because all of these preparations have a large proportion of liquid and fruit juice in them, special treatment is required to keep the texture solid and smooth. Beaten egg whites, marshmallows and gelatin are often used as stabilizers.

When made in the refrigerator, sherbets are stirred once or twice while freezing. This is done before they get too hard; after they are about half frozen, or still mushy. To do this properly, scrape the sherbet from the sides and bottom of the tray or mold with a large spoon; stir, then return to the freezer compartment to continue freezing until half frozen. Then take out the mixture again, turn it into a bowl and beat hard.

⊙━╾ This stirring and beating done at the right time is important, because if the sherbet is stirred too soon, it will invariably return to its original liquid state. If it freezes too hard, it becomes difficult to stir into a smooth mush without beating so hard that the air incorporated with the stabilizer is lost. These operations are not required, of course, when the sherbet is made in an ice-cream freezer, either a hand-operated or electric one. In this case, the rule of packing the freezer with 3 parts ice to 1 part salt applies.

It is important to chill the sherbet mixture before beginning to freeze it. Never fill the mold, the freezer tray or the freezer can more than three quarters full, because the mixture increases quite a bit in bulk when stirred.

Pack any sherbet that is left over in plastic containers, just as for ice cream, and keep stored in the freezer.

Lemon ice

This is a simple ice, made with water and fruit juice. For a variation, use orange or lime juice instead of lemon.

3 cups (750 ml) cold water

1 cup (250 ml) sugar

¾ cup (190 ml) corn syrup

Grated rind of 1 lemon

⅔ cup (160 ml) fresh lemon juice

Place the water, sugar, corn syrup and lemon rind in a saucepan. Stir over medium heat until the sugar is dissolved. As soon as the mixture boils, stop stirring, but boil for an extra 5 minutes. Remove from the heat and cool for 15 minutes. Add the lemon juice, then cool thoroughly.

Pour the mixture into ice-cube trays and freeze until firm.

Remove from the trays, break into chunks, and place in the bowl of an electric mixer, or use an electric hand beater. Beat the ice until it has a mushy consistency. This is important, because the beating will incorporate air into the ice. Return it to the ice-cube trays and cover with foil. Freeze until the ice has the right consistency. Since the ice melts quickly, it should be taken from the freezer only when ready to serve.

Makes about 1 quart (1 L).

Cranberry sherbet

If you have uncooked cranberries in your freezer, this is a dessert you can make all year round. It is particularly delightful served with fruit salad in the summer.

2 cups (500 ml) fresh cranberries

1¼ cups (310 ml) cold water or apple juice

1 cup (250 ml) sugar

1 tsp (5 ml) unflavoured gelatin

¼ cup (60 ml) cold water

Juice of 1 lemon

Cook the cranberries in the 1¼ cups (310 ml) water or apple juice until the skins pop. Pass them through a sieve or food mill to make a purée. Return them to the saucepan and add the sugar; stir over medium heat until the sugar is dissolved. Simmer for 5 minutes. Soak the gelatin in the ¼ cup (60 ml) water for 1 minute, or until the gelatin is dissolved. Add the lemon juice. Stir the gelatin and the lemon juice into the sweetened cranberry purée and cool the mixture. Freeze, beat, then freeze again, in the same way as for Lemon Ice.

Makes about 1 quart (1 L).

Strawberry milk sherbet

This truly delightful sherbet should be made only with fresh strawberries. For a special occasion, serve it topped with crushed baked meringue.

1 envelope unflavoured gelatin

¼ cup (60 ml) cold water

2 eggs, separated

1 cup (250 ml) sugar

¼ tsp (1 ml) salt

1½ tsp (7 ml) vanilla extract or rosewater

2 cups (500 ml) milk or light cream

2 cups (500 ml) crushed fresh strawberries

Soak the gelatin in the water for 5 minutes. Dissolve over hot water, or by setting the bowl in a pan of hot water. Beat the egg yolks well, then beat together with ¾ cup (190 ml) of the sugar, the salt, vanilla or rosewater, milk or cream and crushed strawberries (measure the berries after they are crushed). When well mixed, beat in the dissolved gelatin, mix thoroughly, then freeze in ice-cube trays. When frozen, break into chunks and place in a chilled bowl. Beat with an electric or hand beater until smooth and fluffy. Beat the egg whites until stiff, gradually add the remaining ¼ cup (60 ml) sugar, and then beat until thick. Fold this meringue into the beaten strawberry mixture. Return quickly to trays and freeze until firm.

Makes about 2 quarts (2 L).

Lime milk sherbet

This is an excellent milk sherbet that lends itself to variations. You can replace the lime gelatin with strawberry, cherry or any other flavour you choose.

1 3-oz (80 gr) package lime-flavoured gelatin

1 cup (250 ml) boiling water or ½ cup (125 ml) boiling water and ½ cup (125 ml) fresh lime juice

½ cup (125 ml) sugar

2 cups (500 ml) milk

1 cup (250 ml) light cream

¼ cup (60 ml) lemon juice

1 tsp (5 ml) grated lemon rind

Place the gelatin in a bowl. Pour in the boiling water or boiling water and lime juice. Stir until the gelatin is dissolved. Add the remaining ingredients and mix thoroughly. Freeze. Beat, then freeze again, as in the Lemon Ice recipe.

Makes about 1½ quarts (1.5 L)

Rhubarb sherbet

4 cups (1 L) sliced rhubarb

½ cup (125 ml) water

2 eggs

1 cup (250 ml) sugar

Grated rind and juice of 1 lemon

½ cup (125 ml) orange juice

½ cup (125 ml) maple syrup

½ tsp (2 ml) salt

Wash the rhubarb and cut it into small slices, then measure. Place the pieces in a saucepan with the water. Cover and boil over high heat for 5 to 8 minutes, stirring once or twice to break up the pieces.

Beat the eggs until light and pale yellow, then gradually add the sugar. Beat until very fluffy and pale. This takes 5 to 8 minutes with an electric mixer.

Add the lemon rind and juice, the orange juice, maple syrup and salt to the rhubarb. Stir over low heat until well mixed, then cool as rapidly as possible by placing the bowl in the refrigerator or freezer. ⚷ Quick cooling preserves the deep red colour of the rhubarb. The mixture cools in about 15 minutes.

Remove from the refrigerator and beat in the egg mixture. Pour into ice-cube trays and cover with foil. Freeze, beat, and freeze again, just as for the Lemon Ice.

Makes about 1½ quarts (1.5 L).

CHAPTER 18

Cheese and nuts

CHEESE is made from milk curds that are always drained, sometimes pressed and often fermented. When you realize that a quart (1 L) of sour milk is reduced in cheese making to a small lump of scarcely ⅓ cup (80 gr), you can better appreciate why cheese is so costly.

Milk itself contains organisms and enzymes that help mature the cheese. And some cheeses are made by adding foreign organisms such as Penicillium molds; blue cheeses are an obvious example.

Cheese can be used for any course in a meal. In France, cheese is always served before dessert, but in North America it is generally served before the meal, as an hors d'oeuvre, or with fruit at the end of the meal.

Using cheese

You can do much more with cheese than serve it with crackers or decorate apple pie with it. All kinds of sandwiches can be made with cheese, and many different cheeses can be used for sauces. Grated hard cheese enhances all sorts of dishes — soup, pasta dishes, salads. Cheese added to yeast doughs or quick doughs make delicious bread, rolls or biscuits.

Cheese is a good way to enrich your diet with protein, calcium and vitamin A. Low-calorie diets make extensive use of cottage cheese, especially the skim-milk variety.

Most cheese is salty; it contains the concentrated salt of a large quantity of milk. Remember this when using cheese in cooking.

⚬━┱ Low temperatures are important in cheese cookery. High heat can make the cheese harden on the bottom of the pot instead of blending with other ingredients. ⚬━┱ If you are adding grated cheese to a hot mixture, add it at the very end and remove the saucepan from the heat immediately. The heat retained in the hot mixture will melt the cheese.

It is useful to know that 1 pound (500 gr) of cheese equals about 2 cups (500 ml); 6 ounces (170 gr) of grated cheese will fill 1 cup (250 ml).

CHEESE AROUND THE WORLD

The name of a cheese often indicates its country of origin. Watch for certain prefixes or suffixes to give you a clue. For instance, cheese from Norway or Sweden commonly ends with Ost, which means cheese. Examples are noekklost and gjetost. In Denmark, names carry the suffix bo. Examples: Danbo, Fynbo, Elbo.

A cheese often derives its name from an ingredient. The German Kümmelkäse means cheese studded with caraway (Kümmel) seeds. The French La Grappe is a mild, semi-soft, creamy cheese covered with dried grape seeds.

GREAT BRITAIN

England is the home of Cheddar cheese, and much of the other cheese produced there bears a certain resemblance to Cheddar in texture as well as in flavour.

CAERPHILLY — semi-soft, cream-coloured, salty and tasting of buttermilk. Originally made in Wales but now almost all is made in Somerset.

CHEDDAR — yellow, firm; becomes sharper in flavour when aged.

CHESHIRE — similar to Cheddar, but more crumbly and quite salty.

DERBYSHIRE — firm cheese, mild in flavour.

DUNLOP — white pressed cheese, more moist than Cheddar and tasting more buttery; from Scotland.

GLOUCESTER AND DOUBLE GLOUCESTER — white, hard, similar to Derbyshire. Gloucester is soft-textured; Double Gloucester is somewhat crumbly.

STILTON — cream-coloured with blue-green veins and sharp in flavour.

WENSLEYDALE — soft, white, delicate in flavour when young; when aged it resembles Stilton.

FRANCE

France has a far greater variety of cheeses than any other country because of its wide range of climatic and soil conditions. In addition, it has many breeds of cows, ewes and goats. In France, cheese is much more than a snack or the filling for a sandwich; more often than not it is a meal in itself.

Cream cheeses

BOURSAULT and BOURSIN — rich, creamy cheeses sometimes mixed with crushed black peppercorns or with herbs. They are sold in different shapes.

LA GRAPPE — a bland cheese similar to a creamy Gruyère. It is pasteurized after it is made and covered with grape seeds, but has no grape flavour.

NEUFCHATEL — a small loaf-shaped cheese made of skimmilk, whole milk or milk with cream added. Cheese of this type is mixed with other ingredients, such as pimientos, to make processed soft cheese spreads.

PETIT GERVAIS — similar to Petit Suisse but a little more sour. Both are perfect for desserts.

PETIT-SUISSE — a paper-wrapped, cylindrical, unsalted fresh cream cheese. These come six to a box, with each cylinder individually wrapped.

SAINT-MARCELLIN — a soft cream cheese made from half goats' milk and half cows' milk.

Soft cheeses

BANON — goats' milk cheese made in Provence. These little cheeses usually come wrapped in chestnut leaves. Sometimes they are wrapped in herbs to ripen and have an herb flavour when ready to eat.

BRIE — a round cheese with a fine, delicate flavour. This cheese was known as early as 1500. There are three kinds, all made in Seine-et-Marne. When perfectly ripe, this whole-milk cheese is luscious, melting but not runny.

CAMEMBERT — a world-famous Normandy cheese made from cows' milk; sold in round boxes. French Camembert is definitely seasonal and is at its best from January to April. Like Brie, it should be luscious and melting when perfect.

CARRÉ DE L'EST — soft, slightly salted, milder than Camembert, sold in boxes of various shapes. Sometimes difficult to find in North America.

CHÈVRE — goats' milk cheese, generally strong-tasting. Many types are made in France, but relatively few are imported to North America.

PONT L'ÉVÊQUE — a rich, soft, strong cheese; sold in square boxes. Many regard it as the best cheese of Normandy, and it is one of France's oldest cheeses. It is pale yellow, with many tiny holes. Delicious with red wine or applejack.

SAINT-BENOIT — a soft, creamy, mild cheese from the Loire Valley.

Semi-hard cheeses

BEAUMONT — a large Alpine cheese similar to Reblochon; usually sold by the piece.

MUNSTER — the regional cheese of Alsace, often mistaken for a German cheese. It has a creamy texture and is semi-mild. Sometimes it is rolled in crushed cumin seeds or caraway seeds.

PORT SALUT — a smooth yellow cheese with delicious flavour and aroma; made by Trappist monks since 1850 in the abbey of Port-du-Salut in Brittany and now made in other places as well. This slow-ripening cheese keeps well.

REBLOCHON — a small, round cheese, with creamy texture, from the mountains of Savoie. It is made from the milk of the Tarentais cows. Young Reblochon has the best flavour.

SAINT-PAULIN — another delicious mild cheese with tiny holes, made by the Trappists and other cheese makers.

Blue cheeses

BLEU DE BRESSE — the oldest French blue cheese, the mildest, the creamiest and — many believe — the most delicious.

FOURME D'AMBERT — a blue cheese stronger than Roquefort and quite salty and crumbly; it keeps well.

ROQUEFORT — the best-known blue cheese, made of ewes' milk. The cheese is pungent in flavour and is rather dry and crumbly compared with Danish or American blues, which are more spreadable.

France also produces processed semi-soft cheese of excellent quality, such as La Vache Qui Rit, Bonbel and Baby Bel.

DENMARK

Although cheese for home consumption has been made in Denmark for generations, since the end of World War II the export trade has rapidly expanded. The country's two most important cheeses are the golden and the blue.

The golden carries the suffix bo, and comes mostly from the type Samsoe, which is made from whole milk. A golden, semi-hard cheese with small holes, has a delicious nutty flavour and is rich in body and bouquet.

CREMA DANICA — a creamy, fresh-tasting cheese in a rectangular block. It ripens like Brie but the flavour is more like a cream cheese. Wonderful for breakfast, or with fruits for dessert.

DANBO — a square, creamy, mild cheese.

DANISH BLUE OR DANABLU — a fine blue cheese that is more buttery than Roquefort and sharper in flavour.

ELBO — a brick-shaped cheese; yellow, with a few eyes.

ESROM — deliciously fragrant, sweet and rich; it is a beautiful pale yellow colour.

FYNBO — like Danbo, but nuttier in flavour.

TYBO — shaped like a brick; resembles a Dutch Edam in texture and colour.

SWEDEN and NORWAY

Much cheese from Sweden and Norway is a dark caramel colour and has a special flavour and texture that is almost uncheeselike. Many of these cheeses are made from whey only. They are best served in paper-thin slices; special knives are made in Scandinavia for the purpose. Some cheeses are spiced with cumin-seeds, cloves or caraway seeds.

GJETOST — sweet brown-coloured Norwegian goats' milk cheese, somewhat grainy and very hard; usually served in thin slices, and always served for breakfast in Norway. It looks and tastes like no other cheese.

HABLÉ CRÈME CHANTILLY — a Swedish cream cheese like a French double-crème. Very delicate; for desserts.

HERRGARD — a bland cheese with holes, with a taste similar to Gouda.

JARLSBERG — a bland, buttery cheese with holes.

NOEKKELOST — a firm, dark yellow cheese with caraway seeds, cuminseeds or cloves, or a mixture of all three. For those who like these spices, it is delicious.

NORMANNAOST — a blue cheese similar to Roquefort; less sharp and creamy than Danish blue, but very good.

SVECIAOST — similar to Herrgard.

SWITZERLAND

The Swiss make, eat, and export more pounds of cheese per person than people of any other country.

APPENZELL — a whole-milk cheese, very pale yellow with a brown wrinkled skin and pea-size holes. The flavour is much more delicate than that of the other Swiss cheeses, and comes partly from a bath of wine and spices.

EMMENTHAL — the most imitated cheese, but the real Emmenthal, with its sweetness and hazelnut flavour, remains by far the best. Made from whole milk, it has large holes.

GLARUS — made of whole milk; somewhat like Tilsit, but softer and sweeter.

GRUYÈRE — similar to Emmenthal, but the eyes are smaller, ranging in size from a pea to a hazelnut; also the eye formation is less extensive than in Emmenthal. The famous Swiss fondue is made with half Emmenthal and half Gruyère.

PROCESSED SWISS — made of Emmenthal and Gruyère, and available under many brand names, but recognizable by the way it is packed in foil-wrapped triangular portions. It is different from the natural cheese and keeps for a long time.

SAPSAGO — a hard cheese shaped like a cone with its point cut off. An aromatic clover is added to the mixture, which makes the cheese green. It is not sage, despite its name. The flavour is very distinctive because sour milk and whey are used. This cheese is delicious grated into soups.

SPALEN or SBRINZA — the oldest Swiss cheese, probably known to Julius Caesar. It is hard, with low water content, and is good for grating.

GERMANY

The Germans make many different cheeses, and most are sold in cheese specialty shops. French cheeses are made to be eaten with wine; German cheeses, with their more pungent, strong flavours, are usually eaten with beer.

BIERKÄSE — a white, strong-flavoured cheese intended to be eaten with beer.

HANDKÄSE (Hand Cheese) — strong-tasting little round cheeses originally shaped by hand. They become more pungent with age.

KOCHKÄSE — a slightly fermented pressed cottage cheese, medium mild.

KÜMMELKÄSE — a creamy cheese flavoured with caraway seeds.

LIMBURGER — soft, cream-coloured, with a highly developed flavour and aroma. This cheese originally was made in Belgium and marketed in Limburg. It has a texture similar to Brie.

LIPTAUER — originally a Hungarian cheese from Lipto. The Austrians called the cheese and the spread made from it by the same name. Today, mixtures of cottage cheese and pungent seasonings are given this name.

ROMADUR — similar to Limburger, but milder and less salty.

TILSIT — a semi-hard cheese with many tiny holes. It is mild tasting and especially good in sandwiches.

HOLLAND

Cheese making is an important part of the agricultural economy of the Netherlands. Dutch cheese is mostly semi-hard, nutty-flavoured and usually mild. It keeps its quality exceedingly well for a long time.

EDAM — spherically shaped, with flattened top and bottom; it is often referred to as "Dutch Red Ball." A delicious cheese.

GOUDA — whole-milk cheese, more firm than creamy, with a distinctive flavour. It is pale yellow with a red exterior.

LEYDEN — a spicy cheese flavoured with cuminseeds and sometimes a few cloves.

ITALY

The Italians produce a wide variety of cheeses. Most Italian cheeses are soft or semi-soft and most are very mild. Two of the most famous are Parmesan, a hard cheese, and Gorgonzola, a blue cheese preferred to Stilton or Roquefort by many cheese lovers.

BEL PAESE — uncooked, soft, sweet and mild; very pleasant as a table cheese. This is a trade name, not a cheese type.

CACCIOCAVALLO — very hard grating cheese, shaped like an eggplant. These are tied with strings and dried in pairs. While they are used fresh for eating in Italy, usually only the matured hard cheeses are exported to North America.

FONTINA — ivory-coloured, mild and creamy; often used for fondue and many other cooked cheese dishes. It is not as readily available as most of the others.

GORGONZOLA — a superior blue cheese made from whole milk. It is more creamy than Roquefort and the veins are green rather than blue. There is also a delicious white Gorgonzola, without veins.

MOZZARELLA — the cheese everyone knows as the pizza cheese, it can also be eaten uncooked. It is a very mild, tender and moist.

PARMESAN — the true Parmesan, Parmigiano-Reggiano, is produced in a strictly limited area. It is made according to exact standards and is always aged for at least two years. No copy can equal its flavour and granular quality. While it is usually aged and grated, younger cheeses are delicious for eating.

PECORINO — cheese made of ewes' milk, eaten fresh or grated. It can be found under many different brand names at Italian specialty stores and is often used instead of Parmesan.

PROVOLONE — uncooked cheese made from whole cows' milk. It is a fairly mild cheese and usually comes shaped like a pear with grooves in it. The grooves are caused by the fibre cords with which it is suspended.

RICOTTA — a soft, cooked cheese like cottage cheese, but with a quite different flavour because it is made from whey. Used in lasagna and often used in desserts.

ROMANO — similar to Parmesan but with a more pronounced flavour. The Italians of the South prefer Romano to Parmesan.

GREECE

Most cheese made in Greece is soft and somewhat on the salty side. It is made chiefly from ewes' milk. The best known are Feta, Kasseri and Kefaloteri. Feta, which is crumbly, is often served in salads. Kasseri is made from a mixture of ewes' and goats' milk. Kefaloteri is similar to Parmesan.

CHEESE AND NUTS

CANADA

Cheddar cheese made from cows' milk has been the mainstay of the Canadian cheese industry and has become the standard cheese of North America. It is often referred to, as a matter of fact, as Canadian cheese. In England, it is more specifically called Canadian Cheddar. It comes in white and yellow and is made soft, medium and strong. Some Canadian brands are known the world over, such as Black Diamond and Cherry Hill. These are matured under special conditions and sold as commercial brands.

There is also a Colby type that ripens quickly and is softer and moister, with a more open texture than the regular Cheddar. It does not keep as well as regular Cheddar.

Oka, which used to be made only by Trappist monks at Oka in Quebec, is similar to the Italian Bel Paese, although it is neither as creamy nor as soft, and it has a more pronounced flavour. It is a cooked cheese. Fromage l'Ermite is a blue cheese made by Benedictine monks in Quebec.

UNITED STATES

While every kind of cheese from all over the world is imitated in the United States, some cheeses are American inventions.

BEER CHEESE — a pale, firm Wisconsin cheese like its German original, Bierkäse, with a rather strong taste and aroma. It is delicious with beer.

BRICK — the invention of a Wisconsin farmer; originally, bricks were used to press the curds. Firm, cream-coloured, with small eyes, it has a flavour between Limburger and Tilsit.

COON — a superior Cheddar-type cured by a patented method; crumbly, with a sharp flavour.

COTTAGE CHEESE — actually made of whole milk rather than cream, but creamy in texture. The cheese can be flavoured in countless ways and used in cookery as well as eaten plain.

FARMER CHEESE — fresh cottage cheese or pot cheese, molded or pressed to make it drier. It can be sliced.

HERKIMER — a crumbly yellow cheese similar to Cheddar, made from raw milk. It originated in Herkimer county, New York.

LIEDERKRANZ — creamy soft cheese with a flavour and aroma similar to Limburger, but still very individual. Like the other soft cheeses, it develops its full flavour only when completely ripened and allowed to reach room temperature. Packaged in small foil-wrapped rectangles.

MONTEREY JACK — a mild, pale yellow cheese that originated in California. There is a semi-soft type and a harder one used for grating.

PINEAPPLE CHEESE — invented in Litchfield, Connecticut, in the 19th century. A hard cheese of the Cheddar type, it is matured in a net that impresses a pineapple design on it.

SAGE — a bland white cheese originally flavoured with sage leaves, which gave it a mottled green appearance and herb taste. Today the flavour comes from sage oil and the green bits are other chopped leaves. When this is aged and hard, it is grated.

TILLAMOOK — An Oregon Cheddar type made of raw milk, with a wide flavour range.

VERMONT CHEDDAR — sharp-tasting and almost white, made from raw milk. It keeps well.

Two American cheeses that were designed as "copies" of European originals have become something different. Processed Limburger is a creamy, delicious spread that scarcely resembles the original natural cheese. American Munster is quite different from the Alsatian cheese; it is very mild, fresh-tasting, good in sandwiches and cooking and a fine food for breakfast.

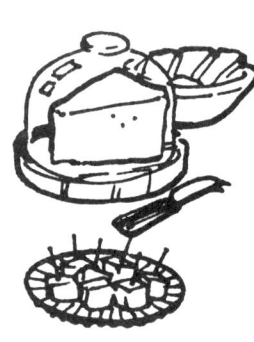

Storing cheese

The length of time cheese may be kept depends largely on its type. Soft cheeses such as Brie and Camembert dry out and spoil rapidly. Hard cheeses such as Cheddar can be kept for much longer without loss of quality. Should a hard cheese develop a mold, simply scrape or cut off the moldy part. Refrigerate all cheese after wrapping it tightly in waxed paper, transparent plastic or foil. However, always remove it in time to serve at room temperature. That's when the flavour and texture of cheese are at their best. Even cottage cheese is better at room temperature.

Do not store cheese in the freezer, for this damages both texture and flavour. The only exception to this rule is grated cheese, which can be kept frozen for up to a year without being affected.

A soft creamy cheese will keep refrigerated for up to two weeks. A semi-soft or hard cheese will keep for as long as nine weeks without loss of flavour.

NUTS

Most people think of nuts as a snack or as a garnish to add, whole or crushed, to other foods. This attitude does scant justice to their nutritional value as a staple food. While there is variation between one type and another, in general they are all rich in fat and protein. Nuts are comparable to meat in the amount and kind of protein they contain, but it is not animal protein, so we cannot substitute nuts for meat and have exactly the same nutritional values. Many nuts are an excellent source of Vitamin B1. Peanuts also contain riboflavin and niacin. Almonds are a good source of calcium. All nuts are a good source of phosphorus, and a most economical source of energy. For example, ¼ cup (50 gr) of roasted peanuts contains 100 calories. If you add to this 1 apple, which contains 60 calories, and 1 slice of ham, which contains 141 calories, you will have a protein lunch containing 301 calories with little effort and no cooking. This is not a recommendation for a steady diet; it is only an example of a protein-rich, sustaining quick meal.

ALMONDS are available in the shell, as shelled whole nuts, unblanched and blanched, and as sliced, slivered or ground blanched and roasted nuts. The most economical way to buy them is shelled and unblanched. Dry-roasted almonds are delicious but expensive.

One pound (500 gr) of almonds in the shell will give you about 1¼ cups (300 ml) shelled nuts. You will lose less than 1 ounce (25 gr) through blanching.

BRAZIL NUTS are not true nuts botanically but seeds that grow in a podlike fruit. Each seed is encased in its own hard shell. They are sold in the shell as well as shelled whole or sliced.

One pound (500 gr) of Brazil nuts in the shell will give you about 1½ cups (375 ml) shelled nuts.

CHEESE AND NUTS

CASHEWS, also the seeds of a tree, have no shells, but grow dangling from the tree fruits. They are sold plain or salted.

CHESTNUTS are true nuts, but they are treated like a vegetable and used most often with vegetables or in desserts. You will find directions for shelling and cooking them in the section on vegetables. They are sold in the shell, and water-packed canned chestnuts are available, as well as French marrons preserved in syrup.

One pound (500 gr) of chestnuts in the shell will give you about 1½ cups (375 ml) shelled nuts.

Dried chestnuts are available, and they will keep in dry storage for a long time. Fresh chestnuts, on the other hand, will keep for only a few months.

COCONUTS are the fruit of the coconut palm, which grows wherever the climate reaches the subtropical level. The tree and the fruit are essential and life-supporting in many areas of the world. Coir (the fibres from the husk), copra (dried meat from the nut) and oil pressed from the fresh nuts and from copra are important in world trade.

Because coconuts seem so different from walnuts or pecans, we do not often think of them as true nuts. They are the largest nuts we use, and have very thick shells. A fully ripe nut with no cracks or holes will be heavy and sometimes make a sloshing sound because of the milk inside. To open a coconut, pierce the three indentations at the flatter end and drain off the liquid. Sometimes a slightly less ripe nut will have a jellied liquid and will not drain. Then bake the nut for about 15 minutes. After that, a few blows with a hammer should crack it. Peel the brown skin from the white meat.

Whole coconuts can be stored for many months, like other nuts in the shell, but after opening use the milk and the meat within a week.

One average coconut will give about 1 cup (250 ml) milk and about 3 cups (750 ml) chopped meat.

FILBERTS or HAZELNUTS are sold both in the shell and shelled. You will have to blanch them yourself. They are at their best and readily available from November to February.

One pound (500 gr) of hazelnuts in the shell will give you about 1½ cups (375 ml) shelled nuts.

MACADAMIA NUTS are another example of a tree seed that we use like a nut. They are almost always husked and shelled before being sold and are very expensive. They are chiefly grown in Hawaii.

PEANUTS are not nuts at all but the fruits of a vine like the green pea vine. The "nuts" are developed under the ground. Peanuts are sold in the shell and shelled. Shelled peanuts come salted and unsalted; unsalted are better from a nutritional standpoint. Dry-roasted shelled peanuts have been oven-roasted instead of deep-fried; as a result, they have fewer calories and are more easily digestible, but they cost more.

PECANS, native American nuts, are sold in the shell, shelled, and roasted, salted or plain. They may also be obtained dry-roasted. Despite the large crop, they are never cheap.

PIGNOLAS or pine nuts are small, elongated, cream-coloured nuts, the fruit of several varieties of pines. They are usually sold shelled and are expensive.

PISTACHIOS are sold in the shell either in natural colour or with the shells artificially coloured red. The natural colour of the nut is pale green. You can sometimes get them shelled, salted or unsalted; they are expensive.

WALNUTS are sold in the shell or shelled. The shells are easy to open. Walnuts make a good dessert served with apples or muscatel raisins.

Storing nuts

Nuts in the shell can be kept at room temperature if you are planning to use them within two months. If you plan to keep them longer, they should be treated like fresh fruits. Since nuts have such a high fat content, they may develop a rancid flavour. Therefore, once a can, jar or bag of shelled nuts has been opened, refrigerate the contents, well covered, or freeze. Unlike most other foods, nuts can be refrozen and do not have to be thawed out before you use them in cooking.

Shelling nuts

Cashews, macadamias and pine nuts are sold without shells. Almonds have such thin shells that they can be shelled with the fingers. Peanuts are also easy to shell. Walnuts and pecans can be shelled by gently applying pressure with a nutcracker; they will usually split neatly. For information on shelling chestnuts, see page 349, Vol. II. Pistachios need to be pried apart; they are usually already split at one edge. Brazil nuts and the hard-shelled wild nuts are very difficult to shell. To help the process, soak them in hot water or boil them for a few minutes, or freeze them and crack them open while still frozen. A nutpick may be needed with some nuts.

Blanching nuts

All true nuts have a close skin inside the hard shell. While this skin is edible, it is sometimes sufficiently tough to make peeling advisable. Cashews, pine nuts and macadamias come without skins. Almonds, Brazil nuts and chestnuts are dropped into boiling water; the skins of almonds will be loose enough in 2 minutes to pop off when you squeeze the nut between thumb and forefinger. It will take 5 minutes or longer to loosen the skins of Brazil nuts. Fresh chestnuts take only a few minutes, but as they get older long soaking is necessary. Peanuts, of course, can be peeled easily. Filberts or hazelnuts have an edible skin, but for some preparations you may prefer them peeled. Either blanch them like almonds, or roast them in a 350°F (180°C) oven for about 15 minutes and then rub them vigorously in a coarse towel. Walnuts and pecans and the wild American nuts have such tight, thick skins that it is difficult to get them off. Blanching tends to soften the nut, so toasting and rubbing as with hazelnuts may work better, but it will never be easy to get rid of all the skin in the hollows.

Nuts with cheese and a glass of Madeira make a perfect conclusion to a meal. Walnuts with port are an old English tradition. Any nut can be served with cheese, fruit or wine as a delicious dessert.

CHAPTER 19

Wine: The cup that cheers

THE GLASS OF WINE is for many people a means of promoting friendship and hospitality, its appeal deriving from its flavour, its aroma or bouquet and its colour. The right bottle of wine can make a good dinner superb, because wine has the wonderful faculty of complementing the flavours of food, thus enhancing the enjoyment of eating. It also sparks conversation and conviviality. Spirits can make one heavy and dull; wine is conducive to gaiety.

Unfortunately, some people are terrified they will make a mistake in the kind of wine they serve, or in the comments they make about a wine served by someone else. This is largely nonsense. The first thing you must understand is that the choice of wine is a matter of personal taste. You are the one to decide which wine to serve with what food. Think of wine as a pleasant beverage with infinite varieties and beautiful colours, and don't be afraid to make a mistake with it.

Basically, wine is the fermented juice of ripe grapes, crushed after harvesting. It can range in colour from deep red to light pink to almost "colourless" white. The colour of the wine depends on the colour of the grape skins, which can be red, black or green, and the length of time they were allowed to stay in the vat when the wine was made.

Although wines can be made of other fruits (and even vegetables), the word "wine" used alone always means an alcoholic drink made from grapes. The magic ingredient that turns the grapes into wine is yeast. Yeast cells are present on the grape skins, and when the fruit is mashed the yeast starts to feed on the sugar in the mash and convert it into alcohol and carbon dioxide. (Grapes normally contain enough sugar to complete this fermentation process, but other fruits and vegetables need added sugar.) When the yeast has ample food, it starts to bud and produces more yeast cells to finish the process. The carbon dioxide bubbles carry the yeast cells through the mash, thus helping to stir and mix it.

A table wine can be dry or sec, semi-dry or demi-sec, sweet or doux. In dry wines, all the sugar in the grapes is converted to alcohol. When the grapes are sweeter, there is more sugar than the yeast can use and some remains to make a sweeter wine.

The most famous wine-growing areas in the world are Bordeaux, Burgundy and Champagne in France. A few other famous regions are the Rhône and Loire valleys and Alsace in France, and the Rhine and Moselle districts in Germany. But wine is made everywhere in the world where grapes can be grown, from Africa to Canada, from Hungary to California.

CLASSIFYING WINES

In France, wine growers have been well organized for a very long time, and French wines must be labeled according to very strict standards. Growers in the Burgundy region have one classification system, those in Bordeaux another, and those in Alsace yet another. No other wine-producing country has anything like the elaborate organization that exists in France. While we may speak of a Chianti or a Soave with a reasonable certainty as to its general character, to call a wine just a Burgundy or a Bordeaux reveals much less about it. The difference between the best and the least in these famous French wines is tremendous. Wines marketed under the name of the region alone will be the least impressive; yet they may be quite pleasant, especially if the year has been a good one. Wines designated as being from a small area within the region, such as the Mâconnais or Côte de Beaune in Burgundy, or Médoc or Saint-Emilion in Bordeaux, will have been produced more carefully. Those wines marked with the name of a specific district, town or even vineyard, or in Bordeaux a château, and identified with appellation contrôlée, are wines that have been produced according to very exacting standards. In France, appellation contrôlée is the mark of authenticity of origin.

Of course, all this does not mean that the wine is good, or that you will like it. Weather, area of production, genius and experience are the ultimate factors the ultimate factors in making it good; a grape will produce only what it has taken from the soil it has grown in, from the sun that has warmed it, from the rain that has washed it. Your taste determines which wine to buy.

Just to confuse the issue further, there are wines produced in the United States, Chile and South Africa that are labeled "Bordeaux" or "Burgundy" or "Riesling" or "Sauternes" or "Champagne". They have no real right to use these regional names, but at least you will recognize that the wine producer intends to sell you a wine of that particular type. A more informative system is to name the wine after the principal grape used in making it (Cabernet Sauvignon for red and Chardonnay for white wines). They are called varietal wines. For instance cabernet sauvignon for red wines, or chardonnay for white wines. Many other wines are named after the places where they are produced.

Judging wines

In all wines there is a delicate balance between acidity and sweetness. This balance depends on the grape and the growing conditions of the year in which it was produced, which in turn determines the wine's ability to improve in the bottle with age. In truly great wine, this balance is just right. Other aspects of good wines are the bouquet (aroma and fragrance), the breed (character or finesse) and the body or substance of the wine.

These characteristics vary not only from type to type but from vineyard to vineyard. So when you are particularly pleased with a wine, take note of the name of the producer on the label. A pommard of one vineyard house can be quite different from that of another. Half the fun in serving wine is discovering what you and your friends enjoy, what best enhances the flavour of the food you serve.

Every type gives a different taste sensation. Only by tasting will you develop preferences.

Vintage

Vintage is the gathering of the grapes, and the particular year when the grapes were gathered and made into wine. It suggests the synthesis of weather and physical conditions of that specific growing season. There are good, poor and in-between years. Vintage is most important in French wines, because Italy, Spain and Portugal do not have the same weather variations. The price you pay for a French wine often depends on the quality of its vintage. Modest-priced wines of a good year may be better than expensive wines of a poor year.

Wine storage

Wines in bottles with corks should be stored lying on their sides. Those with screw caps can stand up. The reason for storing corked wine lying down is simple: When the wine is lying down the cork is moistened by the wine; this means that it remains wet and swollen, and it is airtight. It doesn't necessarily mean that you can't stand corked bottles upright, but you are taking a chance that air might get in and spoil the wine.

Another important thing to remember is that too much heat or too much cold affects wine adversely. Never allow a bottle to remain in the sun or an overheated place or in the freezer.

If you have one or two bottles that you plan to serve within a few days, simply keep them cool — under 60°F (15.6°C), if possible — and in a dark place. If you have bottles that you plan to store for weeks or months, it is important to find a dark spot that is not subject to vibration, is not damp or musty and has a constant temperature of 55° to 60° (12.8° to 15.6°C). If this is impossible, leave the wine in storage with your dealer and take home a few bottles at a time as you need them. Remember, wine continues to mature in the bottle. If you chill it for a long time the process stops. If you keep it at too high a temperature, the process is speeded up and the wine may spoil.

Wine with food

While some wines are best served alone — very sweet or fortified wines, for instance — most wine is the perfect accompaniment to food. Choosing the right wine has developed into a status game, but you should ignore all the nonsense and snobbery and just think of the tastes involved. Suppose that your main dish tonight is chicken in a cream sauce and that you are planning to serve steak tomorrow. You will sense that the same wine will not do for both meals. The white chicken in its creamy, ivory sauce seems to call for a light wine; consider a Sauternes or Graves, a Vouvray, a Moselle if you feel extravagant or a simple Orvieto. But a light red would also be acceptable, such as an Italian Valpolicella or a French Beaujolais. On the other hand, the robust flavour of steak seems to be best accompanied by a full-flavoured red. Such wines include Chambertin, Margaux and the Italian Bardolino. That's all there is to it, save in summer when a lighter, cool red wine will be more appropriate.

Here is a brief outline that may serve as a guide, but do not follow it slavishly.

Serve red wine with beef and lamb roasts, steak, stews, game, duck and goose. Veal and cheese are served with red wine too, although white wines and rosés are acceptable with either.

Serve rosé wine or Beaujolais with salmon, fish stews, kidneys, omelets, soufflés and cold cuts.

Serve white wine with fish and shellfish, chicken, turkey and ham.

Serve Champagne throughout an elaborate meal. It should follow other wines only if a toast is being offered at the end of dinner.

Serve dessert wines — Marsala, Madeira, sweet sherries, Tokay — with fruits, compotes, rich cakes, tarts and pies, mild or creamy cheeses.

After-dinner wines are served at room temperature. Port is the most usual and is often served with a good Cheddar or Stilton cheese. Cognac or brandy and liqueurs are also served after dinner. Serving temperatures are very important for wine appreciation. See later in this chapter.

Generally speaking, wines can be classified in four major categories — still table wines, sparkling wines, fortified wines and apéritif wines.

WINE CATEGORIES

Red wines

A wine is red when the skins of dark grapes are permitted to remain in the juice during fermentation. The alcohol dissolves the colouring of the skins. Sometimes, of course, it is because special wine colourings have been added. A red wine can be pinkish-red, purple-red or even brownish-red.

Red wines of great distinction are produced in Burgundy and Bordeaux in France. In these French reds, the grapes are the crucial element.

The best Burgundy wine is made from Pinot grapes — Pinot Noir and Pinot Blanc or white Chardonnay. However, Gamay grapes are also extensively grown in Burgundy; it is these that produce Beaujolais. A wine that is lighter than most red Burgundies, Beaujolais is prized by many when it is very young. A good quality Beaujolais is excellent whenever you want a lively young red wine. Red Burgundy wines are quite dry, some of them even astringents, and they have a long life. But Beaujolais should be drunk when it is still young. With an excellent roast beef or a broiled steak, you may want a full-bodied red wine; Burgundy is perfect for this.

The Bordeaux area of France includes perhaps the most famous vineyard acreage in the world. It is the land of château wines, and there are hundreds of them. A château is the home or centre of a wine-producing estate. It may be a true château — an old castel house — or it may be simply the office that serves the surrounding vineyards. In some cases, the wine is bottled at the château. In these cases, the legend *mis en bouteille au château* should be stamped on or burned into the cork. (The corks in estate-bottled Burgundies are marked *mis en bouteille au domaine*.) Sometimes the wines from small châteaux are very expensive, but occasionally good wines from small châteaux are quite reasonable.

The great areas producing red Bordeaux wine, or claret as the English call it, include Médoc, Graves, Pomerol and Saint-Emilion. (Graves also produces excellent white wines.) Most Bordeaux grow old gracefully, especially those from vineyards of the 1855 classification and those known as "cru bougeois". It is not uncommon for the best to be delicious when they are 15 to 20 years old, or even more. However, there is no guarantee that the wine you buy will be one of these. Wines of different years have different characteristics and mature at different times.

The Rhône Valley offers several interesting wines, two of which are the Hermitage and the Côte Rôtie, but the best known is Châteauneuf-du-Pape, soft and delicious, purple-red in colour. This wine is a blend of the juices of several grapes, all grown on the slopes near Avignon, where the Romans found wine for their French legions so many centuries ago.

One can find in France, surrounding the three main wine producing regions, a great number of local wines of controlled appellation such as those of LanguedoRoussillon, Southwest Provence or the Loire, quite apart from many red wines blended from the product of several vineyards.

Italy also produces red wines. These do not pretend to compete with the greatest wines of France, but greater vine uniformity, improved techniques and cleaner vineyards are at the root of remarkable progress. Legislation, too, has helped with the creation of DOC's and DOCG's that are standards similar to those used in France. Many wines from Tuscany and Piedmont have won recognition for such names as Sassiscaia, Tignanello and the House of Gaja. The famous Chianti is not always bottled in a straw-covered flask; good brands are available in conventional bottles. True, well-controlled classico Chianti bears the mark of a little black cockerel on the neck of the bottle. Another symbol that indicates excellence is the putto, or little angel, which can also be found on the neck of the bottle. Chianti is an oddity in that it is made from a blend of several different grape varieties.

Valpolicella is a light, delicate red wine that seems to go well with many foods. Barolo and Bardolino are robust red wines.

The vintage of Italian wines does not mean very much. This is not because the wine is inferior to French; in Italy the equitable climate keeps most vintages uniformly good. This is why the producer is so important for quality, uniformity and, most important, continuity: Each time you open a bottle of a specific brand, it will be as good as the others you have tried of this brand.

Spain, Portugal, Hungary, Yugoslavia, Greece and Switzerland all produce red wines, some of which are very good.

The Spanish Rioja wines marked Reserva have been aged until they are quite good, with a fine colour and taste, which is fairly tart. Of Hungary's delicious reds, the best known is the robust Egri Bikavéer (bull's blood of Eger), which is different from all other reds. Greek reds taste of resin, an acquired taste for most North Americans, but they are palatable and especially good with Mediterranean food. The most familiar of the Swiss wines, Dôle, resembles Beaujolais.

North America now produces millions of gallons of wine annually. California is responsible for the largest amount. The generic California wines are all blends, but the varietals must contain at least 51 per cent of the juice of the grape named on the label. Here again, you must know the producer, because the best will bottle only what the label lists. Among the names you will find are Cabernet Sauvignon, Pinot Noir and Gamay — all true wine grapes similar to the same grapes grown in France. The grape grown most widely in California is the Zinfandel.

Smaller amounts of wine come from New York State, Ohio and near Lake Ontario as well as in the eastern townships of Quebec in both the United States and Canada. Most of these eastern wines are made from native American grapes, Vitis labrusca. The word "foxy" has been used to describe these wines; they taste of the grapes, with a fruity-earthy quality. Canadian wines generally are immature and a little raw, but they are perfectly suitable for certain circumstances.

When you travel in wine country, don't miss tasting the *vins ordinaires* or *vins du pays*. These are local or regional wines of the district. Most of them never travel even as far as the next town, for the simple reason that they cannot stand being shipped from one place to another; it would upset their delicate chemistry. And many wine experts believe that even great wines taste better on home ground, served with the local food specialities.

White wines

White wines are made from white grapes, or from dark grapes with the skins removed.

White table wines are generally lighter and less robust in flavour than red wines. Despite this, many people find them more difficult to digest. Certainly they mix badly with spirits.

White wines are served with fish, seafood, egg dishes and certain types of poultry. Italian chicken dishes with tomato sauce are better with a red wine, but a roasted chicken is usually served with a light white wine.

There is a large variety of white wines to choose from. The areas famous for reds — Burgundy and Bordeaux — also produce great white wines, as do the regions of the Loire and Alsace, the Rhine and Moselle valleys and other areas of Germany, Italy and Switzerland. Canada and the United States also produce them.

White Burgundies are dry, full-flavoured, robust. White Montrachet, conceded by connoisseurs to be the greatest white Burgundy, is about the most expensive too. When this great

wine is hyphenated — Chevalier-Montrachet, Bâtard-Montrachet — it is a different wine; it has less quality and is less expensive. Montrachet is a joy to serve on special occasions. Another fine choice is a good Chablis, a lovely wine with a flinty taste. In the case of Chablis, the shipper's name is important, so be sure to note the full information on the label when you find one you like. Meursault wines are soft and delicate, with a wonderful bouquet. Another fine dry white is the ever-popular Pouilly-Fuissé. Here, too, the name of the shipper or producer is important.

White Bordeaux wines are many and varied. Among the best known are Sauternes and Graves. Sauternes are generally not dry, but they are perfect for desserts, or for between meals served with wine biscuits. Château d'Yquem, a Sauternes, is the finest of all naturally sweet wines. Of course, there are many less expensive than this. The wines of Graves are drier and more versatile.

Vouvray is the best known of the wines of the Loire Valley. It can be sparkling as well as still, and even the still wine is naturally a little *pétillant*, or sparkling. Pouilly-Fumé and Sancerre from the upper Loire are also popular. Muscadet from the lower valley is inexpensive, light and delicious, and especially good with fish.

The fragrant wines of Alsace are named after the grapes used — Riesling, Traminer, Gewürztraminer (very perfumed), Sylvaner. They are all somewhat dry and should be drunk when young. In general, they come in a tall bottle known as alsatian.

Many connoisseurs consider German white wines the greatest in the world. They often have a flowery quality quite different from French wines. Rhine wines are rich, Moselle wines light. German wines are attractively bottled in tall thin bottles; the Rhine bottles are brown, the Moselles are green.

German wine terminology is quite different from French. *Spätlese* means "late picked", picked two or three weeks after the normal harvest. *Auslese* indicates wine from even sweeter, very ripe grapes, picked bunch by bunch. *Beerenauslese* is the label on wines made from the ripest and soundest "berries" picked from each bunch. *Cabinet* or *Kabinettwein,* formerly used for the proprietor's own wine, usually stands for a dry wine. *Naturwein* is natural wine, without added sugar.

Among Rhine wines some famous names are Johannisberg and Hochheim (probably the source of the English term "hock"). Bernkastel, Piesport, Brauneberg and Graach are some of the finest Moselle whites.

Drink German wines when they are young — one, two or three years old; they then are at their best.

Italy produces a large number of good white wines, although few are exported for they do not travel well. The most familiar exports are Verdicchio dei Castelli di Jesi, Orvieto, Soave, Frascati, Est! Est!! Est!!! and white Chianti.

Orvieto (sweet or dry) is inexpensive and delicious. Soave from the right producer is good with many Italian dishes. Frascati is a delicious golden dry wine. Est! Est!! Est!!! is more distinguished by its odd name than its quality. White Chianti is not as good as the red, but it is satisfactory for an everyday wine and is excellent in cooking. Many Italian whites produced from the Chardonnay vine have now come on the market.

Spain and Portugal export a few white wines. Alicante is pleasant, and some white wines are made in Rioja, where the best Spanish reds are produced. Other whites from Portugal and Spain can be found; they are usually inexpensive, but unfortunately they are often "green-tasting" and thin, even acid. The peninsula is distinguished for its fortified wines rather than these.

Hungary exports some excellent white wines from Lake Balaton, made from Riesling and Furmint grapes, and from Somlo in western Hungary. Greek whites usually taste of resin like the reds,

but there is a delicate white called Pallini.

Grinzing, a suburb of Vienna, produces the best known Austrian white wine and a Grizinger Spätlese of a good year can taste as delicious as a good Champagne. Gumpoldskirchener is another delicious, somewhat spicy white. These are different from German wines and absolutely different from French wines. Do not expect to keep them for long; they lose aroma and flavour as they age.

The Swiss produce more white wines than red. Fendant, Neuchâtel and Dézaley are fairly well known and there are other wines from Valais canton named according to the grape used. These are particularly good with cheese dishes.

Chile exports delicious and inexpensive Riesling and Rhine wines, bottled in attractive, squat green bottles. South African wines occasionally find their way into North American markets; none is distinguished.

California white wines can be excellent. They are made from Sauvignon Blanc and Semillon grapes (the same kind of grapes that grow in Bordeaux); Chardonnay (like the Pinot Chardonnay of Burgundy) and Pinot Blanc; Chenin Blanc (like the Loire grape), Riesling, Traminer and Gewürztraminer (like the German and Alsatian grapes). Some producers still sell generic wines called Sauterne (without the s in California), Chablis, Rhine and Moselle. New York State white wines are also found under both generic and varietal names.

Rosé wines

Rosé wines are pink or rose coloured, easily distinguishable from the lightest red. They are made by several methods — drawing off the juice from unpressed black grapes; drawing off the juice of grapes before they have fermented very long; or blending red wines with various white wines. Champagne rosé is made by adding a local red wine (bousy) to the unfermented juice.

It has become the fashion to say that rosé goes with anything and can replace a red or white, but that is not strictly true. Generally speaking, rosés are wines of much less distinction than reds and whites. Nevertheless, they are pleasant and seem particularly suited to some foods. They are especially good with omelets.

Among French rosés are Tavel and Lirac from the Rhône Valley, Anjou and Jura; the *vin gris* of Alsace-Lorraine; and several from Provence (one of the best known is Château Ste-Roseline).

Spain produces a few rosés not unlike those of the Rhône, and Portugal has distinguished itself in the production of superior rosés with a light sparkle. The best known in North America are Mateus and Faisca. Chilean rosés are excellent.

Rosés produced in the United States are made principally of Grenache, Gamay and Zinfandel grapes. The colour of the wine varies, as does the taste, which can be dry or fairly sweet (Bloch).

SPARKLING WINES

In still table wines, all the carbon dioxide is released before the wine is bottled. In sparkling wines some of the gas is left in the wine, and that is what makes the bubbles. Extra sugar and yeast may be added so that the wine undergoes a second fermentation in the bottle (Champagne method).

There is no reason sparkling wines could not be served to accompany food just as still wines are, but because they seem so special and generally are so expensive, we tend to serve them less frequently. An expensive vintage Champagne will not be appreciated properly with a simple meal, and a sweet Champagne will not taste best with a roast. All sparkling wines seem especially designed for festive occasions. Champagne is particularly good for large parties or buffet dinners that offer a variety of foods, for it can be served throughout such meals. Sparkling rosés, like still rosés, are much simpler and less rich than the heavy sparkling whites or reds, so they can be served with anything you choose. A dry Champagne can make a good apéritif, especially if you are serving a very elegant hors d'oeuvre such as caviar.

True Champagne is made only in France, in the small area around the city of Reims and epernay on the Marne. No other sparkling wine has the right to use the name, even though some do.

Champagne is costly because making it involves expensive time and labor. Every bottle is first fitted with a temporary cork, then stored cork down in a slanted position for many months. A slight turn is given to each bottle two or three times a week, so that the impurities produced by the fermentation will descend and settle around the cork. Eventually the neck of the bottle is immersed in a brine solution and frozen. The cork is removed with a special kind of pliers, taking the impurities along with it. In the gap left at the top, a small quantity of sugar syrup is added; the amount determines the sweetness or dryness of the finished Champagne. The bottle is then recorked, wired and sealed, and stored for at least a year.

Brut means the driest Champagne; *extra sec* means very dry; *sec*, dry; *demi-sec*, sweet; *doux*, very sweet. Each term indicates a specific percentage of sugar in the Champagne. *Demi-sec* and *doux* Champagnes are good with desserts.

Champagne *Blanc de Blancs* means one made entirely from white grapes, whereas most Champagne are made from a mixture of red and white grapes. All Champagnes are blends, but vintage Champagnes are blends of wines of a single year.

Another bubbly wine is sparkling Burgundy, which can be delicious and certainly looks beautiful. It was originally made in order to use inferior wine, but the end result is a rich wine, splendid in the glass.

Italy also produces sparkling red and white wines; these will have Spumante on the label. Asti Spumanti is well known. A sparkling white wine similar to Champagne is made in Germany; it is called *Sekt*. Spain and Portugal make some excellent sparkling wines. Sparkling rosé wines are made in France and in Portugal.

A few other sparkling French wines are made, including Sparkling Vouvray and Saumur of the Loire Valley.

FORTIFIED WINES

Fortified wines are those to which brandy is added, before or after they have completed their fermentation. Sherry, port and Madeira are the principal examples. Brandy added during fermentation stops the process, and some sugar is left unconverted. This is the method used to make port and muscatel. When the brandy is added after fermentation is complete, it produces a wine such as sherry.

Sherry comes from the area around Jerez de la Frontera in Andalusia in southern Spain. There are two things especially necessary in the making of sherry: One is *flor*, a yeast or bacteria that grows on the surface of the wine while it is aging in the barrel and forms a crust, shutting out any harmful bacteria. The other is the *solera system*, in which casks are arranged in tiers so that sherry of different ages is slowly blended as it passes from top to bottom. Sherry is always a blend of the wines of several years. Wines labeled Amontillado, Fino or Manzanilla are dry, pale and delicate. Serve these cold as apéritif wines. Amoroso, Oloroso or Brown sherries are rich and sweet. Serve these at room temperature after dinner or on the rocks as an apéritif.

When sherry is used in a sauce, as for meats or game, it should be dry or moderately dry. When used for fruits or desserts, the sweet type is the best.

Port comes from Oporto in Portugal. Vintage port is not a blend, but other types are blended. Although one can find port labeled "dry", none of them is really unsweet. White port, made of

white grapes, is the driest and makes a good apéritif. Ruby port is a blend of young wines, fruity, rich in colour and sweet. Tawny port is usually made of older wines and is matured in wood; it is not as sweet as ruby port.

Madeira is made on the island of Madeira. The long, slow process of maturing this wonderful wine means that it is never cheap. It is good served cool in small glasses, with a rich soup at the start of a meal or with a strong cheese at the end of a meal or added to sauces for entrées and desserts. For flavouring meats and fruit desserts it is unequaled.

Sercial Madeira is dry and is perfect served chilled as an appetizer. Bual is rich, and Malmsey is sweet. Rainwater Madeira is very light in colour and texture.

Other good well-known fortified wines are Malaga and muscatel from Spain and Marsala from Sicily. Both Malaga and muscatel are used with game dishes and desserts. Marsala is excellent with cheese dishes and desserts.

Natural sweet wines

Some of the world's most famous wines are the luscious sweet dessert wines. Noted for centuries is the Hungarian wine Tokay; its grapes grow in volcanic soil between two volcanic cones. The wine is golden and delicious and has a reputation for bringing the dying back to health.

Barsac, a subdivision of the French district of Sauternes, produces a very sweet white wine. Other sweet Sauternes include Château d'Yquem, previously mentioned. These wines are exceptionally sweet because of a mold called "noble rot" (*Botrytis cineria*), which attacks the grapes and sucks out the liquid, leaving them shriveled, like raisins, and much sweeter. This added sweetness and the flavour of the mold itself give a special quality to these wines.

APÉRITIF WINES

An apéritif wine results from the addition of an infusion of various herbs, roots and barks to the fermented juice of grapes. The combination of the ingredients used is usually a well-guarded secret.

Vermouth is the best known of all the apéritif wines. It can be dry (French type) or sweet (Italian type).

There are dozens of other apéritif wines, such as Dubonnet, Saint-Raphaël and Byrrh. Choose whichever you prefer. Apéritif wines are usually served cold. A slice of lemon or lime is a very pleasant addition to any of them. Apéritif wines sometimes are served on the rocks as an agreeable and mild substitute for cocktails. In cooking, apéritif wines are often used to flavour desserts, and dry vermouth can be used in meats and sauces just as you would use white wine.

SPIRITS

A spirit is a distilled liquor. These include brandy, liqueurs and cordials, whisky, rum, gin, aquavit and vodka.

Brandy is a spirit distilled from freshly fermented grape wine, or from the juices of other fruits. The most famous of all grape brandies is Cognac, which takes its name from the locality in France where it has been produced for generations. Other brandies are made from apricots, peaches, blackberries, cherries and apples.

Whisky is a spirit distilled from fermented mashes made from malt alone or from a blend of malt and unmalted cereals.

Rum is a spirit obtained by fermenting and then distilling molasses and sugar cane.

Gin derives its name from the Dutch word *genever*, meaning juniper. It is a spirit distilled from rye or barley and flavoured with juniper berries. It is called *schnapps* by the Dutch, although this word is also used in Europe to mean any "hard liquor" taken straight. When Scan-

dinavians say *schnapps*, they mean aquavit. Gin is so extensively made in the Netherlands that it is also called Hollands. Needless to say that the most popular gin is the english dry gin.

Liqueurs and cordials are highly fortified, sweetened spirits flavoured with various herbs, aromatic spices, fruits or extracts. They are served in relatively small glasses and sipped slowly. The most famous are Benedictine, Chartreuse, Grand Marnier, Cointreau, Curaçao, crème de menthe, anisette, kirsch, and kümel.

Aquavit is a spirit distilled from a grain mash or potatoes and flavoured with caraway.

Vodka is a highly alcoholic spirit distilled from a mash of potatoes or cereals.

SERVING WINE

The choice of what alcoholic beverage to serve with a meal depends on personal taste and the food budget, but there are some basic rules.

Cocktails have no place at a formal luncheon or dinner. Their ingredients tend to dull the taste and actually lessen the enjoyment of the food and wine to follow. Choose instead a dry vermouth, a dry sherry or Madeira. If the hors d'oeuvre are highly spiced, a whisky and soda, aquavit or vodka can be served. However, an apéritif is not a necessary introduction to a meal.

A single good dry wine can be served throughout a meal. If two or more wines are to be served, here is the sequence to follow: White wine, generally lighter in body and flavour, should be served before red wine, which is more robust and full flavoured. But in any case, serve a less good wine or a less robust wine before a better or more full-flavoured wine. For instance, serve white wine with the soup or fish and red wine with the meat course. If you are serving two red or two white wines, the younger wine must be served first. For example, a Beaujolais and a Burgundy served at the same meal would be served in that order. When one of the wines you are serving is sweeter and the other is drier, let the dry precede the sweet.

However, at a simple family meal, or with close friends at an intimate little dinner, it is perfectly suitable to serve only a single wine.

A truly sweet wine is served only with dessert. Instead of a dessert wine, you can serve a liqueur or cordial.

Wine is never served with a salad that is dressed with vinegar.

Temperatures for serving wine

In general, white wines and rosé wines should be served chilled, at a temperature between 40° and 50°F (4° and 10°C). Place them in the refrigerator at least two hours before you are going to serve them. However, the flowery white wines of the Moselle and Rhine vineyards are better served not so cold. Champagne and other sparkling wines should be served extremely cold, preferably from a container filled with crushed ice.

A red wine should be allowed to stand upright, not on its side in a basket, at room temperature for an hour or two before being served. Temperatures between 65° and 75° (18° and 24°C) bring out its flavour and bouquet to best advantage. About an hour before dinner, uncork the bottle and let it stand open until you are ready to serve. This permits the wine to "breathe" and enhances the flavour. Avoid alternate cooling and warming of a wine.

Wineglasses

Wine is its own best ornament and attraction. Wineglasses should be colourless, clear and thin, so that the colour and sparkle of the beverage are displayed to the best advantage. And they should be of ample size to allow for the enjoyment of the aroma and bouquet.

The selection of glasses need not be complicated. Choose a 9-ounce (275 ml) bubble-shaped wineglass for reds, an 8-ounce (250 ml) tulip-shape for whites. Or choose one glass in two sizes — a 6-ounce (170 ml) glass for reds, a

WINE: THE CUP THAT CHEERS

5-ounce (150 ml) glass for whites. If you want to use an all-purpose glass suitable for both red and white wines, a stemmed tulip-shaped 8½-ounce (265 ml) wineglass is ideal.

Sherry, Madeira and port are often served in stemmed 4-ounce (115 ml) glasses.

Champagne is served in long-stemmed glasses of coupe shape, sometimes with hollow stems, or in flute-shaped glasses, containing between 5 and 7 ounces (150 and 200 ml). A popular alternative is a tulip-shaped glass containing 8 ounces (250 ml).

Cordials and liqueurs exhale their fine aroma and display their delicate tints in stemmed clear glasses containing 1 to 3 ounces (25 to 85 ml).

Fine brandy, which has its own special body and bouquet, is enjoyed most when held and sipped from a short-stemmed deep glass of ample width.

A few rules on serving wine

A gracious host sees that the glasses of guests are never completely empty, and that they are continually replenished. If a guest declines, however, never insist; always have a non-alcoholic beverage available to serve instead.

The recipient of a toast remains seated and does not drink with the other guests. He or she acknowledges the toast immediately afterward, by rising and expressing appreciation.

Formal dinners should display glassware that is all of the same design. Glasses are set to the right, in the order in which the wines are served. No more than three glasses, including the water goblet, should be set out at one time. If more than two wines are to be served, the additional glasses are placed on the table immediately before the wine is poured. The glasses can be placed in a straight line in front of the place setting,

The correct glassware

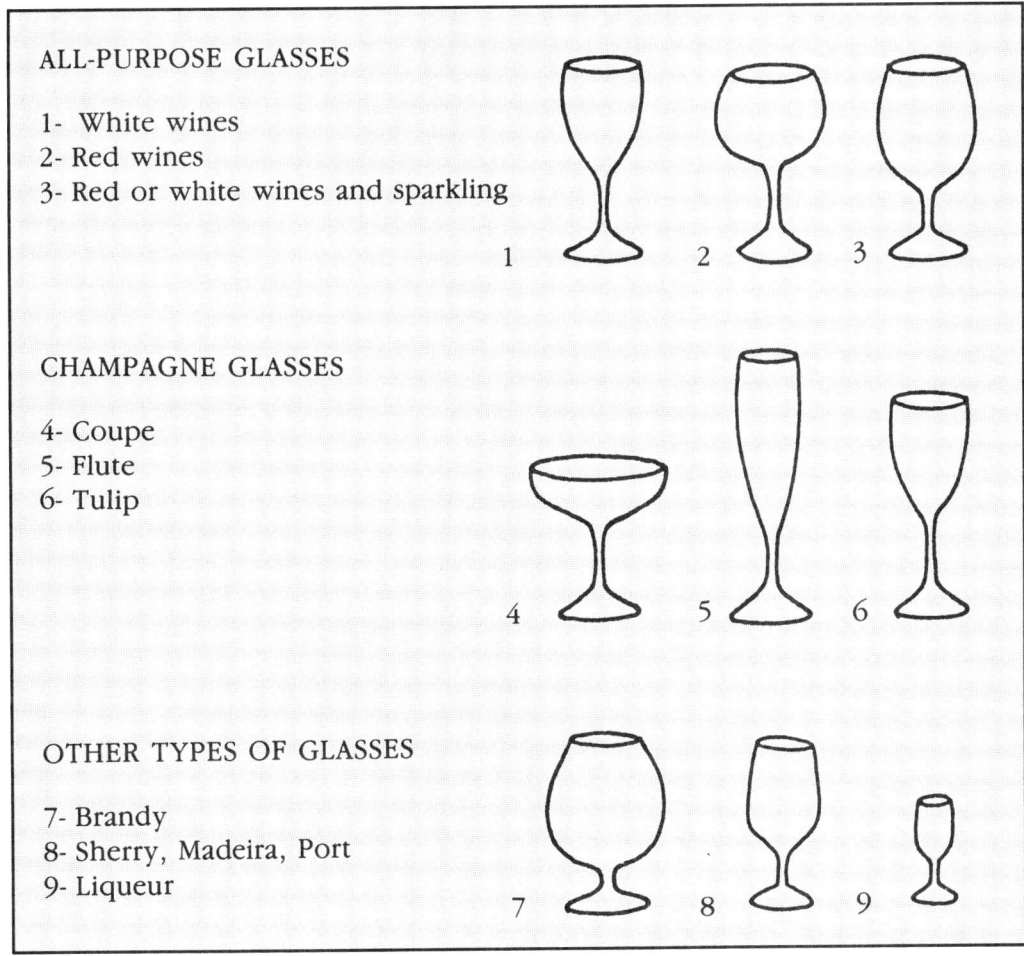

ALL-PURPOSE GLASSES

1- White wines
2- Red wines
3- Red or white wines and sparkling

CHAMPAGNE GLASSES

4- Coupe
5- Flute
6- Tulip

OTHER TYPES OF GLASSES

7- Brandy
8- Sherry, Madeira, Port
9- Liqueur

always beginning with the water goblet, or at an angle in the same order, with the water goblet nearest the centre of the table. To save space, they are sometimes arranged in a cluster above the knives.

A wineglass should never be filled to the brim. If you pour enough to fill it almost to the halfway mark, there will be room in the glass for swirling the wine to release its aroma and give you the pleasure of smell as well as taste.

For the first course, the wine is poured after the food has been served. For succeeding courses, the wine is served as soon as the service for the previous course has been removed.

The wine is poured from its own bottle by the host. The bottle is never passed around.

Wine should be disturbed as little as possible before serving. It should never be shaken. Do not serve a fine wine immediately after buying it. Fine old wines should be stored for several weeks or longer before serving to allow any sediment to settle to the bottom of the bottle.

All bottled still wines, with the exception of light white wines, can be recorked after being partly consumed and served again later, or used for cooking. Champagnes and other sparkling wines must be finished after opening; they lose their effervescence quickly.

Liqueurs and brandies can be served with coffee at the end of the meal.

COOKING WITH WINE

Cooking with wine is as simple as cooking with water, and comparatively little is needed to enhance the flavour of a whole dish. Don't worry about the alcohol content, since the alcohol in the wine evaporates while the food is cooking and only the flavour remains. Not only does wine give a definite flavour to food, but its slight acidity also tenderizes.

To use wine in cooking, follow this general guide: dry red wine with red meat and game; lighter, less-dry red wine with kidneys and stews; white wine with fish, shellfish and chicken. Use dry vermouth just as you would white wine.

But these are not ironclad rules; the famous coq au vin is a chicken dish made with red wine, and there are famous French fish stews made with red wine.

● Wine should never be added to a dish just before serving. It should simmer with the food or in the sauce while it is being cooked, because as the wine cooks it reduces and becomes an extract that flavours. Wine added too late in the preparation will give a harsh quality to the dish.

● When using both wine and herbs in a dish, the final result is better when an infusion or extract is made of both and then added to the food. To do this, add 1 teaspoon (5 ml) of the chosen herb, or ½ teaspoon (2 ml) of each if you are using two herbs, to 1 cup (250 ml) of red or white wine. Simmer for 10 minutes. Add 1 teaspoon (5 ml) of butter and the grated rind of 1 lemon, and simmer for another 5 minutes. The wine and herb extract is then ready to add to whatever food you wish. Use it all at once, or just a tablespoon (15 ml) at a time. Store the remainder in a tightly closed bottle or jar in the refrigerator.

● The colour of a red-wine sauce is sometimes unattractive. By adding a teaspoon (5 ml) of tomato paste or a bit of commercial gravy, you will improve the colour and add richness and body to the sauce.

● Remember that even a little wine adds greatly to the flavour of food.

● Leftover wines should never be thrown away. Keep them in a well-corked bottle, refrigerated. It does not matter if wines of different types are stored in the same bottle. Use the leftovers to flavour a gravy, stew or even stewed fruits or as part of a marinade.

⚬━ A tablespoon or two (15 to 30 ml) of red wine added to French dressing instead of vinegar will work wonders on meat or vegetable salads, but don't use wine on lettuce.

⚬━ If you run short of wine for a recipe that calls for it, substitute an equal quantity of apple juice, or ½ cup (125 ml) water with the juice of 1 lemon for each cup (250 ml) of wine required.

Remember, wine is composed mostly of water. It provides all or part of the liquid you need for the dish you are preparing, plus the subtle flavour that blends so beautifully with meat, fish, fruits or other food. It is used as you would use consommé — to enrich, flavour and moisturize.

It is not true that only a chosen few have the palate or purse to appreciate and to afford cooking with wine. Anyone can enjoy it. All you have to do is buy the occasional bottle and keep it in the refrigerator after opening. Add a bit now and then to your favourite recipes. This is the best and easiest way of learning to cook with wine, and you will be surprised to find how far one bottle will go. Remember not to add too much wine, but just enough to enliven the flavour.

If you want a low-priced dry wine for cooking, you can find inexpensive wines that will do very nicely. But if you are planning to prepare a dish with delicate ingredients, or a haute-cuisine specialty, you will want a wine with more class to it. The better the wine you use, the more delicious your dish will be. Whenever you are in doubt about the type of wine to use in a dish, use the same wine you plan to serve with the meal.

As to the use of fortified and apéritif wines in cooking, think of them as flavouring and seasoning agents. Add them a little at a time, and taste the food as you add until you have the right amount.

FLAMBÉED FOODS

The French word *flamber* means "to be in flame, to blaze." The *plat flambé* is a dish served in flaming brandy, rum, vodka, whisky or liqueur. Flaming is sometimes used during the cooking process to give a finer flavour to meats or fish and to remove the harshness of the alcohol. Generally, however, food is flamed just before serving to give it a different taste and to add glamor to the service.

Plats flambés are not difficult to prepare. First, choose a spirit suited to the type of food to be flamed: Brandy, vodka and whisky are best with meat; light and dark rum and French Cognac with dessert omelets and other desserts. Liqueurs are often used to flambé, but because they contain a good deal of sugar, it is advisable to use rum or brandy for one quarter to one half of the liqueur required.

Whatever type of spirits is used, it must be heated or at least be at room temperature before it is lighted. Never let the alcohol boil. ⚬━ A good trick is to warm the bottle under hot running water.

The food to be served flaming at the table should be arranged on a warmed heat-resistant platter, or in a chafing-dish tray or blazer pan.

You will need 2 to 4 ounces (60 to 125 ml) of hot alcohol to flame a dish yielding 6 portions. First, pour some of the warm alcohol around the edge of the food, not on top, and light with a long match. Ladle the flaming alcohol on top of the food over and over again.

A word of caution: Measure the alcohol or liqueur in a glass or cup. Never pour from the bottle into the pan or around the food. Once a dish is flaming there is a danger that the gases in a bottle of spirits will ignite, causing the bottle to explode.

A SHORT GLOSSARY

ALE: A malt brew, containing about 6 per cent alcohol.

AMER PICON: French bitters used as apéritif wine when mixed with grenadine or cassis.

ANGOSTURA: Rum-based bitters with an infusion of aromatic herbs and plants; used for flavouring cocktails.

ANISETTE: A colourless liqueur flavoured with aniseeds; very aromatic.

APPLEJACK: Apple brandy distilled from fermented cider made from fresh tree-ripened apples.

APRICOT BRANDY: A brandy distilled from apricots, used as an after-dinner liqueur; delicious in desserts.

APRICOT LIQUEUR: A sweet liqueur made from apricots and sweetened brandy.

AQUAVIT or AKVAVIT: A colourless or pale yellow liquor distilled from neutral spirits (grain, potatoes) and flavoured with caraway; the favourite drink in Scandinavian countries.

ARMAGNAC: A brandy produced in Gers, near Bordeaux; it has a drier, heavier taste than Cognac.

B and B: A liqueur made of brandy and Benedictine, the after-dinner drink par excellence.

BEER: A brew fermented from cereals and hops, fermented with yeast; usually contains 4 per cent alcohol or more.

BENEDICTINE: One of the oldest herb-flavoured liqueurs; perfect with after-dinner coffee. A Benedictine monk created the recipe, which is still a secret, about 1510, at the monastery at Fécamp in France. It is now made commercially.

BOTTLED IN BOND: A term meaning that the distiller agrees to store his whisky in bonded warehouses without paying the excise tax until he withdraws the whisky from the warehouses. The law provides that such whisky must be at least four years old and 100 proof; however "bottled in bond" is not a guarantee of quality.

BOURBON: Whisky distilled from grain mashes, not less than 51 per cent of which must be corn. Kentucky is the headquarters of Bourbon production.

BRANDY: Liquor made by distillation of wine or a fermented fruit mash. The term "brandy" used alone refers to liquor made from grape wine.

BYRRH: French apéritif wine flavoured with quinine and fortified with brandy.

CALVADOS: French apple brandy, distilled in Normandy.

CAMPARI: A bitter red liqueur made in Italy; used as an apéritif, mixed with soda, tonic or dry vermouth, and also used as an ingredient in many cocktails.

CANADIAN WHISKY: A liquor made from superior grains and carefully developed yeasts. It is fermented, distilled and aged under strict controls to produce lightness of body and superior flavour.

CHARTREUSE: Green and yellow liqueurs made with herbs and aromatics on a base of brandy. The recipe originated in the Carthusian monastery at Voiron in France, where it is still made.

CLARET: The English name for a dry red table wine from Bordeaux; from the French word *clairet*, meaning "lighter" than the original rather rough red made centuries ago.

COGNAC: Brandy distilled from grapes grown in the region around the French city of Cognac, and aged in casks of Limousin oak. This is the best of all French brandies.

COINTREAU: Colourless sweet liqueur with an orange flavour. Popular for after-dinner sipping as well as for flavouring desserts and fruits.

COLD DUCK: A blend of Champagne and sparkling Burgundy; it can be used as an apéritif or late-evening refreshment.

CRÈME DE CACAO: Dark-brown liqueur made of cocoa beans, spices and vanilla with a brandy base. There is also a transparent colourless variety called "white".

CRÈME DE CASSIS: Sweet dark-red liqueur made from black currants.

CRÈME DE MENTHE: Peppermint-flavoured liqueur, either white or green.

CURAÇAO: Liqueur made from the skins of oranges grown on the island of Curaçao off the coast of Venezuela.

DUBONNET: A French apéritif wine with a slight quinine taste; white and red varieties are made.

EAU-DE-VIE: The French name for a brandy or spirit distilled from fermented juice of ripe fruits; always colourless; literally, "water of life".

FRAISE: An eau-de-vie; a colourless brandy distilled from the juice of strawberries.

FRAMBOISE: An eau-de-vie; a colourless brandy distilled from the juice of raspberries.

GIN: A liquor made with a neutral spirit base, flavoured with juniper berries and other seeds.

GRAND MARNIER: An orange-flavoured liqueur with a brandy base; both red and yellow types are made.

GRENADINE: A sweet red syrup, originally made from pomegranates; now often artificially flavoured.

HOCK: The English name for white Rhine wine, probably from Hochheim, one of the famous Rhine wine towns, actually on the river Main.

IRISH MIST: A liqueur made of Irish whisky, heather honey and herbs.

IRISH WHISKY: Traditionally a blend of straight pot-still whiskies, chiefly made of barley; distinctly different from any other kind.

KAHLUA: Mexican coffee liqueur, good alone or in other drinks and useful in cooking.

KIRSCH: A colourless brandy distilled from black cherries and their pits; it is made in France, Germany and Switzerland.

KÜMMEL: A colourless liqueur distilled from grain alcohol and flavoured with caraway seeds.

MARASCHINO: A liqueur distilled from sour Marasca cherries; made originally in Dalmatia, now in Italy.

MARC: Spirits distilled from the pressings of crushed grapes after wine making.

MAY WINE: A German favourite, medium sweet and aromatic, made from white wine (Moselle or Rhine) flavoured with the herb woodruff.

MESCAL: A colourless Mexican liqueur distilled from fermented roasted leaves of the maguey plant; green tasting and strong.

MIRABELLE: An eau-de-vie distilled from the juice of the mirabelle plum, chiefly in Alsace-Lorraine.

ORANGE BITTERS: English bitters flavoured with the peel of Seville oranges.

PERNOD: Today's substitute for absinthe, which was banned because of the harmful wormwood used in its manufacture. An apéritif flavoured with anise, it becomes cloudy when water is added, like all anise-flavoured drinks.

PISCO: Grape brandy made in Peru, similar to French marc; used in cocktails.

PROOF: The measurement of alcoholic strength; each degree of proof equals ½ of 1 per cent of alcohol; hence, 100 proof equals 50 per cent alcohol.

PUNCH: A hot drink made with spirits, fruits and spices, traditionally served in a bowl and drunk from cups with handles.

QUETSCH: An eau-de-vie distilled from the juice of purple plums, chiefly in Alsace-Lorraine.

RUM: A liquor made from the distillation of fermented sugar cane. There are three popular types — white, gold and dark or Jamaica rum. The darker rums have been fermented by a slower process, and sometimes caramel syrup is added for colour.

RYE: Whisky distilled from grain mashes containing not less than 51 per cent rye, and aged in new charred oak barrels.

SACK: The old English name for sherry, derived from sec, the French word for "dry". Originally sherry was not sweet.

SAINT-RAPHAËL: A French apéritif wine, red, often served with lemon peel.

SCOTCH WHISKY: A liquor distilled from a mash of barley grain, with yeast and water. True Scotch whisky can be made only in Scotland.

SLIVOVITZ: A colourless brandy distilled from purple plums; made in Bulgaria, Czechoslovakia, Hungary and other countries.

SLOE GIN: A cordial made from sloe berries, the fruit of the blackthorn, steeped in gin.

STREGA: A yellow Italian liqueur with licorice flavour; quite sweet.

TEQUILA: A Mexican liquor distilled from the fermented juice of the agave or maguey; also made by redistilling mescal; very dry.

TIA MARIA: Coffee liqueur from Jamaica.

TRIPLE SEC: A colourless liqueur with a slight orange taste, similar to Cointreau.

VERMOUTH: Aromatic herb-flavoured apéritif wines. The dry is light in colour; the sweet is amber-coloured or red, with a bittersweet taste. There also is a colourless very sweet vermouth.

VODKA: The Russian national drink, made from potatoes or grain. Colourless and tasteless, with no after-smell, it can be used in any drink or recipe calling for gin. It is perfect with caviar.

WHISKY OR WHISKEY: This is the general name for liquors distilled from fermented mash of grain and not less than 80 proof. The spelling "whisky" is used in Scotland and Canada, while "whiskey" is used in Ireland and the United States.

CHAPTER 20

Entertaining at home

THE TREND IN ENTERTAINING TODAY is toward small informal dinner parties and buffet-style dining, because they are conducive to relaxed conversation and allow the hosts to enjoy the meal as much as their guests. A successful meal depends as much on the atmosphere as the food and your guests will be relaxed and happy only if you are. It is important to make your guests feel that you are managing everything easily and that you are having as good a time as everybody else. Decide what kind of meal you can serve comfortably and then start your planning.

PLANNING

The first step is to decide what you are going to serve; after that come the plans for shopping, cooking and serving.

The shopping list can be divided into advance buying and the buying of perishables the day before or the morning of the party. The cooking plan should be divided into advance work, same-day cooking and last-minute preparations. The serving dishes should be chosen and set out ahead of time. Try to arrange to have the table set and all the cooking done by the late afternoon of the day of the party. That's when to check on food that has been prepared in advance, arrange food on platters and then relax.

If you make lists and follow them, you will find that everything falls into place.

— Write out your menu

— Make a grocery list of every item and ingredient you will need

— Check off the ingredients already on hand

— Create a cooking timetable

— List the linen, dishes, cutlery and glassware required

— Plan your centrepiece

It can save time and headaches if you keep a list of the stores at which you have found certain items are available. It's also a good idea to keep a list of menus, with the date of the party and who was there, as a reminder of what you have done at other times. If your meal is successful, you will want to serve the same dishes at another time, but you won't want to serve them to the same guests again.

Include in your early planning the clothes you intend to wear, and make sure they are clean and pressed. If you don't think about this until the last minute, you may have to make a hasty switch that can put you completely off your stride.

Also, include a check on household items you intend to use, such as:

— Candles and candlesticks

— Fresh soap, guest towels and tissues in the bathroom

— Cocktail napkins

— Coasters

— Ice, liquor, mixes, wine, openers, corkscrews

— Coat closet space and hangers

Give yourself enough time so you can dress leisurely and relax for at least a few minutes before the party begins.

Table-setting checklist
Check all of these items ahead of time so you will be organized before your guests arrive:

— Tablecloth or place mats

— Napkins

— Plates for each course

— Cutlery, on table or on sideboard

— Candles and holders

— Salt and pepper shakers

— Small dishes for nuts or bonbons

— Serving forks and spoons

— Serving dishes

— Trivets or hot trays for hot dishes

When choosing your tablecloth or place mats, take into consideration your centrepiece and your candlesticks. The menu and the occasion dictate the type of table setting you should use.

A good menu should offer an appetizing variety of flavours, colours and textures, combining the bland and the sharp, the crisp and the soft, the bright and the pale, all at one meal. Your personal touches make the difference.

Formal dinner
For a formal dinner, it is easiest to have the first course already on the table when you and your guests enter the dining room. If the first course is hot, place the soup plate or entrée dish on a service plate at each place. A cold entrée or cold soup does not require a service plate, except for oysters on the half shell or seafood cocktail served in a deep plate of crushed ice.

Forks, knives and spoons should be lined up evenly, about an inch from the edge of the table. Forks should be on the left, with tines upward. Napkins go on the left, next to the forks. Knives should be on the right, cutting edges facing inward. Place soup spoons to the right of the knives. When placing extra knives and forks, the rule is simple: Place them in the order they are to be used, starting from the outside and working in toward the plate. For example, if the first course is soup, the soup spoon goes to the far right, while the larger knife and fork for the main course are next to the plate on either side of it. On the other hand, if the main course is to be followed by a salad, the large knife and fork are placed on the outside and the salad knife and fork nearest the plate.

The dessert fork and spoon are placed on the table when the dessert is served. This keeps the table from being too cluttered with silverware at the beginning of the meal. When possible, set the dessert plates, dessert silver and the dessert itself on a sideboard or service table before dinner, making service easy.

ENTERTAINING AT HOME

If cheese is served, a small bread plate and cheese knife is placed in front of each guest before dessert. You can also have these ready on the service table.

Water glasses go slightly to the right of the plate, above the knives. Wineglasses go to the right of the water glasses. If liqueur and coffee are served at the table, bring in the glasses and the bottles on a tray and bring it in at the same time as the coffee service.

Informal dinner
For informal dinners, keep the table setting simple, but attractive. Create a subtle atmosphere in place of a more obvious elegance.

Have soup or entrée on the table before you sit down. Hot rolls, sauces or any other similar accompaniments can be set on the table ahead of time to simplify the service.

After the soup, serve the main course. Placing the hot course on a hot tray on a sideboard or on a nearby small table before you come into the dining room, will save a lot of coming and going. Coffee can be served informally at the table or in the living room.

For such dinners choose food that can stand waiting and recipes that can be prepared ahead of time so that you save yourself last-minute work.

Formal place setting

1. Salt and pepper shakers
2. Water glass
3. Wineglass
4. Napkin
5. Meat fork
6. Plate
7. Meat knife
8. Soup spoon
9. Cocktail fork

Informal place setting

1. Bread plate and butter knife
2. Water glass
3. Wineglass
4. Napkin
5. Meat fork
6. Salad fork
7. Soup bowl and plate
8. Meat knife
9. Soup spoon

Buffet supper

The buffet supper has come a long way from Victorian days, when the food was left on hot plates in the dining room on the cook's or maid's day off, and people ate when they felt like it by helping themselves. Today, buffet suppers often are more elaborate than a sit-down dinner.

One reason for the popularity of the buffet meal is that it enables us to entertain a maximum number of people in a minimum amount of space. Despite their convenience, they also have their drawbacks; the worst is that they can turn into perpetual-motion affairs — guests helping themselves, sitting all over the place, eating food all over the house, constantly going back and forth for additional courses. I much prefer a buffet supper where guests help themselves to the first course and eat at little tables that have been set out, with the dessert and coffee served to them at their tables. If you are having a buffet for 15 to 25 people, try to have at least one person to help set out the dinner, clear away plates and glasses and clean up.

Try to have food that can be eaten with a fork only, especially if plates have to be balanced on the knees. Consider cold meats, stews, goulashes and casseroles.

Setting the buffet table

The dining table is the natural place to set out the food for your buffet, but you can also use a sideboard or one or two smaller tables placed together. Arrange the table against an imaginative background or set it away from the wall so that people can walk around it easily when they are helping themselves.

Place the dinner plates, silver and napkins nearest to the end where guests will approach the table. If you have room, place the silver in a row and the napkins in a row below the silver. If you don't, wrap the silver in the napkins and place the bundles one next to the other. This makes it possible for a guest to hold plate, fork and napkin in one hand, leaving the other hand free to serve food.

When arranging the food, place the main dish first, followed by the vegetables and hot rolls or bread. If you are serving noodles, rice or a similar food, place this just before the main dish for those who like to pour the sauce over the pasta or rice. Place the condiments after the rolls or bread, and after these the salad, cheese and crackers, and then the glasses for beer or wine. (The glasses can be omitted here if you have someone to help with the serving.)

Utensils such as hot trays, electric frying pans or saucepans and food warmers are almost indispensable at buffet suppers to keep hot food hot. Large serving spoons and forks make it easy for guests to help themselves.

When everything is ready, invite the guests to help themselves; go to the table yourself to direct the traffic and see that things get moving in the right direction. You can even suggest that guests eat the hot dish first and come back later for the salad and cheese. After everyone has served himself, replace the covers on the hot dishes.

When the main course, cheese and salad are finished, place the dessert where the main dish was originally set, with the necessary plates and silver near it. Liqueurs should be at one end of the table. If you have help, it will be easy to organize the clearing of the table while your guests enjoy themselves and relax before eating dessert.

Buffet setting

Wineglasses

Crackers

Cheese

Salade

Butter

Silver and napkins

Centerpiece

Salt and pepper shakers

Bread

Plates

Main dish

Vegetables

BREAKFAST

The comment I hear most often about serving breakfast to guests is that it is a chore to get a good meal on the table on time. It seems there aren't many people who feel bright and efficient the moment they get out of bed. The key is to decide the night before what you are going to serve and get it organized.

Following recipes for my favourite breakfasts, you will find some ideas for lazy breakfasts.

TRADITIONAL BREAKFAST

Bacon and eggs

Panfried bacon: Place as many slices of bacon as you need in a cold frying pan. Cook very slowly over low heat, turning only once. Drain fat as you turn slices.

Broiled bacon: Place slices of bacon on a wire rack. Broil 3 inches (8 cm) from the source of heat, without turning. Cook for 3 to 4 minutes. This is the best method for bringing out the full flavour of the bacon.

Drain the cooked bacon on paper towels and keep hot in a warmer or in an oven heated to 250°F (120°C). At the same time, warm the plates. So many breakfasts are spoiled by being served on cold plates.

Fried eggs: You will find out how to prepare these in Chapter 16. Remember, always cook eggs at a low temperature. You can fry the eggs in the fat left from cooking bacon if you wish, or in butter; use ½ teaspoon (2 ml) butter for each egg. Don't let the butter brown.

Bacon, eggs and fried tomatoes: Panfry the bacon and remove from pan when cooked. Break eggs into the fat. Cut tomatoes into halves and sprinkle with sugar, salt and pepper. Place the tomatoes, cut sides down, in the frying pan. Don't turn them while they cook. When the eggs are cooked, the tomatoes are ready.

Fines-herbes omelet: Follow the recipe in Chapter 16.

Cheese omelet: The night before, shred 1 cup (250 ml) of cheese (Swiss, Dutch or Cheddar) for 2 to 3 eggs. Beat the eggs with 2 tablespoons (30 ml) of cream. Melt 1 tablespoon (15 ml) butter in a frypan and pour the eggs on top. Sprinkle cheese over all. Then cook like an ordinary omelet. Serve with a bowl of chopped parsley.

Lazy breakfasts

If you like to sit down with your guests and let breakfast cook itself, the answer is automatic equipment. I like to call these lazy breakfasts. Prepare your trays and set them near you.

Coffee tray: automatic coffee maker, cups, saucers, spoons, sugar, cream or milk.

Toast tray: toaster, bread, butter, jam or marmalade.

Main tray: this can vary a great deal. If I make my husband's favourite Eggs Landaise, for instance (recipe follows), I place on the tray the automatic electric frypan, sliced sausages on a plate, chopped onion in a closed container (no one wants to smell raw onion before breakfast), ready-cut tomatoes, the eggs in a bowl, grated cheese in another and all the other requirements, plus hot service plates.

Old-fashioned buttermilk pancakes

½ package active dry yeast

2 tbsp (30 ml) warm water

2 cups (500 ml) sifted all-purpose flour

1 tbsp (15 ml) baking powder

1 tbsp (15 ml) baking soda

1 tbsp (15 ml) sugar

½ tsp (2 ml) salt

2 cups (500 ml) buttermilk

2 tbsp (30 ml) melted butter or shortening

3 eggs

½ cup (125 ml) heavy cream

Sprinkle the yeast over the warm water; let stand for 10 minutes; stir. Sift into a bowl the flour, baking powder, baking soda, sugar and salt. Pour in the buttermilk and beat into a smooth batter. Then mix in the well-stirred yeast and the melted butter. Beat the eggs slightly with the cream and add to the batter.

Heat your griddle. Grease the surface with shortening. Pour just enough batter for each pancake from a pitcher all at once. Cook until the pancake looks slightly dry on top and tiny bubbles appear. Flip onto the other side and brown. Never turn more than once. Continue until all the batter is cooked.

Makes 4 to 6 servings.

Eggs Landaise in electric frypan

Cut 2 or 3 pork sausages into thick slices. Chop an onion; peel 2 tomatoes, remove seeds and cut into small pieces. Cook the sausages at 350°F (180°C). When brown, add the onion, then the tomatoes; cook for a few minutes.

Break 4 to 6 eggs on top. Sprinkle with grated cheese to taste. Cover and reduce heat to 200°F (95°C), then cook for 10 minutes, while you chat and become more and more hungry.

Makes 4 servings.

On other mornings you can make Old-Fashioned Buttermilk Pancakes topped with Molasses Lemon Sauce, or French Toast in the same way. Arrange what you need on trays, set them near you, then make pancakes or toast to your heart's content without having to run from the stove to the table to serve.

My mother's French toast

8 slices of bread

3 eggs

Pinch of salt

Pinch of grated nutmeg

½ cup (125 ml) maple syrup

1 cup (250 ml) milk

¼ cup (60 ml) heavy cream

Butter for frying

Cut bread into halves. Beat eggs with salt, nutmeg and maple syrup. When well mixed, add milk and heavy cream. Heat enough butter in an electric frypan at 350°F (180°C) to barely cover the bottom, but do not let it brown. Quickly dip the bread, a piece at a time, into the batter. Fry on both sides. When done, it is crisp on the outside and creamy on the inside. Serve the toast as is, or with sweetened slices of fresh strawberries.

Makes 4 servings.

Molasses lemon sauce

If you like molasses, this is the best pancake sauce.

1½ tbsp (25 ml) cornstarch

½ cup (125 ml) sugar

Pinch of salt

¾ cup (190 ml) water

½ cup (125 ml) molasses

Butter to taste

Grated lemon rind to taste

In a saucepan mix together the cornstarch, sugar and salt. Add water and molasses. Cook over low heat until clear and thickened, stirring all the time. Add butter and grated lemon rind to taste. Serve hot. You can make this the day before.

Makes about 1½ cups (375 ml) sauce.

LUNCHTIME FOOD

Soup and sandwich fun

Soups and sandwiches are a winning team that can be served almost any hour of the day. It's easy to create combinations that tempt both the eye and the appetite.

Soups have justifiably taken on stature as a main-course dish because they can be hearty and nourishing, enough to form the backbone of a meal. Canned soups are excellent and easy to serve, but a homemade soup has real feeling. Don't let the can opener be the master of your soup kettle.

Consider the following reasons why you should make your own soups. First, soups are extremely easy to make and those that need a long cooking time require a minimum amount of pot watching. Second, soups are extremely economical. The principal ingredients in most soup recipes are low-cost foods such as vegetables, milk, bread, rice, cheaper cuts or scraps of meat, and water. Soups can even be meatless and still be marvelous. Even guest-worthy soups will not overtax your budget. Third, soups have a way of providing an endless variety of meals from limited materials.

As for sandwiches, there are endless varieties — man-sized, small-fry, picnic-style, open-faced, square-meal, rich boy or poor boy, smorgasbord, two deckers, three deckers, Dagwoods and baked sandwiches. So why always the same bread, the same filling, served in the same old way? Who wears the same dress for 25 years?

Here are a few soup and sandwich combinations that have flair, yet take a minimum amount of work to prepare.

English Midland soup

1 lb (500 gr) beef, chopped or ground

2 medium-sized carrots, peeled and grated

2 onions, minced

1 10-oz (284 ml) package frozen green peas

1 20-oz (570 ml) can tomatoes

1 tbsp (15 ml) sugar

1 bay leaf

Minced parsley to taste

¼ tsp (1 ml) grated nutmeg

1½ tsp (7 ml) salt

Place the beef in a large bean pot or earthenware casserole. Place on top, in this order, the grated carrots, minced onions, the frozen peas, broken up (not necessary to thaw them); the canned tomatoes and an equal amount of water. Add the sugar, bay leaf, parsley to taste, nutmeg and salt. Cover and cook in a 350°F (180°C) oven for 1 hour.

Serve, placing in each plate some of the meat.

Makes about 6 servings.

English liver and bacon sandwich

Use any type of liver you prefer, including leftovers. Fry slices of bacon until crisp and place on absorbent paper to drain. Add liver slices to the fat left in the pan and brown quickly on both sides; be careful not to overcook. Place liver on absorbent paper with the bacon and sprinkle both with a little crurry powder. Spread the liver with a little chutney or English table sauce. Cool. Butter slices of brown bread; in England, this sandwich is made with Hovis bread, available in many shops on this side of the Atlantic. Crush the bacon and spread on the bread. Cut the liver into slivers and place on top of the bacon. Cover with another slice of buttered bread.

French velouté d'oignon

- 3 tbsp (50 ml) butter
- 2 tbsp (30 ml) bacon fat
- 2½ cups (625 ml) thinly sliced onions
- 3 tbsp (50 ml) flour
- 2 cups (500 ml) light cream
- 1 egg, well beaten
- Pinch of dried thyme
- Salt and pepper to taste
- 1 or 2 celery ribs, cut into tiny, even-sized dice

Heat the butter and bacon fat together and add the onions. Mix well, cover and simmer over low heat for 20 minutes. Beat together until well mixed the flour, cream, egg and thyme. Add to the onions and stir until slightly thickened. Season to taste. Serve as is or make a purée by passing through a sieve or blending in an electric blender for 1 minute. Garnish each cup of soup with 1 teaspoon (5 ml) of the celery.

Makes about 4 servings.

Croque-monsieur

Place a thin slice of cooked ham on a slice of unbuttered white bread. Spread a good French mustard on top and add a thin slice of Swiss cheese. Sprinkle with a little dried marjoram. Top with another slice of white bread. Melt 1 tablespoon (15 ml) butter in a large frying pan or grill. Place the sandwich in the hot butter and brown lightly on both sides over low heat, turning only once. Serve immediately.

Calgary oxtail soup

2 oxtails (1½ to 2 lbs/750 gr to 1 kg each), cut into pieces
3 carrots, diced
2 celery ribs, diced
2 onions, minced
½ tsp (2 ml) dried thyme
1 bay leaf
1 lemon slice, unpeeled
3 whole cloves
1 tbsp (15 ml) salt
8 peppercorns
2 quarts (2 L) boiling water
1 19-oz (590 ml) can tomatoes
½ cup (125 ml) sherry (optional)

Bring everything but the sherry to a boil. Cover and simmer until the meat is tender, 2 to 3 hours. When ready to serve, add the sherry. This soup reheats very well and freezes equally well.

Makes 6 or more servings.

Québec cream of cabbage soup

2 cups (500 ml) boiling water
1 onion, minced
2 carrots, grated
2 celery ribs, diced
1 large potato, peeled and diced
4 cups (1 L) milk, scalded
2 cups (500 ml) fine-shredded cabbage
Salt and pepper to taste
2 tbsp (30 ml) butter

Bring the water to a boil in a saucepan large enough to hold all the ingredients. Add the onion, carrots, celery and potato to the boiling water. Cover and simmer for 20 minutes, or until the potato is tender. Mash the pieces of potato with a fork, right in the saucepan, then add the hot milk and bring to a boil again. Add the cabbage. It is important to have the liquid at a full rolling boil when adding the cabbage, because this keeps it a nice green colour. Season with salt and pepper to taste and cook over low heat for 15 to 20 minutes. When ready to serve, add the butter.

Makes about 6 servings.

Calgary's own sandwich

Break up cold corned beef or pickled beef. Place on a slice of buttered white bread and top with chili sauce and onion rings or fried onions. Cover with another slice of white bread. This sandwich is sometimes dipped into melted beef fat, then browned on a barbecue.

Brittany pumpkin soup

3 tbsp (50 ml) butter

2 lb (1 kg) pumpkin, peeled and diced

¼ tsp (1 ml) grated mace

1 cup (250 ml) water

1 cup (250 ml) milk

½ cup (125 ml) light cream

1½ tsp (7 ml) salt

¼ tsp (1 ml) pepper

½ cup (125 ml) bread croutons, fried

Melt the butter and add the pumpkin and mace. Stir, cover and cook over low heat for 20 minutes. Add water and milk and bring to a boil. Cover and simmer for 10 minutes. Force through a sieve. Add the cream and salt and pepper. Heat just to boiling, but do not boil. Serve with the croutons.

Serves 6.

Sardine treat

1 4-oz (113 gr) can sardines

1 tbsp (15 ml) lemon juice

Grated rind of 1 lemon

1 tbsp (15 ml) minced parsley

1 tsp (5 ml) minced chives or shallots

2 tbsp (30 ml) minced fresh celery leaves

Buttered black bread slices

Open can of sardines and turn them onto a plate. Sprinkle with lemon juice and the grated lemon rind. Mix together the parsley, chives or shallots, and celery leaves. Cover a thickly buttered slice of black bread with sardines. Sprinkle with the herb mixture, salt and pepper, and top with a buttered slice of black bread.

Old French favourite
Butter sliced white bread. Spread with cream cheese, then with honey mixed with a little lemon juice. Add thinly sliced unpeeled apples. Top with a second slice of buttered white bread.

A Canadian Autumn Lunch
(for six)

Ontario mild Cheddar soup
Sage hot bread
Small Quebec tourtières or
Vancouver salmon salad
Maple-sugar shortcake or
Maple-syrup sundae

Sage hot bread
Slice a loaf of crusty French bread. Blend butter with grated lemon rind and crushed sage to taste. Butter each slice. Reshape the loaf of bread and tie together. Heat in the oven before serving.

Ontario mild Cheddar soup

- 5 tbsp (75 ml) butter
- 2 carrots, grated
- ½ cup (125 ml) diced celery
- 1 large onion, minced
- 1 small parsnip, peeled and grated
- 4 tbsp (60 ml) flour
- 4 cups (1 L) consommé
- 2 to 3 cups (500 to 750 ml) grated mild Cheddar cheese
- 2 cups (500 ml) cold milk
- Salt and pepper to taste
- Chopped parsley to taste

Melt 3 tablespoons (50 ml) of the butter in a saucepan. Add the carrots, celery, onion and parsnip. Cover and simmer over low heat for 10 minutes.

Blend the rest of the butter with the flour. Add to the vegetables along with the consommé. Stir together until creamy and continue cooking over low heat for 5 to 8 minutes. Add the cheese and stir until melted. Then gradually add the cold milk. Continue to cook for another 10 minutes, but do not boil after the cheese is added, for this makes the cheese stringy. Season with salt and pepper to taste. Add a big handful of chopped parsley, and serve.

Vancouver salmon salad

- 1 lb (500 gr) canned salmon
- ½ cup (125 ml) diced celery
- 1 19-oz (590 ml) can green peas, drained
- 2 tbsp (30 ml) lemon juice
- 1 tsp (5 ml) minced onion
- ½ tsp (2 ml) salt
- ⅛ tsp (0.5 ml) pepper
- ¼ tsp (1 ml) ground dill
- 1 cup (250 ml) commercial sour cream

Break salmon into bite-sized pieces in a medium-sized bowl. Add celery and green peas. Combine lemon juice, minced onion, salt, pepper, ground dill and sour cream. Pour over the salmon and toss lightly with a fork. Chill for several hours. Serve in lettuce cups. Garnish with chopped chives and lemon wedges if desired.

Small Québec tourtières

1 lb (500 gr) pork, minced

1 small onion, chopped

½ tsp (2 ml) salt

1 small garlic clove, minced

½ tsp (2 ml) crumbled dried savory

¼ tsp (1 ml) ground cloves

½ cup (125 ml) water

¼ or ½ cup (60 to 125 ml) bread crumbs

Pie pastry for a 2-crust 9-inch (23 cm) pie (Chap. 17)

Place together in a saucepan the pork, onion, salt, garlic, savory, cloves and water. Bring to a boil and cook, uncovered, over medium heat for 20 minutes.

Remove from the heat. Add a few spoonfuls of bread crumbs. Let the mixture stand for 10 minutes. If the fat is sufficiently absorbed by the bread crumbs, do not add more. If not, continue in the same manner, adding all the bread crumbs if necessary. Cool.

Line 6 large tart pans with half the pastry. Pour the cooled pork mixture into the pastry-lined pans. Cover with the rest of the pastry. Bake in a 500°F (260°C) oven until the tops are well browned. Serve hot.

Maple-sugar shortcake

1 8-inch (20 cm) sponge cake

1 cup (250 ml) shaved maple sugar

1 cup (250 ml) chopped nuts of your choice

1 cup (250 ml) heavy cream

¼ cup (60 ml) sugar

½ tsp (2 ml) vanilla extract

Cut the sponge cake horizontally into two equal layers. Mix together the shaved maple sugar, chopped nuts and ¼ cup (60 ml) of the cream. Spread this mixture as a filling on the bottom sponge cake layer, then place the second layer on top. Whip the remaining heavy cream; add the sugar and vanilla extract. Spread over the top.

Maple-syrup sundae

1 cup (250 ml) maple syrup

1 tbsp (15 ml) butter

3 tbsp (50 ml) brandy

Vanilla or maple walnut ice cream

Chopped walnuts

Heat maple syrup with butter and brandy. Cool. Pour the sauce over ice cream. Garnish with chopped walnuts.

A Party Tea

Mushroom rolls
Baby lobster puffs
Honeyed Sally Lunn
Cinnamon coffee cake
Oatmeal fruit cookies
Brandied almond-strawberry jam
Arabian tea

Afternoon tea

Afternoon tea was an elegant part of the Edwardian era and it was everything to the emperor of China hundreds of years before that. Today we may not have Oriental chefs with their hundreds of helpers nor a staff of starched and aproned maids and superbly trained butlers, so much a part of the Edwardian age, but we can still have charming tea parties.

Choosing the tea you serve is important, since there is a lot more to tea than a tea bag. Look for the varieties of Chinese, Indian and Ceylon teas, or make a special tea mixture, such as Arabian Tea. Make the tea in a hot earthenware teapot, and serve it with a choice of delicate tidbits and hot cakes.

Arabian tea

Juice of 1 lemon

½ cup (125 ml) honey

½ tsp (2 ml) ground cinnamon

Hot green tea

Blend together the 1 lemon juice, honey and ground cinnamon. Place in a dainty container and serve in place of sugar with a pot of very hot green tea. No milk should be used with this type of tea.

Mushrooms rolls

Prepare these 6 to 12 hours ahead.

2 tbsp (30 ml) butter

1 cup (250 ml) minced mushrooms

1 tbsp (15 ml) cornstarch

½ cup (125 ml) light cream

16 thin slices of fresh bread

Soft butter

Melt butter. Add minced mushrooms and stir over high heat for 3 minutes. Add cornstarch and stir until mixed with the butter. Add cream. Cook, stirring often, until creamy. Remove crusts from bread slices and spread slices with soft butter, then spread with the mushrooms. Roll up the bread slices and fasten with food picks. Refrigerate, covered, until you are ready to serve them.

With a sharp knife slice the rolls on an angle into slices 1 inch (2.5 cm) thick. Brown in a preheated 400°F (200°C) oven for 10 to 15 minutes.

Baby lobster puffs

Puffs and filling can be prepared separately 24 hours ahead. Fill the puffs with the lobster mixture about 1 hour before serving.

1 package small cream-puff shell mix

1 6- or 8-oz (170 or 227 gr) can of lobster

2 shallots, minced

¼ cup (60 ml) minced parsley

¼ cup (60 ml) minced walnuts

½ tsp (2 ml) curry powder or ¼ tsp (1 ml) crushed coriander seeds.

½ cup (125 ml) finely diced celery

Salt and pepper to taste

Make cream-puff shells according to the directions on the package. Bake and cool.

Shred the lobster. Add shallots, parsley, walnuts, curry powder or coriander seeds, celery, and salt and pepper to taste.

Cinnamon coffee cake

This fragrant fluffy coffee cake can be served hot or cold. It will keep fresh for 48 hours.

½ cup (125 ml) butter

½ cup (125 ml) sugar

2 eggs

1 tsp (5 ml) baking soda

1 cup (250 ml) commercial sour cream

1½ cups (375 ml) cups all-purpose flour

1½ tsp (7 ml) baking powder

Pinch of salt

1 tsp (5 ml) vanilla extract

Cinnamon-walnut topping

¼ cup (60 ml) sugar

1 tbsp (15 ml) ground cinnamon

2 tbsp (30 ml) chopped walnuts

Cream the butter with the sugar. Add the eggs, one at a time, beating well after each addition. Mix the baking soda with the sour cream and gradually beat into the butter mixture. When the mixture is light, add the flour sifted with the baking powder and salt. Add the vanilla. Pour half of this batter into a 9-inch (23 cm) square pan. Top with half the cinnamon-walnut topping mixture, then pour on the rest of the batter and sprinkle the remainder of the cinnamon mixture over the top. Bake in a preheated 350°F (180°C) oven for 40 minutes.

Honeyed Sally Lunn

You can buy a Sally Lunn tea loaf at a bakery or pastry shop.

1 Sally Lunn tea loaf

½ cup (125 ml) honey

½ cup (125 ml) butter, softened

Grated rind of 1 lemon

1 tsp (5 ml) lemon juice

Make honey butter by creaming together until light and fluffy the honey, soft butter, grated lemon rind and lemon juice.

Slice the loaf horizontally and butter each round slice with honey butter. Then reassemble the slices in the original shape of the loaf. Place on a baking sheet or pie plate and refrigerate until 20 minutes before serving. Bake in a preheated 400°F (200°C) oven for 20 minutes.

Oatmeal fruit cookies

1½ cups (375 ml) all-purpose flour

1¾ cups (440 ml) sugar

1 tsp (5 ml) baking powder

½ tsp (2 ml) baking soda

1 tsp (5 ml) salt

1 tsp (5 ml) ground cinnamon

3 cups (750 ml) rolled oats

1 cup (250 ml) chopped candied cherries

½ cup (125 ml) chopped walnuts

1 cup (250 ml) melted butter or margarine

2 eggs

½ cup (125 ml) milk

Sift together the flour, sugar, baking powder, baking soda, salt and cinnamon. Add the oats, candied cherries and walnuts. Stir together. Make a well in the middle and add first the melted butter or margarine, then the eggs, finally the milk. Mix until thoroughly blended. Drop by spoonfuls onto an ungreased baking sheet. Leave about 1½ inches (3.75 cm) between the spoonfuls of batter. Bake in a preheated 400°F (200°C) oven for 10 to 12 minutes. Cool on a wire rack. Store in an airtight box.

Makes about 72 cookies.

Brandied almond-strawberry jam

1 jar homemade strawberry jam

½ cup (125 ml) toasted slivered almonds

3 tbsp (50 ml) brandy

Add almonds and brandy to strawberry jam of fine quality. Mix thoroughly, cover and keep at room temperature for 3 days before serving.

ENTERTAINING AT HOME

Late-afternoon guests won't pose a problem if you keep tangy snacks on hand. A cup of good hot tea will always be welcome, and the sweet can be as conservative as lemon poundcake or as rich as a thickly iced chocolate cake.

> **AFTERNOON TEA FOR VIPs**
> (enough to satisfy 4 to 6 VIPs)
>
> Caper crackers
> Deviled almonds and walnuts
> Chicken-liver pâté
> Lemon poundcake
> Double-rich chocolate cake

Caper crackers

1 4-oz (113 gr) package of cream cheese

⅓ cup (80 ml) heavy cream

2 tsp (10 ml) vinegar from a bottle of capers

2 tbsp (30 ml) capers

Cream together the cream cheese, cream and caper vinegar. When smooth, add capers. Spread over small crackers.

Deviled almonds and walnuts

2 tbsp (30 ml) unsalted butter

2 tbsp (30 ml) bottled table sauce or chutney sauce

1 cup (250 ml) walnut halves

1 cup (250 ml) blanched whole almonds

½ tsp (2 ml) salt

Good pinch of cayenne

½ tsp (2 ml) curry powder

Melt butter and stir in table sauce or chutney sauce. Add walnut halves and almonds. Sprinkle with salt, cayenne and curry powder; stir together. Bake in a 350°F (180°C) oven for 15 to 20 minutes, stirring occasionally. Drain on paper towels and serve warm.

Chicken-liver pâté

1 large onion, finely chopped

4 tbsp (60 ml) butter

1 lb (500 gr) chicken livers

1 tsp (5 ml) salt

½ tsp (2 ml) freshly ground pepper

¼ cup (60 ml) sherry or brandy

Brown chopped onion in butter over medium heat. Clean chicken livers and add. Cook over fairly high heat, stirring, until livers are no longer pink. Add salt, pepper and sherry or brandy. Mash and blend until smooth, or purée in a blender. Pour the pâté into a covered dish and refrigerate. Serve spread on Melba toast.

Lemon poundcake

Butter, softened

2 cups (500 ml) sifted pastry flour or cake flour

½ tsp (2 ml) salt

¼ tsp (1 ml) baking powder

⅔ cup (160 ml) butter, softened

1 cup (250 ml) fine fruit sugar

4 eggs

1 tsp (5 ml) grated lemon rind

1½ tbsp (25 ml) lemon juice

Brush the bottom and sides of a loaf pan (4½ by 8½ inches/11.25 by 21.25 cm) with soft butter. Line the bottom with a single thickness of waxed paper, then brush the paper with butter.

Sift together the flour, salt and baking powder. Cream the ⅔ cup (160 ml) soft butter and gradually beat in the sugar. Continue to beat until light and fluffy. Add the eggs, one at a time, and beat well after each addition. Beat in the lemon rind and juice.

Sift together the dry ingredients and add a little at a time, to the creamed mixture, combining lightly after each addition. Spread the batter evenly in the prepared pan. Bake in a preheated 350°F (180°C) oven for 1 to 1½ hours, or until a straw inserted in the centre comes out clean. Cool in the pan on a rack for about 10 minutes. Loosen around the edges with a knife and remove from the pan. Peel off the paper and cool completely on a rack.

Double-rich chocolate cake

2 cups (500 ml) sifted pastry flour or cake flour

1 tsp (5 ml) baking soda

¼ tsp (1 ml) salt

½ cup (125 ml) butter

1¼ cups (310 ml) fine fruit sugar

2 eggs

3 squares (3 oz/90 gr) unsweetened chocolate

1 cup (250 ml) milk

1 tsp (5 ml) almond extract

***Chocolate frosting* (recipe follows)**

Sift the flour again with the baking soda and the salt. Cream the butter and gradually add the sugar. Beat together until light and fluffy. Add the eggs, one at a time, beating well after each addition. Melt the chocolate and cool it. Add it to the butter mixture and mix thoroughly. Add the almond extract to the milk. Add the sifted flour mixture to the butter-chocolate mixture, gradually, alternating with the milk mixture. Butter two 8-inch (20 cm) layer-cake pans. Divide the batter between them. Bake in a preheated 350°F (180°C) oven for 25 to 30 minutes. Unmold and cool. Fill and frost.

ENTERTAINING AT HOME

Double-rich chocolate frosting

2 eggs

2 cups (500 ml) sifted icing sugar

Pinch of salt

1 tsp (5 ml) vanilla extract

¼ tsp (1 ml) almond extract

¼ cup (60 ml) milk

5 ounces (5 squares) unsweetened chocolate

2 tbsp (30 ml) butter

Break the eggs into a bowl and add the icing sugar and salt. Add the vanilla, almond extract and milk. Beat until smooth and creamy. Set this bowl in a larger bowl filled with ice cubes. Now melt the chocolate with the butter. Add this gradually to the sugar and egg mixture. Continue beating with a hand beater until very thick, 8 to 10 minutes. Use to fill and frost the cake.

Simplicity and a true respect for good food are the themes of this fine dinner.

The marinated cheese is simple to make and is an interesting new way to serve cheese as an appetizer; serve it with a cool dry sherry. The glorious beef dish is in reality a beef stew. But it is prepared according to the rules of French haute cuisine, it yields tender beef morsels in a velvety brown sauce. Coupled with hot crusty French bread and a good vintage Burgundy, it can be a perfect main course. The green peas are also from the classic French repertoire.

The flan can be prepared 24 to 48 hours ahead. It is cool, light and superbly flavoured. Finish your meal with café noir and Cognac.

> **A PERFECT LITTLE DINNER**
> (for the sheer pleasure of entertaining 4 guests)
>
> Marinated Swiss Cheese
> Dry sherry
> Boeuf bourguignon
> Red Burgundy
> Green peas à l'étuvée
> Chocolate flan de Nevers
> Café noir
> Cognanc

Marinated Swiss cheese

1 lb (500 gr) Swiss cheese (Gruyère)

Grated rind of ½ lemon

2 tbsp (30 ml) lemon juice

4 tbsp (60 ml) salad oil

Salt and pepper to taste

2 tbsp (30 ml) minced fresh parsley

¼ tsp (1 ml) minced fresh marjoram

Dice the cheese and add the other ingredients. Place in an attractive container that can be covered. Refrigerate for 4 to 6 hours. Serve with dry sherry.

Boeuf bourguignon

The meat for this superb stew must be lean beef — top round or meaty short rib — of the very best quality. It must be browned in melted salt pork. Use small whole onions if you can't get shallots, but shallots are better. To make an authentic dish, do not add celery, carrots or potatoes.

Use red Burgundy for the liquid; in this case, the better the wine, the better the dish. You can prepare this early and reheat it carefully when you are ready to serve it.

3 lbs (1.5 kg) lean beef (top round or meaty short rib)

½ lb (250 gr) salt pork (more fat than lean)

24 shallots or small white onions

1 tsp (5 ml) sugar

2 tbsp (30 ml) flour (optional)

Freshly ground pepper

2 garlic cloves, crushed

3 inches (8 cm) of orange peel

2 bay leaves

¼ tsp (1 ml) dried thyme

Grated mace or nutmeg

4 sprigs parsley

½ tsp (2 ml) minced marjoram

½ bottle dry red Burgundy

2 tbsp (30 ml) butter

1 cup (250 ml) white button mushrooms

½ cup (125 ml) minced parsley

1 cup (250 ml) croutons, browned in butter

Cut beef into 2-inch (5 cm) cubes. Slice the salt pork onto 1-inch (2.5 cm) cubes and melt in a heavy enameled cast-iron pan or Dutch oven until crisp and brown. Remove the pieces of pork, leaving the fat.

Add the shallots or onions to the fat and sprinkle with the sugar; brown over light heat. Remove onions from the fat and set aside.

Add the pieces of meat, just enough at one time to cover the bottom of the pan. Brown the meat evenly on all sides, removing each batch as it browns. When all the meat is browned, return it to the pan and sprinkle with the flour if you want a creamy sauce; if you prefer a clear sauce, omit the flour. Then sprinkle with freshly ground pepper.

Tie the crushed garlic, orange peel, bay leaves, thyme, mace or nutmeg, parsley sprigs and marjoram in a piece of cheesecloth. Add this to the meat. Heat the wine and pour it over the meat. Do not add salt to this dish. There should be just enough wine to barely cover the meat, so use more or less as needed. Cover the pan tightly and cook in a 250°F (120°C) oven for 1½ to 3 hours. Open only once or twice to check the meat's tenderness. If more liquid is needed during cooking, add a little hot red wine or beef consommé.

At 20 minutes before the end of the cooking time, add the browned onions and the browned salt pork. Melt the butter and sauté the mushrooms in it until delicately browned. Stir them into the stew just before serving. Then sprinkle with the minced parsley and the croutons.

Green peas à l'étuvée

The flavour secrets of this dish are the very low heat used throughout the 30 minutes of cooking and the fact that you add no salt. Of course, it is especially delicious made with fresh green peas. In that case, use 2 pounds (1 kg) of fresh peas.

3 tbsp (50 ml) butter

1 head lettuce, chopped into long shreds

2 10-oz (284 gr) packages frozen peas

½ tsp (2 ml) sugar

1 bunch green onions, minced

2 tbsp (30 ml) water

Melt butter. Add lettuce shreds to the butter. Top with frozen peas. Sprinkle with sugar and minced green onions. Add water. Cover the saucepan and cook over low heat for 30 minutes, stirring 3 or 4 times. Do not add salt.

Chocolate flan de Nevers

4 tbsp (60 ml) fine granulated sugar

6 egg yolks

1¼ cups (310 ml) hot milk

8 oz (227 gr) semi-sweet chocolate

1 cup (250 ml) unsalted butter

30 small ladyfingers or small almond macaroons

Place the sugar and egg yolks in the top part of a double boiler; mix thoroughly. Add the hot milk and mix well again. Cook over hot water, stirring often, until the mixture is thick and creamy. Pour this custard through a fine sieve and let it cool.

Melt the chocolate over hot water. (Use the same double boiler in which you made the custard; no need to wash it.) Add the butter and stir until well blended. Pour the chocolate into the cooled custard and beat with a rotary beater until smooth.

Line a buttered mold at the sides and bottom with ladyfingers or macaroons. Gently pour the chocolate cream into the mold. Cover the top with more ladyfingers or macaroons and a sheet of foil. Refrigerate for 8 to 24 hours. To serve, unmold and garnish with cold Custard Sauce (Vol I, page 140) or with chocolate curls.

> **AUTUMN WILD DUCK DINNER**
> (for 6 friends)
>
> *Carco wine consommé*
> *Glazed ducklings*
> *Pungent brown rice*
>
> *Carrots Ninon*

A domestic duck can be given a wild taste, but nothing can domesticate the elegant wild duck. If you don't have the three wild ducks called for in the recipe for Glazed Ducklings, replace them with two domestic ducks to prepare a dinner for six persons.

Roast duck is delicious served with apple sauce. As a variation, add segments of orange or pitted candied cherries. Fresh pineapple cut into fingers and heated in butter with a bit of curry makes a very tasty fruit sauce with duck, especially with wild duck.

Carco wine consommé

3 10½-oz (300 ml) cans undiluted condensed consommé

1¼ soup cans cold water

1 cup (250 ml) red wine

Lemon peel strips

Heat together the undiluted consommé and cold water. When boiling, add red wine; choose a dry claret type. Let the mixture simmer for a few minutes, but do not let it boil again. Garnish each cup with a few long thin slivers of lemon peel.

Glazed ducklings

These ducklings are not only beautiful and delicious, they are easy to prepare.

3 wild ducks or 2 domestic ducks

Salt and pepper to taste

¼ tsp (1 ml) dried rosemary or dried sage

¼ cup (60 ml) corn syrup or maple syrup

¼ cup (60 ml) fresh orange juice

1 cup (250 ml) orange juice

1 cup (250 ml) black-currant jelly

1 cup (250 ml) consommé

1 tbsp (15 ml) grated fresh gingerroot
or ½ tsp (2 ml) ground ginger

1 tsp (5 ml) curry powder

¼ tsp (1 ml) grated nutmeg

Clean the ducks and place them on a rack in a roasting pan. Sprinkle inside and out with salt and pepper. Rub dried rosemary or sage inside each duck. Roast in a 400°F (200°C) oven for 30 minutes to the pound (500 gr), or until done. Pierce the skin all over once during the cooking period so that the fat will run out. The ducks are done when the drumsticks wiggle easily when moved.

Thirty minutes before the birds are done, stir together the corn syrup or maple syrup and ¼ cup (60 ml) of the fresh orange juice. Pour off the fat from the roasting pan and brush the ducks with the orange-juice mixture. Let them continue to cook until tender and beautifully glazed. Remove the ducks from the roasting pan when they are done and keep in a warm place.

ENTERTAINING AT HOME

To the juice in the pan add 1 cup (250 ml) orange juice, black-currant jelly, consommé, gingerroot or ground ginger, curry powder and grated nutmeg. Boil over direct heat, while stirring, until the sauce has reduced and thickened slightly. Carve the ducks (see right), or cut into individual portions with a pair of kitchen shears. Cover with very hot sauce.

Carving duck

Carving a duck is more difficult than carving a chicken because the joints are tougher. Before you begin to carve, make sure to remove all the juices from the inside of the duck by standing the bird upright and letting the liquid flow out. Add the juices to the sauce.

First remove the legs by making a circular incision with the point of a knife where the legs join the body. Insert the fork in the thigh and with a quick movement lift the leg towards you and cut through the joint. Separate the legs from the thighs by cutting through the joint between thigh and leg.

Insert the fork in the lower part of the carcass to get a good grip and begin to carve slices from the breast on one side, beginning at the wing and finishing against the breastbone. A large duck should yield 4 to 6 slices on each side. The choicest slices are those from the breast.

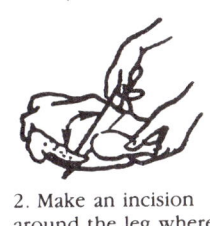
1. Lift up the duck and let any juices from the inside flow out; add these juices to the sauce.

2. Make an incision around the leg where the leg joins the body.

3. Insert a fork in the thigh, lift the leg towards you, and cut through the joint.

4. Carve slices from the breast, beginning near the wing and finishing against the breastbone.

Pungent brown rice

- 2 cups (500 ml) brown rice
- 2 tbsp (30 ml) butter
- 1 large onion, thinly sliced
- ¼ cup (60 ml) chutney
- ¼ cup (60 ml) brandy
- ½ cup (125 ml) commercial sour cream
- Salt and pepper to taste

Cook brown rice according to the directions on the box; or follow one of the methods in Volume 2. Melt butter and add onion. Sauté until golden brown. Add chutney, brandy and sour cream. Add this mixture to the cooked rice. Stir together. Season and serve.

Carrots Ninon

8 to 12 carrots, thinly sliced

1 cup (250 ml) seedless raisins

Juice of 1 lime of ½ a lemon

1 tbsp (15 ml) butter

Salt and pepper to taste

Peel carrots and slice into thin diagonal slices. Steam or pan-cook until just tender but still a little on the crispy side. Drain well and add raisins, lime or lemon juice and butter. Sprinkle with salt and pepper to taste.

Lemon mousse

Grated rind of 1 lemon

½ cup (125 ml) fresh lemon juice

4 eggs, separated

½ tsp (2 ml) salt

1 cup (250 ml) sugar

1 envelope unflavoured gelatin

¼ cup (60 ml) cold water

1 cup (250 ml) heavy cream

Place the lemon rind and juice in the top part of a double boiler. Add the egg yolks, salt and ½ cup (125 ml) of the sugar. Cook over boiling water, stirring most of the time.

Soak the gelatin in the cold water for 5 minutes, then add to the cooked egg-yolk mixture. Stir until the gelatin has dissolved. Refrigerate until cool.

In a large bowl, beat the egg whites until stiff and gradually add the remaining ½ cup (125 ml) of sugar, beating until the whites hold a peak. Whip the cream and pour it over the egg whites. Fold in the cooled lemon mixture and fold all together with a wire whisk or a rubber spatula. Pour into a cut-glass bowl. Refrigerate.

To serve, top with a single autumn leaf or a chrysanthemum. Serve with thin buttery wafers.

ENTERTAINING AT HOME

This superb dinner has one great advantage: Almost all of it can be prepared the day before. However, you will have a great deal of cooking to do to get everything ready. Begin with a careful shopping list, of course, and finish with an elegant centrepiece. Serve this in the proper setting with lace cloth, silverware, your best crystal, candlelight and flowers.

> ### GRAND DÎNER
> (a very special dinner for 16 guests)
>
> *Tapénade de Nice avec les crudités*
> *Champagne*
> *Melon Alcantara*
> *Xérès*
> *Paupiettes de sole à l'écossaise*
> *Chablis, Premier Cru*
> *Jardinière de légumes*
> *Salade de cresson*
> *Brioches*
> *Pêches dijonnaise*
> *Café filtre*
> *Liqueur française*

Tapenade de Nice

The tapenade sauce can be prepared two or three days ahead of time. Keep it refrigerated until you are ready to serve it with the raw vegetables and canned artichoke hearts.

1 slice of dry bread

1 garlic clove, peeled

3 tbsp (50 ml) red-wine vinegar

¼ lb (125 gr) pine nuts (pignolia)

3 tbsp (50 ml) capers

4 anchovy fillets

2 hard-cooked egg yolks

12 black olives, pitted

¼ cup (60 ml) minced parsley

1 cup (250 ml) olive oil

Salt and pepper to taste

1 cucumber

1 green pepper

2 carrots

1 16-oz (500 ml) can artichoke hearts

Remove the crust from the bread. Cut the garlic into halves and rub both sides of the bread with the garlic pieces. Break up the bread in a bowl and pour the vinegar on top. Work bread and vinegar with the fingers until mushy.

At this point, the work can be done in a blender or the ingredients can be put through a food chopper. Place in the blender the bread mixture, garlic pieces, pine nuts, capers, anchovy fillets, hard-cooked egg yolks (save the whites for Salade de Cresson), black olives and parsley. Add ½ cup (125 ml) of the olive oil. Blend until creamy. Gradually add the balance of the olive oil. When well blended, add salt and pepper to taste. The procedure is the same when using a food chopper; add the oil gradually as the food is chopped. Pour the mixture into a glass dish that can be fitted into an elegant bowl filled with ice.

Make small sticks of the cucumber, green pepper and carrots. Drain the artichoke hearts, and spread on absorbent paper until thoroughly dry.

Place the prepared vegetables on the ice around the dish of *tapenade* sauce. Serve with glasses of cold champagne.

Melon Alcantara

2 cantaloupes

1 Spanish melon

Salt and pepper

Freshly grated nutmeg

¼ lb (125 gr) butter

1 tbsp (15 ml) grated fresh gingerroot

4 limes

Make balls of cantaloupe and Spanish melon, counting a mixture of 5 to 7 per serving. Put each portion in an individual ovenware dish. Salt and pepper each one. Grate a dash of nutmeg over each. Cut the butter into small dice and divide evenly among the dishes. Mix the grated gingerroot and the lime juice and sprinkle on top of the melon. Cover and refrigerate, overnight if convenient.

Shortly before serving, place in a preheated 350°F (180°C) oven for 20 minutes. Serve with dry sherry.

Scottish sole paupiettes

This dish can be prepared in the early morning to be served for evening dinner. It will only need to be warmed at the last minute.

2 lbs (1 kg) fresh salmon

2 eggs

½ cup (125 ml) minced parsley

1 tsp (5 ml) minced tarragon, fresh or dried

1 tsp (5 ml) salt

½ tsp (2 ml) pepper

18 fillets of sole

Salt and pepper to taste

Grated rind of 3 lemons

1 bottle dry white wine

5 tbsp (75 ml) butter

½ cup (125 ml) flour

1 cup (250 ml) heavy cream

½ cup (125 ml) milk

3 tbsp (50 ml) brandy

½ tsp (2 ml) sugar

Salt and pepper to taste

1 lb (500 gr) fresh mushrooms, thinly sliced, or 1 14-oz (435 ml) box imported *chanterelles*, drained

1 green onion, finely chopped

Fillet the salmon and pass it through a food chopper twice. Add the eggs, parsley, tarragon, salt and pepper. Beat with a whip or a wooden spoon until creamy and well blended.

Spread the sole fillets on a table, sprinkle each one lightly with salt and pepper, and sprinkle a pinch of lemon rind on each. Spread each fillet with some of the salmon mixture. Roll the fillets and tie each one with a thread.

Warm the white wine in a large frying pan, but do not let it boil. Place half the rolled fillets in the wine and simmer over low heat for 10 minutes, basting constantly with the hot wine. Remove the fillets to a deep ovenproof serving platter, arranging the rolls one next to the other. Cook the rest of the rolled fillets in the same manner. Strain the cooking wine and set it aside.

In the same frying pan, melt 4 tablespoons (60 ml) of the butter and add the flour. Stir until very well blended. Pour the strained wine into the roux and add the cream and milk. Cook over medium heat, stirring constantly with a wire whisk, until you have a smooth velvety sauce. Then add the brandy, sugar, and salt and pepper to taste. Stir again for a few minutes. Adjust season-

ENTERTAINING AT HOME

ing. If sauce is too thick, add a little milk or cream gradually while stirring, until the consistency is right. Set aside.

Melt the remaining 1 tablespoon (15 ml) butter. When light brown add the mushrooms and chopped green onion. Stir over high heat for ½ minute. Arrange the mushroom mixture around the fish. Spoon the sauce evenly over the rolled fish fillets leaving some of the mushrooms uncovered.

Shortly before serving, place the platter in a preheated 400°F (200°C) oven for 15 to 20 minutes.

Makes 16 servings.

Jardinière de légumes

Make a dish of any mixture of fresh vegetables you choose. Blanch according to the basic method (Vol. II) and roll in creamed butter. Mix and serve.

Salade de cresson

Wash and drain equal amounts of watercress and Bibb lettuce. For 16 servings you will need about 4 bunches of watercress and 6 heads of Bibb lettuce. At serving time, toss with a plain French dressing and garnish with shredded hard-cooked egg whites that are left over from making *Tapenade de Nice*.

Pêches dijonnaise

8 peaches

1 cup (250 ml) fresh orange juice

Grated rind of 2 oranges

½ cup (125 ml) black-currant syrup

1 cup (250 ml) sugar

1 cup (250 ml) water

Praline

2 cups (500 ml) sugar

Juice of ½ a lemon

1 cup (250 ml) blanched almonds

1 cup (250 ml) unblanched hazelnuts

Wash the peaches but do not peel them. Place the orange juice and grated rind, the black-currant syrup, sugar and water in a large frying pan with a cover. Bring to a fast rolling boil, while stirring. Place the unpeeled peaches in the syrup, cover, lower the heat and simmer for 25 minutes, turning once. Remove from the heat. Uncover. While the peaches are cooking, prepare the praline mixture.

Place the sugar and lemon juice in a saucepan. Stir constantly over medium heat until the mixture has turned to a light golden syrup. Add the nuts and stir until well mixed. Pour the mixture into a jelly-roll pan with sides, spreading it as quickly as possible. Set aside until cold, about 1 hour. Then, either crush gradually in a blender at high speed, removing the blended portion each time before adding more, or butter a rolling pin and crush a few pieces at a time over a wooden board. Set aside.

Peel the cooled peaches and cut into halves. Place a half, with rounded side up, in an individual heatproof custard cup or soufflé dish. Sprinkle 2 tablespoons (30 ml) of the praline over the top of each peach half. Then make the French cream.

French cream

5 whole eggs

4 extra egg yolks

1 cup (250 ml) sugar

4 cups (1 L) light cream

1 cup (250 ml) milk

1 vanilla bean

Beat together lightly the whole eggs, extra egg yolks and sugar. In the meantime, warm the cream and milk with the vanilla bean. When hot, remove the vanilla bean. Beat the hot liquid into the egg and sugar mixture. Divide equally among the peaches.

Set the individual dishes in a pan of hot water. Bake in a preheated 350°F (180°C) oven until the blade of a knife comes out clean. Cool, then refrigerate overnight, or until ready to serve. Serve with Dijon syrup.

Dijon syrup

1 cup (250 ml) sugar

1½ cups (375 ml) water

4 tbsp (60 ml) vanilla extract

4 tbsp (60 ml) coffee liqueur

1 tbsp (15 ml) brandy

Place the sugar in a frying pan and stir over medium heat until it turns into a light golden syrup. Remove from heat. Add the cold water, 1 tablespoon (15 ml) at a time. When all is added, return to the heat and cook, stirring occasionally, until the mixture has formed a light syrup. Remove from heat and cool. Then add the vanilla, coffee liqueur and brandy. Mix well. Place in a jar and refrigerate until ready to pour some over each dessert. This sauce can be kept refrigerated for 2 to 3 weeks.

Makes about 3 cups (750 ml) syrup.

ENTERTAINING AT HOME

BUFFET SUPPER

This kind of party is the solution for the busy host, with little or no help, who wishes to entertain six or more guests. The food can be prepared entirely in advance; the table can be set early in the day; and the guests can serve themselves. When you arrange it with elegant little touches, a casserole buffet supper can impress even a true connoisseur. If you are entertaining 12 guests, double the recipes.

Shopping and checking of staples on hand should be done two days before the party. The sherry and wine or beer are optional, of course; dinner can be served without them and still be a success.

Prepare as much as you can ahead of time, leaving as little work as possible to do on the day of the party.

If you follow the procedure outlined for this menu, you will find everything is accomplished neatly and without fuss.

A CASSEROLE BUFFET
(for 6 or 12 guests)

Chopped chicken livers
Hot crisp bread
Dry sherry

Swiss chicken casserole
Swiss light white wine
or
East Indian shrimp curry
Red wine or cold beer

Baked long-grain rice

Green-bean salad

Fresh lemon granité with strawberry sauce
Café noir

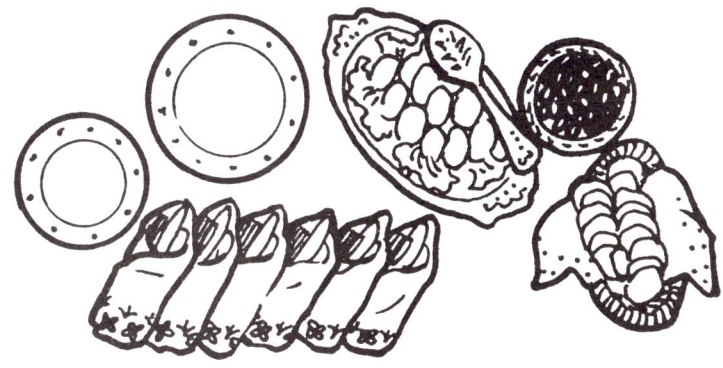

Chopped chicken livers

2 tbsp (30 ml) butter

2 tbsp (30 ml) chicken fat

2 medium-sized white onions, chopped

¼ tsp (1 ml) dried tarragon

½ lb (250 gr) chicken livers

2 hard-cooked eggs, chopped

¼ cup (60 ml) chopped parsley

Salt and pepper to taste

The day before heat together the butter and chicken fat (removed from the chicken used for the casserole). When the chicken fat is melted, add chopped onions and sauté until golden. Add dried tarragon. Add cleaned chicken livers and stir over high heat until red juices cease to run. Do not overcook. Place the cooked livers on a chopping board or in a bowl, add hard-cooked eggs and pour whatever fat and onions remain in the pan over this. With a sharp knife, chop the whole mixture until fine and well mixed. Add chopped parsley and season with salt and pepper to taste. Place in an attractive bowl and refrigerate until serving time.

Hot crisp bread

The day before, cut thin slices of rye bread or crusty French bread, about 3 slices per person. Do not remove the crusts. Butter each slice and sprinkle with celery salt. Place on a baking sheet. Cover with foil and refrigerate until just before serving.

The day of the party, place the sheet of bread slices in a preheated 450°F (230°C) oven for 10 minutes, or under the direct heat of a broiler for 3 minutes. Watch closely when under the broiler.

Put a small spreader in the liver paste, set the bowl in a basket, and surround with hot, crisp bread. Let each guest spread his own while you serve the sherry.

Refrigerate the sherry for at least 3 hours before serving, as an apéritif sherry should always be served cold. The liver paste, sherry and glasses can be set in the living room just before the guests arrive.

Swiss chicken casserole

- 1 5-lb (2.5 kg) chicken or boiling fowl
- ½ cup (125 ml) all-purpose flour
- ½ tsp (2 ml) salt
- ¼ tsp (1 ml) pepper
- 1 tsp (5 ml) paprika
- 4 tbsp (60 ml) butter
- 1 cup (250 ml) water
- ½ cup (125 ml) white wine or lemon juice
- 3 tbsp (50 ml) minced fresh parsley
- 2 green onions, minced
- 1 garlic clove, minced
- 2 whole cloves
- ½ bay leaf
- ¼ tsp (1 ml) dried basil
- 1 cup (250 ml) grated Swiss cheese
- 2 tbsp (30 ml) flour
- ¼ cup (60 ml) light cream

The day before, cut chicken into individual portions; save the fat for the chopped chicken livers. On a large plate mix the flour, salt, pepper and paprika. Roll the chicken pieces in this.

Melt the butter in a large frying pan. Brown the chicken over medium heat. Add the water, white wine or lemon juice, parsley, green onions, garlic clove, cloves, bay leaf and dried basil. Cover and simmer over low heat until tender. Cool and refrigerate.

Grate Swiss cheese; wrap and refrigerate.

The day of the party, warm the chicken over low heat. Remove 3 tablespoons (50 ml) fat from the surface and place in a small frying pan. Lift the chicken pieces to a plate and strain the cooking liquid. Add the 2 tablespoons (30 ml) flour to the fat, mix well and add the strained liquid and the cream. Cook, stirring all the time, until the sauce is smooth and creamy. Season to taste.

Place half the sauce in an attractive shallow casserole. Sprinkle half the cheese over the sauce. Place pieces of chicken on top. Sprinkle with the rest of the cheese and pour on the remaining sauce. Keep at room temperature until ready to bake. Bake in a preheated 425°F (220°C) oven for 30 minutes.

ENTERTAINING AT HOME

East Indian shrimp curry

There are many types of curry and the ways of cooking with it vary from region to region in India. This shrimp curry is easily prepared and, like all curries, has the wonderful quality of being even better when reheated. The dish can be prepared the day before the party; when ready to serve it, just reheat. Use 2 pounds (1 kg) of shrimp for six guests and 3 pounds. (1.5 kg) if you double the recipe for 12 guests.

2 lb (1 kg) uncooked shrimps

3 tbsp (50 ml) butter

2 medium-sized onions, thinly sliced

2 tbsp (30 ml) curry powder

2 garlic cloves, crushed

3 tbsp (50 ml) water

Juice of 1 lemon or 2 limes

1 tbsp (15 ml) freshly grated gingerroot

or 1 tsp (5 ml) ground ginger

1 tsp (5 ml) ground turmeric

1 19-oz (540 ml) can tomatoes

1 tbsp (15 ml) tomato paste

Salt to taste

1 cup (250 ml) diced celery (optional)

Peel the uncooked shrimps by cutting the under-shell with scissors and pulling out the meat. If the shrimp are frozen, soak in cold water for 1 hour, then peel. Clean and set aside.

Melt butter in a large saucepan. When golden brown, add sliced onions. Once browned, remove the onions with a slotted spoon to a plate. Add curry powder to the butter remaining in the pan. Stir until well mixed.

Place crushed garlic in a small bowl with the water and lemon or lime juice. Add fresh gingerroot or ground ginger, and ground turmeric. Stir well.

Return the browned onions to the curry and butter; heat. Pour in the water and lemon-juice mixture all at once; stir quickly. Add tomatoes and tomato paste and bring to a boil while stirring. Then let simmer, uncovered, for 30 to 40 minutes.

At this point add the shelled shrimps, salt to taste and add to taste up to 1 cup (250 ml) diced celery. Remove immediately from the heat. Pour into a dish, cover and refrigerate.

The day of the party, place the curry in a chafing dish, or in an electric frying pan set at 300°F (150°C) to reheat at the table, or place in a casserole to reheat uncovered in a 300°F (150°C) oven. Do not let it boil; just allow it to get hot.

If you wish, with the shrimp curry serve little dishes of chutney, whole or chopped cashews, small cubes of cantaloupe and toasted coconut. Let your guests help themselves to these accompaniments.

Baked long-grain rice

- 2 tbsp (30 ml) butter
- 4 green onions, minced
- 2 cups (500 ml) uncooked long-grain rice
- 2 10½-oz (300 ml) cans condensed consommé and enough water to make 4 cups (1 L) or 2 chicken bouillon cubes dissolved in 4 cups (1 L) boiling water
- ½ tsp (2 ml) crumbled dried basil or ¼ cup (60 ml) minced fresh parsley

The day before, melt butter, add green onions and stir until limp. Add uncooked long-grain rice and continue to stir over medium heat until the rice is glossy and light golden brown. Place in a casserole with a cover. Pour over the condensed consommé and water or bouillon cubes in boiling water. Mix in crumbled dried basil or fresh parsley. Cover and refrigerate until 40 minutes before serving.

The day of the party, preheat oven to 375°F (190°C) and bake the rice, covered, for 40 minutes.

Green-bean salad

- 1 lb (500 gr) fresh green snap beans
- Pinch of sugar
- ½ cup (125 ml) salad oil
- 2 tbsp (30 ml) cider vinegar or tarragon vinegar
- ½ tsp (2 ml) salt
- ½ tsp (2 ml) sugar
- ½ tsp (2 ml) paprika
- ¼ tsp (1 ml) dry mustard
- 1 tsp (5 ml) grated onion
- Few drops of table sauce
- ½ tsp (2 ml) crumbled dried basil
- 1 garlic clove
- 2 hard-cooked eggs
- ¼ cup (60 ml) slivered toasted almonds

The day before, wash green beans and cut each into 2 or 3 pieces, or split lengthwise. Place in a saucepan with a pinch of sugar. Cover with boiling water and cook over high heat for 8 minutes. Drain and rinse under cold water. Refrigerate.

Make an herb French dressing; put in a glass jar the salad oil, cider or tarragon vinegar, salt, sugar, paprika, dry mustard, grated onion, table sauce, crumbled dried basil and peeled garlic clove.

Hard-cook 2 eggs.

Sliver ¼ cup (60 ml) toasted almonds.

The day of the party, add enough dressing to the cooled beans so they are well coated. Place in a salad bowl and garnish the edges with quartered hard-cooked eggs. Sprinkle the centre with a mixture of minced parsley and green onions. Top with slivered almonds.

ENTERTAINING AT HOME 515

Fresh lemon granité

1 6-oz (170 ml) can evaporated milk
or 1 cup (250 ml) heavy cream
2 eggs, separated
½ cup (125 ml) sugar
⅓ cup (80 ml) fresh lemon juice
Grated rind of 1 lemon
¼ cup (60 ml) sugar

One or two days before the party, pour evaporated milk into a metal ice-cube tray and chill until crystals start to form around the sides. Whip until thick. Or whip heavy cream.

Mix the egg yolks with sugar, lemon juice and grated lemon rind. Beat until light and foamy. Beat the whites of the eggs stiff, add sugar and beat again until the consistency of meringue. Fold into the egg-yolk mixture. Add the whipped evaporated milk or cream. Pour into a metal ice-cube tray and let set in the freezer for 6 to 8 hours. When frozen, cover the granité with foil to keep it from drying at the surface.

To serve, cut into 2-inch (5 cm) sections. Let each guest help himself to strawberry sauce to pour over the granité.

Strawberry sauce

1 10-oz (284 gr) package frozen strawberries
¼ cup (60 ml) port wine
2 tbsp (30 ml) cornstarch
Juice and grated rind of 1 orange

The day before, thaw frozen strawberries. Place in a saucepan with port wine. Mix cornstarch with the orange juice and grated rind. Add to the hot strawberries and stir over medium heat until creamy and transparent. Pour into a dish, cover and refrigerate until ready to serve.

OUTDOOR PARTIES

Comfort and originality are important factors in the success of an outdoor party. Being in the open, of course, always adds to the general spirit of relaxation, but for people to be comfortable everyone should have something to sit on and the food, naturally, should be good.

As for any other party, try to have most of the food ready to be cooked, or the cooked food ready to be served and set on platters. When it is not a barbecue party, consider having colourful trays, one for each guest, set with plates, cutlery and glasses. Serve the main course onto each tray in the kitchen and have someone pass them around, or ask the guests to come to the kitchen to pick up their trays. Once the food has been eaten, clear away the trays. Then dessert, cheese and coffee can be brought out to a table set with the necessary plates and cutlery.

There should only be a few courses at an outdoor meal to keep the work of serving and cleaning up to a minimum.

Remember, part of the charm of an outdoor party lies in the setting and visual appeal, so the decorations should blend into the setting, which is, of course, nature itself. Use inexpensive pottery or wooden utensils, or anything close to the earth, and decorate with the leafy or flowery offerings of the outdoors.

Barbecues are good for the dinner hour, but picnics are great fun for lunchtime. All kinds of convenience foods can be used, and many things can be prepared ahead of time and kept well wrapped and ready to go. If you own a freezer, you can do a large part of your cooking days or even months ahead. Portable ice chests or insulated containers will hold perishable foods and keep drinks ice cold or piping hot. Plastic plates, tumblers and food boxes are very helpful.

An Elegant Victorian Picnic

Picnic hors d'oeuvre

Oxford sausages

Shooters' loaf

English cold beef and kidney pie

Pickled damson plums

Rose-geranium poundcake

Perry cup

White-wine cup

They used to go to such lengths to create memorable picnics around the turn of the century! I have vivid memories of the days when my family used to carry picnic food in large wicker hampers filled with delightful enameled boxes, sandwich tins and sometimes even a copper kettle with a spirit lamp for making hot tea or toddy. If you really want to enjoy a Victorian picnic, find yourself such a hamper or basket (a few can still be found in antique shops) if you weren't lucky enough to have inherited one.

Here are a few ideas for food you can carry to a faraway spot, or eat in your own garden.

Picnic hors d'oeuvre

This tray of appetizers can be a real tableau. At Victorian picnics it was often the centrepiece, set on a large white damask cloth that had been spread on the grass.

Clean a bunch of radishes, leaving on a few of the little green leaves, and place them in a glass jar filled with water; refrigerate until ready to put in the basket. Fill another glass jar with equal quantities of stuffed green olives and ripe black olives; add a bay leaf and a whole green onion; do not refrigerate. Boil 6 to 12 eggs, remove the shells and refrigerate them, well covered, until ready to pack. Clean and wrap a box of whole small tomatoes.

Bring along a pepper mill, a salt shaker, several lemons, butter packed in a covered earthenware crock and a loaf of crusty bread.

To serve, arrange all these ingredients on a long oval dish or a teak tray. The eggs can be cut into halves or, if a small slice is removed at the thicker end, the eggs can be placed standing up. Cut the lemons into quarters and slice the bread. These, and Oxford Sausages (recipe follows), are enough to make a beautiful picnic for six people.

ENTERTAINING AT HOME 517

Oxford sausages

In Victorian times, these delicious sausages were often made with venison or partridge instead of pork. They then were referred to as Hunters' Sausages. The best cut of meat to use is pork fillet. For the suet, ask your butcher to give you beef kidney fat if possible.

1 lb (500 gr) lean pork, ground

1 lb (500 gr) beef suet, ground

Grated rind of 1 lemon

1 tsp (5 ml) minced sage (fresh, when possible)

½ tsp (2 ml) minced marjoram (fresh, when possible)

½ tsp (2 ml) ground mace

1 tsp (5 ml) black pepper

1 tsp (5 ml) coarse salt

Milk

3 cups (750 ml) fine dry breadcrumbs

Melted beef fat or bacon fat

Mix the ground pork and suet together and add the grated lemon rind, herbs, spices and salt. Blend thoroughly. Take a spoonful of the mixture and shape into a small sausage on a floured board. Roll in milk, then in breadcrumbs. Cook slowly in the fat until browned on all sides. Cool on absorbent paper.

These sausages can be rolled in very thin slices of ham that have been spread with mustard. Either way, they should be served cold.

Serves 6 or more.

Shooters' loaf

1 large thick first-quality steak or half a beef fillet

3 tbsp (50 ml) butter

1 tsp (5 ml) dry mustard

¼ tsp (1 ml) powdered garlic

Salt and pepper to taste

1 long loaf crispy bread, unsliced

Cream the butter with the dry mustard and powdered garlic. Spread half this mixture on top of the steak or fillet. Preheat the oven to 400°F (200°C) and place the meat on a shallow dripping pan. Roast for 20 minutes, then turn, spread the other side with the rest of the butter mixture and roast for another 20 minutes.

While the meat is roasting, take the loaf, preferably a narrow one, and cut off a thick slice at one end. Pull out a good part of the inside of the loaf, enough to make a hole that can take the piece of meat.

When the meat is ready, sprinkle with salt and pepper to taste and without delay push the hot meat into the hollowed-out loaf; replace the end of the loaf. Wrap in a double layer of waxed paper and tie securely with string. Wrap again with another layer of waxed paper and tie again. Place something heavy on the bread and let it stand on the kitchen counter for 1 hour. Then refrigerate the loaf, with the weight still on top, for another 5 to 6 hours.

Place the loaf in the picnic basket without unwrapping. When ready to serve, unwrap, place on an attractive wooden board in a nest of greens and cut into thin slices. Serve with a good chutney.

English cold beef and kidney pie

Beef and kidney pie, served with pickled damson plums, was another "must" as Victorians picnicked on the grass.

1 beef kidney, trimmed and diced

1 cup (250 ml) beef kidney fat, diced

1 lb (500 gr) stewing beef, diced

3 onions, chopped

3 cups (750 ml) hot water

1 tsp (5 ml) salt

½ tsp (2 ml) black pepper

1 tsp (5 ml) dry mustard

½ cup (125 ml) browned flour

½ cup (125 ml) cold water

Pie pastry for a large 2-crust pie

Melt the kidney fat until crisp. Add the diced kidney and stewing beef and brown over high heat for 2 minutes. Add the onions and continue to brown over high heat for another 2 minutes. Pour the hot water and seasonings over the meat and onions. Bring to a boil. Cover and cook over low heat for 2 hours, or until the kidney is tender.

When the kidney is cooked, thicken the broth; stir the browned flour into the cold water and stir into the stew. Pour the thickened stew into a pastry-lined casserole. Cover with another layer of pastry, crimp the edges and make a hole for the steam to escape. Bake in a 400°F (200°C) oven until the crust is brown. Cool.

Unmold the pie from the casserole, cover with a cloth, and keep at room temperature until ready to pack. Then wrap the pie in a clean white linen cloth and tie the four corners of the cloth on top.

To serve, cut into thick slices and garnish with a few pickled damson plums.

Makes 6 to 8 servings.

Pickled damson plums

These are sometimes called Italian plums. The smaller they are, the more attractive they will look when pickled. Make several days ahead.

2 lb (1 kg) damson plums

1 cup (250 ml) brown sugar

1 cup (250 ml) cider vinegar

3 whole cloves

1 bay leaf

Rinse the plums under cold running water and rub dry with a cloth. Make a few holes in each plum with the point of a knitting needle, then place them in an earthenware or glass jar.

Boil the sugar and vinegar together, stirring until the sugar is completely dissolved. Add the cloves and bay leaf. Pour this mixture, boiling hot, over the plums. Cover and let stand until the next day. Pour off the syrup into a saucepan. Bring it to a fast rolling boil and pour it again over the plums. Cover and let stand another day. Repeat this process a third time and let the plums stand a day longer. Then pour the syrup and plums into a saucepan and bring just to the boil without stirring. Pour into jars and cover the jars.

Victorian picnic sweets included rose-geranium pound-cake, glacéed or candied fruit, small bitter Neapolitan chocolates wrapped in gold paper and, if the season was right, large clusters of fresh grapes.

ENTERTAINING AT HOME

Rose-geranium poundcake

Rosewater can be purchased in drugstores. If you can't find a rose-geranium plant, you can bake the cake without the leaves; it will still be a good poundcake.

1 cup (250 ml) unsalted butter, softened

1 cup (250 ml) sugar

¼ cup (60 ml) clear honey

5 eggs

2 cups (500 ml) cake flour, sifted

Grated rind of ½ a lemon

1 tsp (5 ml) rosewater

2 tsp (10 ml) lemon juice

5 fresh leaves of rose geranium

Cream the butter and sugar until very light and creamy. Add the honey and mix well. Add the eggs, one at a time, beating well after each addition. Gradually add the cake flour, blending thoroughly after each addition. (If using an electric mixer, do this at moderate speed.) Add the lemon rind, rosewater and lemon juice. Stir well.

Grease a loaf pan (5 by 9 inches/13 by 23 cm) and line the bottom with the rose-geranium leaves. If these are unavailable, line the pan with waxed paper and grease the paper. Pour the batter over the leaves or greased paper in the pan and bake in a 350°F (180°C) oven for about 1¼ hours.

When the cake is baked, place the pan on a cake rack and let it stand for 15 minutes. Unmold. Cool completely, then wrap in a double layer of foil.

This cake will keep fresh without refrigeration for 2 to 3 weeks and requires no icing. Icing sugar can be sprinkled on top just before serving.

Favourite drinks at Victorian picnics were iced sherry and bitters, perry cup and white-wine cup. The bottle of sherry was kept cool by being wrapped in sheets of wet newspaper. You can put yours on ice. Add a few drops of bitters to the sherry and drink while cold.

Perry cup

The name of this drink came from a delicately flavoured cider made from pear juice. A modern version can be made with apple cider. The Victorians placed a sprig of borage in each glass before serving. This can be replaced by a thick slice of cucumber peel, which has the same flavour.

3 slices brown bread, toasted

½ nutmeg, grated

3 tbsp (50 ml) sugar

1 tsp (5 ml) ground ginger

Grated rind and juice of 1 lemon

1 cup (250 ml) sherry

4 to 6 cups (1 to 1.5 L) soda water

Cucumber peel slices for garnish

Place toasted bread in a gallon jug. Grate nutmeg into a bowl and add sugar, ground ginger, grated lemon rind and juice and sherry. Pour over the bread in the jug and seal the jug.

When ready to serve at the picnic, add 4 to 6 cups (1 to 1.5 L) of cider and an equal quantity of soda water. Shake thoroughly and serve.

Makes 4 to 6 servings.

White-wine cup

This was perhaps the most popular of all drinks at Victorian picnics. In each large glass put a piece of cucumber peel, a piece of orange peel, a leaf of borage and 2 lumps of sugar. Pour a liqueur glass of brandy over this and let stand for 20 minutes. Fill the glass half full with white wine and add soda water to taste. Add a cube or two of ice just before serving.

A ROMANTIC PICNIC FOR TWO

Cold salmon superb
Twisted cucumber in sour cream
New potatoes in chive butter
Crisp celery and radishes
Chocolate cake à la rose
White-wine fizz

The romantic picnic has never gone out of fashion; when you are part of it you'll feel that this is the best of all possible worlds. Gather a few field flowers or a flowering branch to arrange attractively around the food.

New potatoes in chive butter

Boil new potatoes in their jackets. If possible, use small round ones. Drain and peel, then place while hot in a container. Top with a good-sized piece of butter, sprinkle with salt and pepper to taste and add as much minced chives as you like. The heat of the potatoes is enough to melt the butter. If you prepare these in the morning, keep them at room temperature until ready to pack. Shake the container before serving. Serve them tepid. They're delicious!

Chocolate cake à la rose

2 squares (2 oz/50 gr) unsweetened chocolate

½ cup (125 ml) butter

1 cup (250 ml) icing sugar

1 tsp (5 ml) grated lemon rind

2 eggs, well beaten

½ cup (125 ml) all-purpose flour

Pinch of salt

½ tsp (2 ml) baking powder

¼ cup (60 ml) hazelnuts, minced

½ tsp (2 ml) vanilla extract

Place the chocolate in the top of a double boiler. Melt it over hot water and let it cool. Cream the butter until very light. Gradually add the icing sugar and lemon rind, stirring constantly. Then add the eggs and the cooled melted chocolate. Beat until well mixed. Sift together the flour, salt and baking powder. Add in 3 portions to the creamed mixture, stirring well each time. Blend in the hazelnuts and vanilla. Pour into a well-buttered and floured 8-inch (20 cm) square cake pan. Bake in a 350°F (180°C) oven for 30 minutes. Do not unmold this brownie-like cake. Cool in the cake pan placed on a wire cake rack.

Bring to the picnic in the pan. Top with rose petals or wild flowers.

Cold salmon superb

2 lb (1 kg) salmon

⅓ cup (80 ml) melted butter

⅓ cup (80 ml) dry vermouth or lemon juice

Salt and pepper to taste

Place the salmon on a piece of heavy-duty aluminum foil, large enough to make an envelope to enclose the fish; lift the edges all around to form a dish. Pour the melted butter over the salmon and add the vermouth or lemon juice. Sprinkle with salt and pepper. Fold the edges of the foil together and seal with a double fold so the juices cannot escape. Place the packet on a dripping pan and bake in a 350°F (180°C) oven for 40 minutes.

When cooked, remove from the oven, but do not open the foil. Let the fish cool, then keep it in the refrigerator for at least 12 hours. The juices, when cold, will form a most delicious jelly. Carry to the picnic in an insulated cold box or portable refrigerator.

Twisted cucumber in sour cream

Ridge 1 or 2 cucumbers by pulling the prongs of a fork lengthwise all the way around. Then slice as thinly as possible. Place the slices in a dish, sprinkle with salt and pepper, and top with ice cubes. Let stand for 1 hour.

Drain off the water by twisting the cucumbers in a cloth. Place the drained cucumbers in a bowl, cover, and keep refrigerated until ready to leave for the picnic.

Just before leaving, add barely enough commercial sour cream to cover. Stir with a fork to mix and sprinkle with pepper. Place in an attractive jar and cover.

White wine fizz

Take along a bottle of white wine and a bottle of soda. Buy ice cubes along the way, or bring them with you if you can. Bring attractive tall glasses. Mix half wine, half soda in each glass and add 1 or 2 ice cubes. Swirl and serve.

A PICNIC IN THE CAR
(for 4 grown-ups and 2 noisy children)

Celery clam chowder in a vacuum jar

Tokyo beef roulade

Rye bread or crisp French bread

Chopped salad

Buttermilk spice cake

Basket of fresh fruits

Coffee in a vacuum flask

Soft drink

Once the weather turns crisp, it's cosy to have a picnic in the car. Open the windows, spread out your surprises and relax while you are eating them, with only the birds to watch you with envy.

Pack a small box for each traveler; put in it paper napkins, a mug for soup, a paper plate, a paper cup for coffee, a small soup spoon and a fork. You can initial the boxes or, if you're in a whimsical mood, you could even write little personal note in each, to add to the fun of the occasion.

Tokyo beef roulade

1½ lb (750 gr) chopped beef

Salt and pepper to taste

¼ tsp (1 ml) ground thyme

4 to 6 thin slices cooked ham

Mustard to taste

3 eggs

½ cup (125 ml) milk

1 tbsp (15 ml) butter

1 tsp (5 ml) curry powder

Salad oil

Flour

Red wine or tomato juice for basting

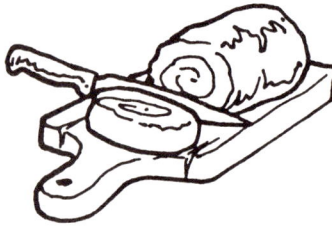

On a floured board or on a sheet of waxed paper spread chopped beef into a rectangle 12 by 16 inches (30 by 40 cm). Sprinkle with salt, pepper and ground thyme. Top with slices of ham.

Spread mustard to taste on the ham.

Beat eggs with milk. Add salt and pepper to taste. Melt butter in a large frying pan and add curry powder. Stir until well blended. Add the eggs and cook into a thin, lightly browned omelet. Remove and place on top of the ham slices.

Roll up the meat, jelly-roll fashion, with the chopped beef on the outside. Do this carefully to keep the beef layer from breaking; if it does, pat it together gently. If you have spread the meat on waxed paper, use the paper to help you make the roll. Arrange the seam side on the bottom. Sprinkle with salad oil and lightly with flour. Place in a meat-loaf pan or an 8-inch (20 cm) cake pan. Bake in a 400°F (200°C) oven for 20 minutes. Baste once or twice with red wine or tomato juice.

Let the roulade cool and cut it into ½-inch (1.25 cm) slices. Wrap each slice in foil. Accompany with buttered bread, also wrapped in portions.

Celery clam chowder

Heat condensed cream of celery soup with an equal amount of milk and 1 can (7 ounces/200 ml) undrained, minced clams for each 10-ounce (284 ml) can of soup. Season to taste. Add chopped parsley or chives. Pour into a vacuum jar. Serve in mugs.

Chopped salad

This mixture will be crisp even after a few hours in a sealed container.

1 cucumber, peeled and diced

1 small bunch radishes, thinly sliced

2 tomatoes, diced

1 green pepper, seeded and diced

3 green onions, chopped

1 small head lettuce, shredded

Juice of 1 lemon

4 tbsp (60 ml) salad oil

Salt and pepper to taste

Mix prepared vegetables together and add the lemon juice, salad oil and salt and pepper to taste. Toss well. Refrigerate for at least 1 hour before packing.

ENTERTAINING AT HOME

Buttermilk spice cake

This cake can be made ahead of time and stored in its baking pan in your freezer. Bring it along in its pan, wrapped and frozen. It will be just right when you are ready to eat it.

- 2¼ cups (560 ml) all-purpose flour
- 1½ cups (375 ml) sugar
- 1½ tsp (7 ml) baking soda
- 1 tsp (5 ml) baking powder
- ¼ tsp (1 ml) salt
- 1 tsp (5 ml) ground cinnamon
- ½ tsp (2 ml) ground cloves
- ½ cup (125 ml) melted butter or margarine
- 1½ cups (375 ml) buttermilk, at room temperature

Sift together in a mixing bowl the flour, sugar, baking soda, baking powder, salt, cinnamon and cloves.

Cool the melted butter and stir into the flour mixture along with the buttermilk. Mix vigorously until the batter is very smooth. (There is no mistake about having left out the eggs. There aren't any in this cake.)

Grease a tube cake pan and dust lightly with granulated sugar. Pour in the batter and bake in a preheated 325° to 350°F (160° to 180°C) oven for about 1 hour, or until a cake tester comes out clean. Cool on a cake rack for 15 minutes in the pan. Unmold.

To freeze, cool for at least 3 hours, then wrap and freeze. To carry the cake to the picnic, put it back into its baking pan.

To serve, slice thinly.

With the cheers still ringing in your ears, the tang of burning leaves in the air and a brisk autumn wind nipping at your nose, this is the time for a jovial, informal, after-game snack.

> **AFTER-FOOTBALL SNACK**
> (for 4 good friends)
>
> Mushroom-ham casserole
> Hot herb rolls
> Cheddar cheese, apples, toasted walnuts

Hot herb rolls

- 2 tbsp (30 ml) butter
- 1 tbsp (15 ml) parsley flakes or
- ¼ tsp (1 ml) dried tarragon or dried marjoram
- 8 to 12 rolls

Cream butter with parsley flakes or dried tarragon or marjoram. Spread the tops of the rolls with this butter. Refrigerate.

To serve, heat in a 400°F (200°C) oven for 10 minutes. (You can heat them with the casserole.)

Mushroom-ham casserole

Prepare this early in the morning and bake just before you are ready to serve.

2 6-oz (170 ml) cans button mushrooms

½ lb (250 gr) cooked ham

½ tsp (2 ml) curry powder

Juice of ½ a lemon

3 tbsp (50 ml) butter

3 tbsp (50 ml) flour

2 cups (500 ml) milk

2 egg yolks

2 to 4 tbsp (30 to 60 ml) sherry

Breadcrumbs

Drain mushrooms and place in a buttered casserole. Dice cooked ham and arrange over the mushrooms. Sprinkle with curry powder and lemon juice. Make a white sauce by mixing together and heating the butter, flour and milk. When smooth and creamy, season to taste. Beat egg yolks with sherry. Add to the hot sauce, stir well, and pour over ham and mushrooms. Sprinkle the top with breadcrumbs. Bake in a 400°F (200°C) oven for 25 minutes.

Makes 4 servings.

Cheddar cheese, apples, toasted walnuts

This is a delightful combination. Put a large wedge of Cheddar — mild, medium or strong — in the centre of a large tray. Arrange crisp polished apples on one side and toasted walnuts on the other.

To toast the walnuts, crack them in the morning, but leave them in their shells. Heat them in a 400°F (200°C) oven until they are golden brown. (They can be heated with the casserole, too.) Mound them, shells and all, on the dish with the cheese. Plenty of coffee and hot buttered rum will be welcome with this hearty snack.

Corn-husking bee (épluchette de blé d'Inde)

At harvesttime, give a truly old-fashioned, homespun, fun party called an épluchette de blé d'Inde. It's as traditional in French Canada as a barn raising is in the West. When the fields are full of ripe sweet corn, gather family and friends together for a hearty party in your backyard, at the summer cottage or on a picnic.

Have lots of corn, at least 4 ears per person. Part of the fun is to fill a large basket with corn and let your guests husk it.

Fill a large kettle with water and place it over a hot fire in a stone pit or barbecue. Add 1 cup (250 ml) of sugar per gallon (4.5 L) of water. Bring the water to a fast rolling boil and add the ears of corn one by one. Keep the fire red hot and let the corn boil for 10 minutes.

Have plenty of beer and ginger ale, to be mixed half and half for shandygaffs, as well as non-alcoholic drinks.

Have lots of paper napkins handy to hold the corn. Let the guests help themselves to whipped butter and relish.

Beat soft butter with a hand beater until creamy white. Divide into 3 bowls. Leave one plain, but top the second with a thick layer of minced chives and the third with minced parsley. Refrigerate until ready to serve or take along.

Mix 1 cup (250 ml) mayonnaise with 2 cups (500 ml) relish. Serve in a bowl with a small spoon. This makes a nice change from butter on the corn.

To complete the food, have a basket of celery and olives and, of course, salt and pepper shakers. The traditional dessert at an épluchette is blueberries with sugar and cream.

ENTERTAINING AT HOME

As a light-hearted touch in keeping with the occasion, prepare a card for each guest containing a few lines of love poetry. Ask the guests to read their cards aloud.

A pale-pink organdy or linen cloth is an attractive table decoration for an engagement party. If you use an organdy cloth, it will need a petticoat, so make one of a slightly deeper shade of pink, preferably of a material that has enough body to hold out the organdy like a bouffant dress. With this, use shocking-pink or pale-green napkins, white dishes, a few rose-patterned serving plates and 2 or 3 clear crystal and ruby-coloured bowls for nuts.

As a centrepiece, fill a cut-crystal vase with deep-red roses, or a deep-ruby jar with pale-pink roses. On each side of the flower arrangement place a low jar or bowl filled with grapes. They should hang over the edges a bit. Use black grapes in one bowl and green in the other.

To set the table, put the tea service at one end; if you're serving coffee as well, you can place the coffee tray at the other end. Ask the mothers of very close friends of the bride-to-be to pour tea and coffee. Have the guests serve themselves all the other foods. It will make things much easier if you use two sets of serving dishes, one on each side of the table.

If you wish to serve an engagement cake, make a presentation of it to give the cake and the occasion extra drama. It can be set on a small table or tea wagon in a different room.

Be sure to have the happy bride-to-be cut the cake. It's good practice for her wedding day.

A TEATIME ENGAGEMENT PARTY
(for 20 happy guests)

Stuffed hot biscuits
Apple muffins
Buttered nut bread
Chicken-salad puffs
Apricot delight

Stuffed hot biscuits

Bake as many 1½-inch (3.75 cm) tea biscuits as you think you'll need, using your favourite recipe or a ready mix. This filling will be good for 24 biscuits.

1 cup (250 ml) walnuts, finely chopped

½ cup (125 ml) candied orange peel, finely chopped

Honey

½ cup (125 ml) butter, creamed

Mix together walnuts and candied orange peel. Moisten with honey and blend with creamed butter. Split the biscuits and fill each with a bit of this mixture. Wrap them and place in the freezer 8 to 10 days ahead of time.

To serve, put the frozen biscuits on a cookie sheet and heat in a preheated 400°F (200°C) oven for 8 to 10 minutes.

Apple muffins

½ cup (125 ml) sugar

4 tbsp (60 ml) butter

1 eggs, lightly beaten

2½ cups (625 ml) all-purpose flour

3½ tsp (17 ml) baking powder

½ tsp (2 ml) salt

¼ tsp (1 ml) grated nutmeg

1 cup (250 ml) milk

Grated rind of 1 lemon

1½ cups (375 ml) coarsely grated apple

1 tbsp (15 ml) sugar

1 tbsp (15 ml) brown sugar

½ tsp (2 ml) ground cinnamon

Cream sugar with butter. Add lightly beaten egg and beat until smooth. Sift together the flour, baking powder, salt and nutmeg. Add to the creamed butter alternately with milk. Add the grated lemon rind. Beat until well blended. Fold in grated apple. Spoon into small greased muffin tins, filling them only half full. Mix together the sugar, brown sugar and cinnamon and sprinkle the top of each muffin with some of it. Bake in a preheated 425°F (220°C) oven for 15 to 20 minutes.

These freeze beautifully. To serve, reheat without thawing first.

Buttered nut bread

1 cup (250 ml) whole wheat flour

2 cups (500 ml) all-purpose flour

4 tbsp (60 ml) sugar

2 tbsp (30 ml) baking powder

1 tsp (5 ml) salt

1 tsp (5 ml) baking soda

¼ tsp (1 ml) ground marjoram

4 tbsp (60 ml) honey

2 cups (500 ml) milk

½ cup (125 ml) chopped walnuts

¼ cup (60 ml) chopped pecans

Sift together 3 times whole-wheat flour, the all-purpose flour, sugar, baking powder, salt, baking soda and ground marjoram (marjoram enhances the nutty flavour). Mix honey into milk; pour all at once over the flour mixture. Add chopped walnuts and chopped pecans. Mix just enough to blend. Spoon into a greased loaf pan (9 by 5 by 3 inches/23 by 13 by 8 cm). Bake in a preheated 375°F (190°C) oven for 50 minutes. The bread is done when a straw comes out clean.

This bread freezes very well. Take it from the freezer 24 hours before using. Slice it thinly and spread with a mixture of half butter and half cream cheese. Set on a silver tray and garnish with watercress. Do not use this bread for sandwiches.

ENTERTAINING AT HOME

Chicken-salad puffs

Fill small cream-puff shells purchased from a baker with chicken salad.

- 2 warm barbecued chickens
- 1 cup (250 ml) celery, finely diced
- ¼ cup (60 ml) capers
- 4 hard-cooked eggs, finely chopped
- 1 tsp (5 ml) salt
- 3 green onions, minced
- ½ tsp (2 ml) crumbled dried basil
- ¼ cup (60 ml) minced fresh parsley
- ½ cup (125 ml) mayonnaise
- 3 tbsp (50 ml) salad oil
- Juice of ½ a lemon

Remove the skin and bones from the barbecued chickens. Cut the meat into small pieces. Add celery, capers, hard-cooked eggs, salt, green onions, dried basil and fresh parsley. Add mayonnaise, salad oil and lemon juice. Blend together thoroughly. Use the mixture to fill cream-puff shells.

Apricot delight

- ⅔ cup (170 ml) butter
- 2 cups (500 ml) icing sugar
- 4 egg yolks
- 1½ cups (375 ml) canned apricots, well-drained and mashed
- 2 cups (500 ml) finely crushed vanilla wafers or caramel wafers
- 1 tsp (5 ml) almond extract
- 2 tsp (10 ml) vanilla extract
- 1 envelope unflavoured gelatin
- ¼ cup (60 ml) orange juice
- 2 cups (500 ml) heavy cream
- Ladyfingers
- Whipped cream for garnish

Cream butter and icing sugar. When light, add egg yolks. Beat again until creamy. Stir in apricots, wafers, almond extract and vanilla extract. Cook over low heat, stirring until smooth and creamy. Do not boil.

Soak gelatin in orange juice for 5 minutes. Add to the hot mixture and stir until dissolved. Cool.

Whip heavy cream and fold into the cooled apricot mixture. See that it is well mixed. Then pour into a springform pan that has been lined with ladyfingers. You can make a pattern on the bottom of the pan by cutting some ladyfingers into halves. Let stand in the refrigerator for 24 to 48 hours before unmolding. Unmold and serve with a bowl of sweetened whipped cream.

SHOWER FOR BABY

Sandwiches in a circle

Marinated mushroom canapés

Bee's Kiss Torte, or De Luxe Charlotte russe

Coffee

A shower for baby should have an atmosphere of gentleness and quiet charm. Keep the decorations simple, mostly white and pastel shades. Make the mother-to-be feel like a queen. When all the guests have arrived, bring out a tray of your best glasses with a decanter of cooled sherry. Pour it and toast the new maman. Offer the gifts and serve a simple snack.

Sandwiches in a circle

Remove both ends of a crusty roll. Pull out the inside until you have a hole large enough to fill. Fill to capacity with your choice of one of the following fillings. When filled, wrap each roll in foil and refrigerate for 12 hours.

To serve, slice the rolls with a sharp knife into thin round pieces. This way you get crust all around with filling in centre.

Egg filling

Combine:

5 hard-cooked eggs, chopped or grated

1 tbsp (15 ml) minced celery

2 green onions, minced

¼ cup (60 ml) minced fresh parsley

¼ tsp (1 ml) curry powder

3 to 4 tbsp (50 to 60 ml) mayonnaise

1 tbsp (15 ml) soft butter

Salt and pepper to taste

Ham filling

Combine:

½ lb (250 gr) cooked ham, ground

1 2¼-oz (75 gr) can deviled ham

1 tsp (5 ml) horseradish mustard

3 tbsp (50 ml) soft cream cheese or grated mild Cheddar cheese

1 to 2 tbsp (15 to 30 ml) mayonnaise

Salt to taste

Cream-cheese filling

Combine:

4 oz (113 gr) cream cheese, softened

2 tbsp (30 ml) butter

1 tbsp (15 ml) light cream

½ cup (125 ml) minced walnuts or pecans

¼ cup (60 ml) minced fresh parsley

Salt and pepper to taste

ENTERTAINING AT HOME

Marinated mushroom canapés

½ lb (250 gr) mushrooms

4 tbsp (60 ml) olive oil

2 tbsp (30 ml) cider vinegar or white wine

½ tsp (2 ml) salt

⅛ tsp (0.5 ml) pepper

2 green onions, minced

French bread

Chop mushrooms, stems and caps finely. Add olive oil, cider vinegar or white wine, salt, pepper and green onions. Mix together and let stand for 1 hour before using. Spread on thin rounds of French bread or toast.

Bee's Kiss Torte Cake

¼ cup (60 ml) butter

⅓ cup (80 ml) fruit sugar

1 egg

1 tsp (5 ml) vanilla extract

½ tsp (2 ml) almond extract

2 cups (500 ml) pastry flour or cake flour

2 tsp (10 ml) baking powder

½ tsp (2 ml) salt

3 tbsp (50 ml) milk

Cream together until light the butter, fruit sugar, egg, vanilla extract and almond extract. Sift together the flour, baking powder and salt. Add to the creamed mixture alternately with the milk. The batter should have the texture of a hot bread batter.

Divide between two 6-inch (15 cm) round cake pans, generously buttered. Use pans that have a piece of metal attached to the bottom that can be turned to loosen the cake. Pat the batter in the pans as evenly as you can.

Topping

½ cup (125 ml) butter

½ cup (125 ml) sugar

½ cup (125 ml) slivered blanched almonds

2 tsp (10 ml) vanilla extract

2 tbsp (30 ml) milk

Melt butter in a saucepan. Add sugar, almonds, vanilla extract and milk. Stir continually over low heat until the sugar is dissolved and the mixture is thick and lumpy. Divide equally and spread over the tops of the 2 uncooked cakes. Bake in a preheated 400°F (200°) oven for 30 minutes. Unmold and cool on a wire rack.

Cream filling

1 cup (250 ml) light cream

¼ cup (60 ml) sugar

3 tbsp (50 ml) cornstarch

3 tbsp (50 ml) cream

½ cup (125 ml) butter, softened

2 tbsp (30 ml) vanilla extract

Bring light cream and sugar to a boil. Blend cornstarch and cream, then use this mixture to thicken the sweetened milk. Stir until the mixture is very thick and transparent. Cover and refrigerate until quite cold.

Beat butter with vanilla extract until creamy. Add the cold milk mixture and beat with an electric mixer until light and fluffy. Spread it on one cake. Place the second cake on top and serve.

De luxe Charlotte Russe

This most festive of desserts is almost as much fun to make as it is to eat.

2 tbsp (30 ml) unflavoured gelatin

¼ cup (60 ml) cold water

2 cups (500 ml) milk, scalded

½ cup (125 ml) sugar

4 eggs, separated

½ tsp (2 ml) rosewater or

1 tsp (5 ml) vanilla extract

Pinch of salt

2 cups (500 ml) whipping cream

Soak unflavoured gelatin in cold water for 5 minutes. Add to it hot scalded milk and stir until dissolved. Add sugar and stir until dissolved. Beat egg yolks, add a few spoonfuls of the hot milk mixture, stir and pour into the rest of the hot milk. Cook over medium heat, stirring all the time, until the mixture coats the spoon. Add rosewater (available from your druggist) or vanilla extract. Remove from heat. Beat egg whites with a pinch of salt until stiff and fold into the cooled custard. Whip whipping cream until stiff and fold into the custard. Line 12 individual molds or 1 large mold with ladyfingers. Pour the custard into the molds.

Refrigerate for 12 to 24 hours.

DESSERT AND COFFEE FOR AN AFTERNOON COMMITTEE MEETING
(for 8 to 10 committee members)

Lemon snow eggs
Burnt-sugar rice pudding
Jiffy strawberry trifle
Black coffee

Jiffy strawberry trifle

1 sponge cake or angel-food cake

1 10-oz (284 ml) package frozen sliced strawberries, thawed

1 cup (250 ml) heavy cream

Icing sugar

½ tsp (2 ml) vanilla extract or almond extract

Cut the sponge cake or angel-food cake horizontally into 3 layers. Place the bottom layer of the cake in a cut-glass fruit bowl and spread half the thawed strawberries and juice over this. Then add the second layer and the rest of the berries. Cover with the top layer and refrigerate for 12 hours.

At serving time, spread attractively with heavy cream, whipped, sweetened with icing sugar and flavoured with vanilla or almond extract.

Lemon snow eggs

4 eggs, separated

Grated rind of 1 lemon

2 tbsp (30 ml) sugar

2 tbsp (30 ml) cold milk

3 cups (750 ml) milk

½ cup (125 ml) sugar

Small piece of lemon peel

Beat egg whites stiff, then add grated lemon rind and 2 tablespoons (30 ml) sugar. Whip until the sugar is well blended in. Beat the yolks into the cold milk. Bring 3 cups (750 ml) milk to a boil and add ½ cup (125 ml) sugar and lemon peel. Drop spoonfuls of the beaten egg whites into this hot milk, being careful not to let one dollop touch another. Poach for a minute, then turn over carefully and poach for another minute. As each "snow egg" is done, lift it out with a perforated spoon and set on a serving platter.

Beat the egg yolks. When all the snow eggs are cooked, remove the milk from the heat and stir in the beaten yolks until the mixture is slightly thickened. If necessary, put this mixture over heat again to thicken the custard, but do not boil. Remove lemon peel and pour custard over the snow eggs. Refrigerate until ready to serve.

Burnt-sugar rice pudding

This dessert is especially good served with a jug of rich cream sweetened lightly with maple syrup and flavoured with a bit of rum.

3 cups (750 ml) milk

1 cup (250 ml) seedless raisins

1¼ cups (310 ml) cooked rice

¼ tsp (1 ml) salt

¼ tsp (1 ml) grated nutmeg

1 tsp (5 ml) grated lemon rind

1 tsp (5 ml) almond extract

3 eggs, lightly beaten

6 tbsp (100 ml) brown sugar

1 cup (250 ml) brown sugar

2 to 3 tbsp (30 to 50 ml) shredded almonds

Bring to a boil the milk, raisins and rice. As soon as the mixture reaches the boil, take it off the heat. Add salt, nutmeg, grated lemon rind and almond extract. Beat eggs lightly with 6 tablespoons (100 ml) brown sugar. Add to the rice mixture, stirring all the time. Pour into a buttered baking dish. Set the dish in a pan of hot water and bake in a preheated 350°F (180°C) oven for 1 hour. Cool. Then refrigerate until completely cold.

Sprinkle 1 cup (250 ml) brown sugar and shredded almonds on top of the chilled pudding. Put it under the broiler to caramelize. Do not walk away, for it takes only 1 or 2 minutes to brown. Chill again before serving.

COOKING FOR A CROWD

Most recipes can be multiplied to provide enough food for a crowd, but some dishes are better made according to the recipe; when you need a large quantity, simply make the recipe several times. For example, a soufflé is never successful when made in too large a dish; the centre will still be uncooked while the outside will be overcooked.

To make a large amount of coffee

If your regular coffeepot is too small for the number of cups of coffee you have to serve, the following method produces perfect coffee.

Use an enamelware saucepan. Put into it as many cups of water as you need cups of coffee. For mild coffee, use an 8-ounce (250 ml) measuring cup; for stronger coffee, fill the 8-ounce (250 ml) cup two-thirds full. For each cupful of water put in 1 rounded tablespoon (15 ml) of medium-grind coffee. The cold water and coffee should start cooking over very low heat. As it warms, increase the heat. When it comes to a gently rolling boil, let it simmer for another 5 minutes. Remove from the heat, then add ½ cup (125 ml) cold water. Let the coffee rest for a minute to settle the grounds. No matter how much coffee you have, you'll need only ½ cup (125 ml) water to settle the grounds.

> PLUM PUDDING, COFFEE AND BRANDY PARTY
> (for 6 congenial friends, or as many as you like)

There are so many delicious things to eat at Christmas dinner that guests often manage only a few mouthfuls of the pudding so lovingly and painstakingly prepared. So make an event of enjoying plum pudding, by presenting it at a party when everyone will be hungry enough to really enjoy it. Give your party on Christmas Eve, or any time between Christmas and New Year's Day. The beauty of such a party is that you don't have to wait until the day before or the day of the party itself to make your pièce de résistance. Plum pudding improves with age, because it requires a few weeks to ripen and mellow. And what could give a party a more dramatic note than the moment when the pudding is set ablaze?

For a festive touch, set your table with a lace cloth. Centre the pudding on a round silver tray and place a ring of holly around the platter.

Spray the leaves of a large pineapple with gold spray paint, then give it a coating of bronze, for an antique look. Be sure to wrap the base of the pineapple itself with waxed paper before the spraying so the fruit does not get splattered. Fill a large glass bowl with oranges, lemons and limes; tuck a few large green leaves in here and there. (You can buy leaves from a florist.) Place the gilded pineapple in the middle of the bowl with the other fruit around it. Use the fruit bowl as a centrepiece for the table or sideboard.

Add dessert plates, dessert spoons and forks, a tray with the coffee service along with cups and saucers, and another tray with a bottle of Cognac and glasses.

Making pudding is greatly simplified by organization. If you don't have a mold with a cover, you'll need some foil or parchment paper and a piece of cotton cloth to tie over the rim of the pudding bowl or mold. Be sure you have a saucepan large enough to hold the mold comfortably. ☛ A folded newspaper placed under the pudding dish will keep it from moving around while cooking.

These are some important things to remember:

☛ If you have the butter, eggs and liquid at room temperature, mixing will be much easier.

☛ Eggs, liquids and essences or flavourings are always added to the batter before adding the fruits.

☛ As in cake, too much liquid or fat can spoil the texture. Be sure to measure ingredients carefully.

Plum pudding

1½ lb (750 gr) seedless raisins

2 oz (50 gr) mixed candied fruit peel, diced

1 cup (250 ml) orange juice, brandy or red wine

1 cup (250 ml) finely chopped beef suet

1½ cups (375 ml) fine breadcrumbs

1 cup (250 ml) all-purpose flour

1 tsp (5 ml) ground cinnamon

½ tsp (2 ml) ground allspice

½ tsp (2 ml) ground cloves

1 tsp (5 ml) salt

½ cup (125 ml) sugar

3 eggs, well beaten

1 cup (250 ml) molasses

3 unpeeled apples, grated

Grated rind of 1 lemon

1 cup (250 ml) chopped almonds or walnuts

Soak the raisins and diced peels in the orange juice, brandy or red wine overnight, or for at least 12 hours. This soaking plumps and flavours the fruit and also prevents its drying out during the cooking period.

The next day, rub together the beef suet and breadcrumbs. Sift together 3 times the flour, cinnamon, allspice, cloves, salt and sugar. Add to the suet and breadcrumbs.

Drain the soaked raisins and peel over a bowl, pressing out as much liquid as possible. Mix the liquid with the eggs and molasses. Add the liquid to the dry mixture.

Add the grated apples, lemon rind and the chopped almonds or walnuts to the drained, soaked fruit. Stir the fruit and nuts into the batter. Blend everything together. You'll find it easier to do this by hand because the dough will be heavy.

Give the mold a good coating of salad oil; or use sweet almond oil, which you can buy at a drugstore. Fill the mold three quarters full with the pudding mixture. Place a piece of foil or wet parchment paper on top. Cover the mold with its own lid, or with a piece of cotton cloth tied on securely with string.

Put water into the saucepan that will hold the mold; the water level should be about halfway up the sides of the pudding mold, and it should remain at the same level throughout the cooking period. Bring the water to a boil; it must be boiling before you set in the pudding. Keep a kettle of water at hand in case you need to add more water to keep it at the right level. Be sure it is boiling before you add it, because the cooking must continue without interruption. When the pudding is in the saucepan, adjust the heat so that the water is at a constant simmer; do not let it boil rapidly, or it will boil away, and simmering over constant low heat gives a lighter pudding. Cover the saucepan and cook from 4 to 9 hours, depending on the size of the pudding. An average 2-quart (2 L) mold will require 6 hours.

While it is necessary to open the saucepan to check on the water level and to add more boiling water from time to time, never open the pudding mold until the cooking is complete, or the pudding will be heavy instead of light.

When finished, lift out the mold onto a wire rack to cool. Then open the mold and let it stand until completely cold. Recover and refrigerate until ready to serve. The pudding will gain in flavour through ripening for 2 to 6 weeks.

To warm up a refrigerated pudding, prepare the same saucepan, with a piece of newspaper in the bottom, and add enough boiling water to come halfway up the mold. Steam for 2 hours.

Hard sauce

¼ lb (125 gr) unsalted butter

1 cup (250 ml) icing sugar

3 tbsp (50 ml) rum or brandy

or 1 tbsp (15 ml) vanilla extract or lemon juice

Cream the butter. ⚊ Creaming the butter until it is almost like whipped cream is the secret of a perfect hard sauce. Gradually beat in icing sugar, 1 tablespoon (15 ml) at a time. Work until it is absolutely smooth. Gradually add rum or brandy, or vanilla extract or lemon juice. Beat all the while. Heap into a glass or silver bowl.

Caramel sauce

1¼ cups (310 ml) brown sugar

⅔ cup (160 ml) corn syrup or maple syrup

¼ cup (60 ml) boiling water

¾ cup (190 ml) light cream

Grated nutmeg or vanilla extract to taste (optional)

Put brown sugar, corn or maple syrup and boiling water in a saucepan. Warm over low heat, stirring until the sugar is dissolved. Add light cream and cook until smooth, stirring often. ⚊ Long cooking over low heat makes this sauce velvety. It is good just as it is, but it can be flavoured with a dash of grated nutmeg or a small spoonful of vanilla extract.

Decorating the pudding

It is an old English tradition to decorate the plum pudding with spiced prunes. Before flaming the pudding, arrange the prunes around it on a bed of holly.

4 cups (1 L) brown sugar

1 cup (250 ml) vinegar

5 cups (1.25 L) water

2 cinnamon sticks

12 whole cloves

2 tbsp (30 ml) dark honey

1 lb (500 gr) large prunes

½ orange, unpeeled and thinly sliced

½ lemon, unpeeled and thinly sliced

Walnuts, almonds or almond paste

3 pieces of candied ginger

¼ cup (60 ml) rum (optional)

Mix together in a saucepan the brown sugar, vinegar, water, cinnamon sticks, cloves and dark honey. Boil for 15 minutes. Add prunes and orange and lemon slices. Boil for 1 hour. Let the prunes cool.

Remove the pits carefully and stuff each prune with a walnut, an almond, or a ball of almond paste. Place the stuffed prunes, the fruit slices and candied ginger in a glass jar. Pour rum over the prunes and fill the jar with the boiling syrup. Seal, cool and refrigerate.

How to flame

There are many ways to flame the Christmas pudding. My favourite is easy and reliable, and I like to do it right at the table. Set up a small tray with a bowl of sugar cubes, a dish of butter and a small jug of slightly heated rum or brandy. A word of advice: Don't use a fine old brandy or rum. A less expensive "young" alcohol flames better.

Place the pudding on a silver or flameproof glass platter. It is important to have the pudding on a hot platter. The hotter the platter, the longer the alcohol will keep warm and the longer the flaming will last.

Place a good-sized pat of butter on top of the pudding. Add 6 or 8 cubes of sugar, then pour on the brandy or rum. Light it and start basting. Keep pressing the sugar gently with the back of the spoon and continue to baste until the flames die out naturally. The more you baste, the more the pudding will flame.

No plum pudding seems complete without hard sauce or a caramel sauce. Either can be prepared 6 to 10 days ahead of time and kept covered in the refrigerator.

My Grand-Maman's Christmas Dinner
(for 12 to 16 guests in a merry mood)

Quebec roasted turkey with potato stuffing
Nuns' chicken pie
Pork in jelly
Pork pies
Crown of turnip with green peas
Aniseed sweet bread
French colonial fruitcake
Old-fashioned poundcake ring
Creamy pumpkin pie
Maple-syrup pie
Applesauce mousse
Spiced hot red wine
Marzipan fruits

When you're young, Christmas can be the most exciting time of the year, and Christmas dinner with its sumptuous array of good things to eat the feast of the year. I can still shut my eyes and see the groaning tables of my childhood, with all the delectable food that made Christmas so memorable, and all the family and friends who were so happy on that day.

My grand'maman really believed in Christmas plenty — the food and wines overflowed from the table onto the sideboard, which was laden with pies, cakes, cookies, homemade bonbons and baskets of apples, bananas and oranges. She would go to endless trouble to make every dish particularly wonderful — unusual enough and good enough so that it would be remembered all year long.

Grand'maman's menu was for the most part traditional, but sometimes she had surprise desserts. Of course, this dinner can be served buffet style, or a choice of dishes can be offered.

Québec roasted turkey with potato stuffing

Potato stuffing

Turkey giblets

4 tbsp (60 ml) butter

3 large onions, minced

1 garlic clove, minced

8 to 12 cups (2 to 3 L) cooked potatoes, depending on size of turkey

1½ tsp (7 ml) crumbled dried savory

1 tbsp (15 ml) salt

½ tsp (2 ml) pepper

½ tsp (2 ml) dry mustard

3 tbsp (50 ml) butter, softened

1 thick dry crust of bread

¼ small onion

Butter

Turkey

1 whole nutmeg

½ lemon

½ cup (125 ml) butter

2 tbsp (30 ml) dry mustard

1 tbsp (15 ml) salt

½ tsp (2 ml) pepper

3 tbsp plus 1 cup (300 ml) all-purpose flour

Thin slices of salt pork

Grind or mince the heart, liver and gizzard of the turkey. Melt the 4 tablespoons (60 ml) butter and add onions and garlic. Stir until well coated with butter, then cover and simmer over low heat until onions are soft. Add minced giblets and stir over high heat until brown. Mash the hot cooked potatoes in a large bowl and add the browned onions and giblets. Stir until well blended, then add all the other ingredients. Use to stuff turkey cavity.

Rub the dry crust of bread with the onion, then butter generously. Place inside the opening in the turkey, then sew it closed.

Place the turkey in the roasting pan. Rub the skin all over with the nutmeg. Grate the nutmeg occasionally to draw out the oil. Next rub the skin with lemon. Cream together the butter, mustard, salt, pepper and 3 tablespoons (50 ml) of the flour. Rub this paste all over the turkey's breast and legs. Wrap the legs with the slices of salt pork. Do not cover or add water. Place in a 325°F (160°C) oven and cook for 20 to 25 minutes per pound (500 gr) for a 6- to 10-pound (2.7 to 4.5 kg) bird; for 18 to 20 minutes per pound (500 gr) for a 10- to 16-pound (4.5 to 7.25 kg) bird.

Do not baste during the cooking period as opening the oven tends to dry out the turkey. The paste coating protects the surface and makes it selft-basting.

Transfer the cooked bird to a warm platter and keep warm while you make gravy. The bird will make 10 generous servings.

ENTERTAINING AT HOME

Turkey gravy

This is the way I learned to make gravy as a very young girl and I know of none better.

1 cup (250 ml) fat from the turkey roasting pan

1 cup (250 ml) flour

2 cups (500 ml) cold tea

1 cup (250 ml) consommé or red wine

Salt and pepper to taste

Remove the turkey from the pan. Remove the required turkey fat and put it into a frying pan. Add to this the flour and stir and cook together until the flour is medium brown. Then cook over low heat for 10 minutes. In the meantime, bring the remaining drippings in the roasting pan to a boil. Add the cold tea. Stir until all the brown specks attached to the pan are dissolved. Add the consommé or wine, and the flour mixture. Stir over medium heat until creamy and smooth. Season to taste.

Pork in jelly

2 cups (500 ml) white vinegar or cider vinegar

1 cup (250 ml) sliced onions

1 tsp (5 ml) pickling spices

2 garlic cloves

1 tsp (5 ml) sugar

4 lb (1.8 kg) shoulder of pork

2 lb (1 kg) pigs' knuckles

1 tbsp (15 ml) salt

2 hard-cooked eggs, sliced

1 cup (250 ml) green peas

Mix the first 5 ingredients in a bowl. Add the shoulder of pork and pigs' knuckles. Stir until the meats are well coated with the vinegar mixture. Cover and refrigerate for 48 hours.

Drain the vinegar from the meat and place the meat in a saucepan. Pour on just enough boiling water to cover and add the salt. Bring to a boil, cover and simmer until the meat falls off the bones. Let everything cool slightly. Remove the bones and shred the meat, but not too finely. Reduce the bouillon to 3 cups (750 ml) by boiling.

Cover the bottom of a mold with the egg slices and fill the gaps with green peas. Pack the meat on top. Pour the strained bouillon over all. Cover and place in the refrigerator until set.

Serve garnished with pickled beets.

Pork pies
See Small Québec Tourtières (p. 495). Bake in 6 individual tart pans or in one 9-inch (23 cm) pie pan. These pies can be baked in advance and frozen. To serve hot, heat in a slow oven until the crust is crisp and the filling is hot in the centre.

Nuns' chicken pie

1 boiling chicken (5 to 6 lb/2.2 to 2.7 kg)

1 tbsp (15 ml) salt

½ tsp (2 ml) pepper

1 cup (250 ml) celery leaves

1 large onion, quartered

½ tsp (2 ml) crumbled dried savory or thyme

1 bay leaf

6 cups (1.5 L) boiling water

3 cups (750 ml) sliced carrots

2 cups (500 ml) diced celery

12 to 24 small onions

¾ cup (190 ml) butter

¾ cup (190 ml) all-purpose flour

2 cups (500 ml) milk

1 cup (250 ml) heavy cream

1 tbsp (15 ml) lemon juice

½ cup (125 ml) minced parsley

Pie pastry for a large 2-crust pie

Place the chicken in a large saucepan with the next 7 ingredients. Bring to a boil. Cover, then simmer over low heat until the chicken is tender, from 1½ to 2 hours. When done, leave the bird in the bouillon until cool enough to handle.

Remove the chicken skin, pull the meat off the bones, and place the meat in a large bowl. Pass the skin through a meat grinder and mix it with the chicken.

Meanwhile, boil the bouillon, uncovered, until reduced to two-thirds of the original quantity. Strain the bouillon over the chicken. Cover and keep in the refrigerator overnight.

The next day place the carrots and celery in a bowl and completely cover with boiling water. Let stand for 1 hour, then drain. Peel the onions and boil for 15 minutes, then drain.

Heat the chicken just enough so the bouillon can be strained off. Measure 3 cups (750 ml) of the bouillon. (If there is more than this, save it for some other recipe.) Melt the butter, add the flour and stir until well blended. Add the milk, cream and strained bouillon and cook until the sauce is creamy. Add the onions, carrots and celery to the sauce. Then add the chicken pieces, lemon juice and parsley. Season to taste.

Line a pudding dish with pastry and pour in the chicken mixture. Top with more pastry, crimp or flute the edges, and make a few holes for steam to escape. Bake in a preheated 400°F (200°C) oven for 40 to 50 minutes, or until golden brown. This chicken pie freezes very well and reheats beautifully.

ENTERTAINING AT HOME

Crown of turnip with green peas

1 large turnip

¼ tsp (1 ml) sugar

¼ tsp (1 ml) ground sage

2 slices lemon, unpeeled

1 cup (250 ml) applesauce

3 tbsp (50 ml) butter

Salt to taste

Green peas

Peel the turnip and cut into thin slices; do this just before you are ready to cook. Place in a saucepan with the sugar, sage and lemon slices; cover with boiling water. Boil for 15 minutes. Drain and remove the lemon.

Place the turnip in the bowl of an electric mixer and beat at medium speed until mashed. (Mash by hand if you haven't a mixer.) Add the applesauce and butter, then salt to taste. Form into a ring on a hot vegetable dish. Fill the centre with buttered hot green peas.

Aniseed sweet bread

These galettes are a little tricky to make, but they are delicious.

2 eggs

½ cup (125 ml) sugar

Juice and rind of 1 lemon

¼ tsp (1 ml) vanilla extract

1¾ cups (440 ml) all-purpose flour

1 tsp (5 ml) baking powder

½ cup (125 ml) minced almonds

¼ cup (60 ml) creamed butter

Aniseeds

Icing sugar

Beat the eggs until light. Then add the sugar and continue beating. Add the lemon juice and rind, the vanilla and 1 cup (250 ml) of the flour mixed with the baking powder. Mix well. Add the almonds. Blend in the creamed butter and remaining flour.

Dust some additional flour on a table and turn out half the dough on it. Quickly shape it into a long loaf about 2 inches (5 cm) thick. Place it quickly on a buttered baking sheet sprinkled with aniseeds. Shape again if necessary. Repeat the procedure with remaining dough. Bake in a 350°F (180°C) oven for 20 minutes.

Remove from the oven, cool for 20 minutes, and cut while still warm into slices 1 inch (2.5 cm) thick. Turn each slice flat on the pan. Put back into the oven for about 20 minutes, or until golden brown. Cool and sprinkle with icing sugar.

French colonial fruitcake

This cake will keep well if you brush it with brandy now and then and keep it wrapped in greased paper or aluminum foil.

1 cup (250 ml) butter

2½ cups (625 ml) dark brown sugar

4 eggs

4 cups (1 L) all-purpose flour

½ tsp (2 ml) ground ginger

½ tsp (2 ml) allspice

½ tsp (2 ml) cloves

1 tsp (5 ml) ground cinnamon

1 tsp (5 ml) grated nutmeg

1½ tsp (7 ml) salt

1 tsp (5 ml) baking soda

1 cup (250 ml) prune juice or orange juice

⅓ cup (80 ml) brandy

1½ cups (375 ml) chopped dried prunes

1½ cups (375 ml) chopped dried apricots

2 cups (500 ml) chopped almonds or walnuts

¼ cup (60 ml) butter

1 cup (250 ml) brown sugar

2 tbsp (30 ml) brandy

Cooked whole dried prunes and apricots

Almonds

Cream the butter and sugar until light and creamy. Add the eggs and beat until very creamy. Sift together the flour, spices, salt and baking soda. Mix the fruit juice and brandy together. Place the chopped fruits and nuts in a bowl. Sprinkle with ½ cup (125 ml) of the spiced flour. Add the rest of the flour alternately with the liquid to the creamed mixture. Stir well until thoroughly mixed. Add the fruit and nuts and blend in.

Now, prepare the topping for the cake.

Melt the butter, add the sugar and brandy, and stir until well mixed. Spread on the bottom of 2 bread pans or 1 long loaf pan. Arrange prunes and apricots on the sugar mixture and place almonds in between.

Spoon the fruitcake batter on top, taking care not to disturb the arranged fruit. Bake in a 325°F (160°C) oven for 2 hours, or until done. Let cool on a wire rack for 20 minutes. Invert and let stand for 10 minutes. Then carefully remove the pan.

Old-fashioned poundcake ring

- 3 cups (750 ml) pastry flour or cake flour
- 2 tsp (10 ml) baking powder
- Pinch of salt
- ½ tsp (2 ml) ground mace or cinnamon
- 1 cup (250 ml) unsalted butter, softened
- 1½ cups (375 ml) fine granulated sugar
- 3 eggs
- ½ cup (125 ml) milk
- 1 tsp (5 ml) brandy or vanilla extract
- Icing sugar
- Red sugar (sucre rose)*

Sift together 3 times the flour, baking powder, salt and mace or cinnamon. With the electric mixer set at medium speed cream the butter, sugar and eggs together until light and fluffy, about 4 minutes. Add the brandy or vanilla to the milk. Blend in the sifted flour by hand, alternating with the milk mixture. Beat after each addition.

Pour into a well-greased 2-quart (2 L) ring mold 11 inches (27.5 cm) across. Bake in a preheated 350°F (180°C) oven for 50 to 60 minutes, or until done. Cool on a wire rack for 10 minutes before unmolding. Loosen all around with a knife and remove from the pan. Cool.

Dust with icing sugar and sprinkle with red sugar (sucre rose).

* Make red sugar (sucre rose) by adding a few drops of red vegetable colouring to granulated sugar and rubbing it with the back of a spoon until the sugar is uniformly coloured. (My grandmother used concentrated beet water.)

Creamy pumpkin pie

- 2 eggs, lightly beaten
- 2 cups (500 ml) mashed pumpkin or squash
- ½ cup (125 ml) sugar
- ¼ tsp (1 ml) salt
- ¼ tsp (1 ml) ground ginger
- ¼ tsp (1 ml) nutmeg
- 1½ tsp (7 ml) ground cinnamon
- 1½ cups (325 ml) milk
- ¼ cup (60 ml) molasses
- 2 tbsp (30 ml) melted butter
- Pie pastry for a 1-crust 9-inch (23 cm) pie

Beat the eggs. Add all remaining ingredients except the pastry and mix thoroughly. Line a 9-inch (23 cm) pie plate with the pastry and crimp or flute the edges. Pour in as much of the pumpkin custard as possible. Do not cover the pie. Bake in a preheated 375°F (190°C) oven for 1 hour. Cool. Serve topped with unsweetened whipped cream, molasses or ice cream.

If you have custard left over, pour it into custard cups. Bake for 40 to 50 minutes.

Maple-syrup pie

Pie pastry for a 2-crust 8-inch (20 cm) pie

1 cup (250 ml) pure maple syrup

½ cup (125 ml) water

3 tbsp (50 ml) cornstarch

2 tbsp (30 ml) cold water

¼ cup (60 ml) chopped walnuts

1 tbsp (15 ml) butter

Line an 8-inch (20 cm) pie plate with half the pastry. Roll out the rest into a round large enough to cover the pie.

Boil the maple syrup and ½ cup (125 ml) water together for 5 minutes. Thicken with the cornstarch mixed with the 2 tablespoons (30 ml) cold water. When creamy and clear, add the chopped nuts and butter. Pour into the pastry-lined pie plate and top with the second round of pastry. Bake in a preheated 450°F (230°C) oven for 30 minutes, or until the crust is golden brown.

Applesauce mousse

2 medium-sized apples

1 cup (250 ml) sugar

1 cup (250 ml) water

2 lemons

1 tbsp (15 ml) unflavoured gelatin

2 egg whites

Peel and core the apples and cut them into thin slices. Heat the sugar and water together in a saucepan until the sugar is dissolved. Toss in the apple slices and cook until the fruit is transparent and the syrup slightly thickened.

While the apples cook, grate the rinds from both lemons and extract the juice. Add enough water to the lemon juice to make 1 cup (250 ml). Sprinkle the gelatin over ¼ cup (60 ml) of this liquid. Remove the apples from the heat and stir in the lemon rind, the softened gelatin and the remaining lemon and water mixture.

Let it cool, then refrigerate until it becomes as thick as unbeaten egg white.

Whip the egg whites until stiff enough to hold a peak. Beat the apple mixture until the slices are broken down into little chunks. Gently mix in the stiff egg whites. Refrigerate the mixture again, this time for 2½ to 3 hours, or until the dessert is reasonably firm; it will never become really solid.

Serve plain, or with sweetened whipped cream or a thin custard sauce.

ENTERTAINING AT HOME

Spiced hot red wine

2 cups (500 ml) water

1 cup (250 ml) sugar

1 tbsp (15 ml) whole cloves

3 cinnamon sticks

1 tbsp (15 ml) whole allspice berries

1 lemon, unpeeled and sliced

2 quarts (2 L) red wine

Place the water, sugar and spices in a saucepan. Simmer until the sugar is dissolved. Add the lemon, cover and simmer for 10 minutes. Add the wine and stir to mix. Remove the whole spices. Serve hot with a lemon slice in each glass.

Makes 15 punch-size servings.

Marzipan fruits

1 cup (250 ml) almond paste

2 egg whites

3 cups (750 ml) icing sugar

½ tsp (2 ml) vanilla extract or rum flavouring

Food colouring

Put almond paste in a large bowl and knead by hand. Add unbeaten egg whites and mix well. Add icing sugar, 1 cup (250 ml) at a time. Continue kneading and add vanilla extract or rum flavouring. Mix for about 15 minutes. At the proper consistency, the marzipan will feel like a heavy pie dough. Separate the marzipan into as many portions as there are different fruits you wish to make.

For peaches and pears, add a very small quantity of yellow colouring and knead to obtain an even pale colour. For bananas, add a little more yellow than for peaches. For carrots and pumpkins, mix yellow and red food colouring to obtain an orange colour. For apples, add a delicate green. For new potatoes, no colouring is added. Place the coloured portions of dough in the refrigerator to chill for about 1 hour before shaping.

To make peaches, pears, bananas, carrots and pumpkins: Dust work area with cornstarch to prevent sticking. To give a uniform size to your pieces, roll out the coloured marzipan into a long narrow length ¾ inch (2 cm) in diameter. Cut it into 1¼-inch (3 cm) lengths. Shape. To make potatoes, roll the shaped pieces in cocoa. Make small dents for the eyes of the potatoes. To make strawberries, roll the shaped pieces in red sugar. Use these as part of the centrepiece. They look nice when attractively arranged on top of an evergreen wreath set flat on the table.

Table of Contents

Chapter 16   The Versatility of Eggs

- page 380   Basic Methods of Cooking Eggs
- 384   Omelets. Recipes
- 394   Dessert or Sweet Omelets
- 397   Soufflés. Recipes
- 406   Meringues. Recipes

Chapter 17   The Magic of Pies and Ice Cream

- page 417   Pastry Ingredients
- 418   Mixing and Rolling Piecrust
- 420   How to Solve Some Pastry Problems
- 421   Basic Pastries. Recipes
- 429   Puff Pastry
- 430   Vol-au-vent
- 432   A Few Favourite Pies
- 437   Ice Cream. Technique and Recipes
- 446   Sherbets. Recipes

Chapter 18   Cheese and Nuts

- page 453   Cheese Around the World
- 460   Nuts. Nomenclature

Chapter 19   Wine, the Cup that Cheers

- page 466   Classifying Wines
- 468   Wine Categories
- 474   Serving Wine
- 476   Cooking with Wine
- 477   Flambéed Foods
- 478   Glossary

Chapter 20   Entertaining at Home

page 483	Planning
487	Breakfast. Recipes
490	Lunchtime Food. Soup and Sandwiches
494	A Canadian Autumn Lunch. Recipes
496	A Party Tea. Recipes
499	Afternoon Tea for VIPs. Recipes
501	A Perfect Little Dinner. Recipes
504	Autumn Wild Duck Dinner. Recipes
507	Grand dîner. Recipes
511	A Casserole Buffet. Recipes
516	An Elegant Victorian Picnic. Recipes
520	A Romantic Picnic for Two. Recipes
521	A Picnic in the Car. Recipes
523	After-Football Snack. Recipes
524	Corn-husking Bee
525	A Teatime Engagement Party. Recipes
528	Shower for Baby. Recipes
530	Dessert and Coffee for an Afternoon Committee Meeting. Recipes
532	Plum-Pudding, Coffee and Brandy Party. Recipes
535	My grand-maman's Christmas Dinner. Recipes

INDEX

Acid, 76-78
effects on food, 77-78
examples of uses
    fruits, 77
        gelatine dishes, 354
    meats, 77
    milk and cream, 78
    sauces, 77
    vegetables, 77
interchangeability in recipes, 77

Afternoon tea, 496-501
party tea, 496-498
engagement party, 525-527
for VIPs, 499-501

Ajinomoto (MSG), 81

Algerian stuffed cabbage leaves, 317

Allen, Ida Bailey, 299

Allspice, 103

Almond(s), 460
celery amandine in casserole, 334
garnish for French-style beans, 320
marzipan fruits, 543
and walnuts, deviled, 499

American pie meringue, 412

American salad dressing, 138

American-style French dressing, 137

American vanilla ice cream, 439

Anglaise, à l'anglaise, 363

Anise, aniseed, 98
sweet bread, 539
tisane (herb tea), 98
uses for, 98

Anised sweet bread, 539

Appellation contrôlée, 466

Apple(s)
baked (to freeze), 151
(with) Cheddar cheese, toasted walnuts, 524
corer, 61
in frozen pies, to prevent darkening, 168
muffins, 526
old French favorite (sandwich), 493
pie, country, 433
    Scandinavian, 432
    upside-down, 432
sliced (to freeze), 150-151
uncooked whole (to freeze), 150

Applesauce
mousse, 542
pink (to freeze), 151
(with) spearmint or lemon verbena, 96-97

(in) Swedish mayonnaise, 132
to freeze, 151

Apricot(s)
delight, 527
purée (to freeze), 154
to freeze, 152

Aquavit, 474

Arabian tea, 496

Artichoke(s), 332-333
dressing, hot or cold, 333
to avoid discoloration, 332

Ascorbic acid, see VITAMIN C, 15, 43
for freezing fruits, 149

Asparagus, 336-337
ends for sauces, soups, 336
Sabatini, 337

Aspic, 353-358
adding gelatine to stock, 118
basic, 355
chaud-froid, 353
    to chill, 354-355
clarifying stock for, 118
gelatine base, to chill, 354
gelatine for, 353
liquids for, 353
mathematics, 354
measuring molds, 58
mixtures, chilling, 354
molds for, 57, 353
mousse, to chill, 354
sweet, for dessert, 358; for recipes see JELLIED DESSERTS
testing for jelling, 118
to unmold, 354

Aspic dishes
chicken aspic mousse, 357
chiffon aspic (crabmeat), 357
fish aspic, 357
galantine de porc, 537
jellied canapés, 355
meat aspic, 356
pork in jelly, 537
Scottish molded salmon, 261
tomato vegetable aspic, 356

Aunt Amelia's tomato soup, 343

Aurore sauce, 124

B

B.C. basting sauce, 284

B.C. special (sandwich filling), 167

Bacon
broiled, 487
(with) eggs and fried tomatoes, 487
husband's preference (sandwich filling), 167
and liver sandwich, English, 491
panfried, 487

Bahamian mustard, 101

Baking
with dry heat, 300
fish, 252-254

Balcom apple upside-down pie, 432

Bamboo shoots, 349-350
stir-fried, 349

Banana
ice cream, 440
purée (to freeze), 154

Barbecue, Barbecueing, 279-292
broilers, golden glazed, 290
    split, 290
butterfly leg of lamb, 286
calf's-liver brochettes, 286
club steak, 285
corn, roast, hot buttery, 292
equipment, 279
fire control, 280
fish, 281; see also SEAFOOD SAKANA, 292
    whole, charcoal-baked, 290
halibut steaks, grilled, 291
ham, glazed, 289
    steak, 289
hamburgers, 286
how to build and control the fire, 279-280
importance of a good draft, 280
lamb, chops, 287
    lambburgers, 286
    steak, 286
lobster, see SEAFOOD SAKANA, 292
marinades and basting sauces, 282-284
meat cuts for, 281
Persian kebab, 287
pork, chops, 288
    roast, rolled, crisp-crusted, 287
poultry, 281
rumaki, 350
salmon, Indian, 291
seafood sakana, 292
shrimps, see SEAFOOD SAKANA, 292
spareribs, 288
starting the fire, 279-280
    my old-fashioned way, 280
steak, 284
timing of cooking, 280-281
trout, fresh, 291-292
what can be barbecued, 281
wieners, 286

Barley, 325-326
pilaf, 326
with chicken, 326

Basil, 89
baked tomatoes with mushrooms, 89
broiled tomato slices, see PARMESAN BROILED TOMATOES, 344

Basting sauces for barbecue, 283-284; see also MARINADES; SAUCE, ENTRÉE AND HORS D'OEUVRE
B.C., 284
for barbecued ham steak, 289
for chicken, 290
garlic marinade, 283
lemon, 283
    butter, 284
Texan style, 207

Bateman, Ruth Conrad, 319

Batter
anglaise, à l'anglaise, 363
for batter-fried fish, 365
coating for sautéing and panfrying, 224
for fried oysters, 267
for fried shrimps, clams, mussels, see FRIED SHRIMPS, 272
tempura, 363

Bay leaf, 87

Bean(s)
green snap beans, 320-321
    French-style, with amandine garnish, 320
    Greek-style, 320
    Mennonite, 321
    salad, 322, 514
    nasturtium flavoring for, 96
lima beans, 322
    in cream sauce, 322
    purée, 322
    succotash, 322
wax snap beans, Scandinavian, 321

Béarnaise sauce, 130

Beating, 72

Béchamel sauce, 123-124
variations, 124-125

Beef
boeuf bourguignon, 502
brisket, poached, 227
carbonnade, Belgian, 228
chuck roast, braised, 221
    pot-roasted, 221
    rolled, garnished, 204
club steak, barbecued, 285
cuts, 189
    for barbecueing, 281
    for broiling, 215
    for roasting, 195
hamburger(s), barbecued, 286
    mixture, my favorite (to freeze), 162
heart, basic preparation and cooking, 233
and kidney pie, English, cold, 518
kidneys, basic preparation and cooking, 233
liver, basic preparation and cooking, 233
rib(s), ribs of, roast
    rolled, with pan-browned potatoes, 201-202
    standing, with Yorkshire pudding, 200
    temperature for serving, 76

roasting, timetables, 193
roulade, Tokyo, 522
salad, cold, 204
sandwich, 492
shooters' loaf, 517
short ribs, braised, 222
  pot-roasted, 222
sirloin steak, broiled, perfect, 217
steak, barbecued, 284
tenderloin of, roast, with mushroom sauce, 202
  Wellington, 203
teriyaki, world-famous Hawaiian, 217
tongue, basic preparation and cooking, 234
tripe, basic preparation and cooking, 234
  to freeze, 161
wholesale, for freezing, 161

Bee's kiss torte, 529

Beet(s), 309-311
baked (with dry heat), 300
mashed, 310
relish (raita), 310
salad, 311
steam-baked, 300

Belgian beef carbonnade, 228

Belgian endives, braised, 330

Benne seeds, see SESAME

Bercy omelet, 387

Bercy sauce, 126

Berry omelet, 396

Beurre manié, 122

Beverages
aniseed tea, 98
apricot purée, frozen, 156
Arabian tea, 496
coffee, to make a large amount, 532
lemon-balm iced tea, 94
lemon-verbena tea, 94
mint lemonade, 86
necessary supplies, 66
plum purée, frozen, 156
sage tea, 88

Beverages, Alcoholic; see also names of wines and spirits in: Serving wine, 474
lovage cordial, 95
Normandy tarragon liqueur, 92
perry cup, 519
shandygaff, 524
spiced hot red wine, 543
spiced hot red rine, 543
white-wine cup, 520
  fizz, 521
wine, 465-77
wineglasses, 474-475; illus, 475

Bias or diagonal cutting, 74

Blackberry pie, see GLAZED STRAWBERRY PIE, 434

Blanching and refreshing (vegetables), 298

Blender, 63

Blending, 72

Blueberry pie, see GLAZED STRAWBERRY PIE, 434

Boeuf bourguignon, 502

Bones for stock, cracked, 116

Borage, 92
flowers, sugared, 92-93

Bordeaux hollandaise, 130

Bordeaux wines, red, 465
white, 470

Bottle opener, 62

Bouquet garni, 87

Brain(s)
basic preparation and cooking, 234
calf's-brain salad, 236
storage, 190
to freeze, 161

Braising
casserole for, 56
meats, 219-223
vegetables for, 220

Brandied almond-strawberry jam, 498

Brandy, 473, 478
glasses, 475; illus, 475
in a soufflé, 405
vanilla sauce, 139

Brazil nuts, 460

Bread; see also BREADS
amount to serve daily, 18, 19
and baked products (to freeze), 165
-crumb topping (for fish), 252
croûtons, buttered (to freeze), 165
crumbs as thickener for sauces, 123
(and) lemon stuffing, 243
pans for, 57
(for) poultry dressing (to freeze), 165
sauce, English, 133
for toast (to freeze), 165

Breads
biscuits, stuffed hot, 525
bread
  aniseed sweet, 539
  honeyed Sally Lunn, 498
  hot crisp, 512
  nut, buttered, 526
  sage, hot, 494
  sweet, aniseed, 539
muffins, apple, 526
rolls, herb hot, 523

Breakfast, 487-489
lazy, wife-helpers for, 488
traditional, 487

Bretonne sauce, 126

Brittany pumpkin soup, 493

Broccoli, 315-316
divan à la moderne, 319

Broiling
fish, 254-255
meats, 214-219
  cuts for, 215
pan, 57
quadrillage or checkering, 215, 219

Brose, 325

Brown sauce, 127
for freezing or refrigerator storage, 127
variations, 127-128

Broyage, Swiss, 410

Brussels sprouts, 316
and chestnuts, 317

Burgundy, wines, red, 468
white, 469

Burnt-sugar rice pudding, 531

Butter, see also BUTTERS
amount to serve daily, 18
beurre manié, 122
for finishing sauces, 123
nutrient value, 23
for pie pastry, 418
for puff pastry, 429
salted and unsalted (to freeze), 166
to thicken sauces, 122

Buttercream meringue, 411

Buttermilk pancakes, old-fashioned, 488

Buttermilk spice cake, 523

Butters, see also SAUCE, ENTRÉE and HORS D'OEUVRE
chervil, 93
herb, 274, 286
nasturtium, 96
seasoned, 285
tarragon, 91

Butterscotch ice cream, 443

C

Cabbage, 315-317
family, 315-319
leaves, stuffed, 317
red, bruxellois, 316
soaking, 295, 315
soup, cream of, 492

Cake(s)
bee's kiss torte, 529
buttermilk spice, 523
chocolate, double-rich, 500
cinnamon coffee cake, 497
filling cake pans, 58
(with) frostings and fillings (to freeze), 166
French colonial fruit cake, 540
fruitcake, 540
  to freeze, 166
maple-sugar shortcake, 495
old-fashioned poundcake ring, 541
pans for, 57
pans, measuring, 58
poundcake, lemon, 500
  rose-geranium, 519

Calcium, 16
foods, 17, 21

Calf's brain, see BRAINS; VEAL

Calf's liver, see LIVER; VEAL

Calgary oxtail soup, 492

Calgary's own sandwich, 492

Calories, 20
in foods, chart, 21-23

Canada's Food Guide, 19

Canadian autumn lunch, 504-506

Canadian cheese, 459

Canadian salmon, 258-262

Can opener, 62

Caper(s), 99
crackers, 499
sauce, 125

Capons, 239

Capsicum Peppers, see PEPPER(S), CAPSICUM

Caramel sauce, 534

Caraway, 99
cheese appetizer, 99

Carbohydrates, 14

Carco wine consommé, 504

Cardamom, 103

Cardoons, 332

Carrots, 305-307
French fried, 301
glazed, chef's, 307
  golden (to freeze), 156
Irish colcannon, elegant, 307
Ninon, 506
steam-baked, 300
vegetarian casserole, 306
Véronique, 306

Cashews, 461

Casseroles, ready-cooked (to freeze), 167

Cassia, 103

Cauliflower, 318-319
French fried, 301
golden, 319

Caviar
Russian mayonnaise, 132
muscovite sauce, 131

Cayenne peppers, 107

Celeriac (celery root or celery knob), 311
hors d'oeuvre, 311
with potatoes, 311
salad, 311
to prevent discoloration, 311

INDEX

Celery, 333-334
amandine in casserole, 334
clam chowder, 522
freezing, 145
glazed, see CHEF'S GLAZED CARROTS, 307
leaves, dried, 333
leaves, fresh, uses for, 333
smoked salmon celery, 335
to prevent discoloration, 333

Celery knob, see CELERIAC

Celery root, see CELERIAC

Celery seeds, 99

Centigrade temperatures for sugar boiling, 68

Cereal grains, 323, 325-329
amount to serve daily, 18, 19
necessary supplies, 65

Champagne, 471-472
Blanc de Blancs, 472
glasses, 475; illus, 475
terminology for sweetness, 472
when to serve, 467

Chaud-froid, 353, 354

Checkering (in broiling), 215, 219

Charlotte russe, de luxe, 530

Cheese, 453-460
best temperature for serving, 76
from Canada, 459
Cheddar, (with) apples, toasted walnuts, 524
cream-cheese filling, 528
cream-cheese pastry, Viennese, 426
Danish dressing, 137
from Denmark, 456
from France, 454-455
from Germany, 457
from Great Britain, 454
grated (to freeze), 166
from Greece, 458
from Holland, 458
how to buy, 42
from Italy, 458
mild Cheddar soup, Ontario, 494
natural, 42
from Norway, 456
nutritional values, 42
omelet, 488
processed, 42
Roquefort dressing, 138
soufflé, 400
ingredients (to freeze), 160
storing, 460
straws, 436-437
from Sweden, 456
Swiss, marinated, 501
from Switzerland, 457
(as) thickener for sauces, 123
from United States, 459

Chemistry of cooking, 75

Cherry(ies)
sweet or sour (to freeze), 152

sweet, stewed (to freeze), see STEWED PRUNE PLUMS, 153
and wine aspic, 358

Cherrystone clams, 269

Chervil, 93
butter, 93

Chestnut(s), 349, 461
and Brussels sprouts, 317
fresh, to prepare, 317
purée, 349
roasted, 349
stuffing, see SAUSAGE-MEAT STUFFING, 243

Chicken
aspic mousse, 357
baked, golden, 244
with barley pilaf, 326
basic ways to cook, 241
basting sauce for, 290
broiled, my favorite, 244
Scandinavian, 245
broiler-fryer, 239
broilers, golden glazed, 290
split, barbecued, 290
buying, 239
capons, 239
casserole, 512
croquettes, 364
deviled, 245
dressed poultry, 240
eviscerated oven-ready, 239-240
fricassee of, 248
marinade for, 114
pie, nuns', 538
poached, 246
my way, 246
preparing for cooking, 240
ready-to-cook, 239-240
roasted, 242
roasting, timetable, 242
salad Oriental, 350
salad puff, 527
soufflé, 401
soup, see POACHED CHICKEN, MY WAY, 246
squab, 239
stewing, 239
stock, see FRICASSEE OF CHICKEN, 248
to cut up, 240-241
to stuff, 240
to test for doneness, 241
to truss, 240
two in a pan, 242
types, 239-240
unstuffed, flavoring, 240

Chicken liver(s)
chopped, 511
omelet, 388
pâté, 499
rumaki, 350
soufflé, 402

Chiffon, 353
aspic, 357
citrus pie, 436

Chiffonade, 73

Chiffonade dressing, 137

Chili peppers, 107

Chinese deviled chicken, 245

Chinese fried rice, 328

Chinese stir-frying, 299-300

Chives, 93, 314
fines herbes with chives, 93
fresh-chives omelet, 386
to cut, 73
uses for, 93

Chocolate
-butterscotch ice cream, 443
cake, double-rich, 500
for dessert sauces, 140
Dutch chocolate ice cream, 442
flan de Nevers, 503
frosting, double-rich, 501
ice cream, 441, 442
rich, 444
mocha sauce, 140
necessary supplies, 66
piecrust, 426
soufflé, 404

Cholesterol Content, 23

Chopping block and boards, 61, 63

Choron sauce, 131

Christmas dinner, my grand-maman's, 535-543

Cider, perry cup, 519

Cinnamon, 103-104
cassia, 103
coffee cake, 497
rolls, 437
-walnut topping, 497

Citrus
chiffon pie, 436
dressing for stuffed roast pork, 212
fruits, as acids, 77
as source of Vitamin C, 15, 17, 43

Clam(s), 269
celery clam chowder, 522
Cherrystone, 269
(for) chowder, 269
fried, see FRIED SHRIMPS, 272
Littleneck, 269
quahogs, 269
soft-shell, 269
steamed, 269
to freeze, 165
storage, 165
uses of, 269

Clarifying
stock for aspics, 118
used fat, 362

Cloves, 104

Coatings for fried foods, 224, 365

Cod, pickled, 265
pink, garnished, 265

Coffee
in beans or ground (to freeze), 167

coffee makers, 56
double-coffee ice cream, 443
grinder, electric, 63
ice cream, perfect, 441
mocha chocolate sauce, 140
soufflé, 403
to make a large amount, 532

Coffee cake, cinnamon, 497

Colcannon, Irish, elegant, 307

Concord grape whip, 356

Condiments, 81

Confections
marzipan fruits, 543
praline, 509

Container sizes, guide to, 67

Convenience foods, 38

Cookies, oatmeal fruit, 498

Cooking for a crowd, 531-532

Cordial(s), 474
glasses, 475; illus, 475
lovage, 95

Coriander, 104
leaves, uses for, 104
seeds, uses for, 104

Corkscrew, 62

Corn, 337-338
boiled, 524
-husking bee (épluchette de blé d'Inde), 524
on the cob, frozen, to cook, 160
roast, hot buttery, 292
squaw, 338
succotash, 322
to cook, 160, 337
whole kernel (to freeze), 157

Cornell method for baking fish fillets, 253

Cornflake crust, 424

Country apple pie, 433

Court-bouillon for fish, 257

Crab(s), Crabmeat, 272-273
chiffon aspic, 357
seafood ramekins, 273
soft-shell, 272
to clean, 272
to freeze, 165
storage, 165

Cranberry(ies)
raw (to freeze), 152
relish (to freeze), 152
sherbet, 447

Crawfish, see Rock lobster

Cream
acid with, 78
filling, 529

for finishing sauces, 123
frangipane, 413
French, 510
for ice cream, 438
light and heavy (to freeze), 166
mustard cream sauce, 134
to sour, 78
to thicken sauces, 122
whipped, 140
   use of lemon juice to stabilize, 78
   wire whisk for, 72

Creamy pumpkin pie, 541

Crêpes, 413

Croque-monsieur, 491

Croquettes
basic method, 364
chicken, 364
fish, 364
meat, 364

Croûtons, buttered (to freeze), 165

Crown of turnip with green peas, 539

Cucumber(s), 338-340
purée (to freeze), 157
salad, Finnish, 339
sour-cream sauce, 259
Spanish, 339
and spinach salad, 331
and tomato salad, 345
to prepare, 338
twisted, in sour cream, 521
and yogourt salad, 340

Cumin, cuminseeds, 99-100

Curried, Curry
eggs with saffron rice, 97
mayonnaise indienne, 133
powder, 110
sauce, 125
shrimp, East Indian, 513
uses for, 110

Custard dishes, dessert
charlotte russe, de luxe, 530
chocolate, flan de Nevers, 503
cups for, 57
custard sauce, 139
French cream, 510
lemon snow eggs, 531

Daily food needs, see CANADA'S FOOD GUIDE, 17-19

Dairy products, 17, 19, 21 (to freeze), 166

Dandelions, 330

Danish cheese, 456

Danish dressing, 137

Deep-frying, 361-366
clarifying used fat, 362
coatings for, 363
fats for, 361
fish, 256
how to fry, 363
pan for, 361
storing used fat, 362
temperatures for, 362
thermometer, 62
to coat food, basic method, 363
vegetables, 300-301

Dessert (or Sweet) omelets, 394-396
basic technique, 394
fresh-berry, 396
how to glaze the top, 395
how to flame, 395
macaroon, 396
marmalade, 396
sour-cream, 395

Dessert sauces, 139-140; for recipes see SAUCES, DESSERT

Deviled almonds and walnuts, 499

Deviled appetizers, 436

Deviled chicken, Chinese, 245

Diable sauce, 128

Dicing, 74

Dijon syrup, 510
Dill, 88
sauce, 125
   for lamb, 89

Dinner
Christmas, my grand-maman's, 535-543
grand dîner, 507-510
perfect little, 501-503
wild duck, autumn, 504-506

Diplomate sauce, 126

Doughnuts
the very best I know, 366
to freeze, 165

Dressings
for meats, poultry, fish, see STUFFING
for salads, see SALAD DRESSING

Duchess potatoes, 303

Duck(s), Duckling(s), 247
carving, 535
glazed, 504
marinade for, 115
wild duck dinner, 504-506

Dutch cheese, 458

Dutch chocolate ice cream, 442

Dutch mustard, 101

E

East Indian shrimp curry, 513

Egg(s), 379-396; see also CUSTARD DISHES; MERINGUE; SOUFFLÉ
basic cooking methods, 380
beater, 61
and bread crumbs (coating for sautéing and panfrying), 224
coating, 224, 363
in cocottes, 382
composition, 380
cooked (to freeze), 160
and crumb coating (for deep-frying), 363
curried, with saffron rice, 97
effect of cooking heat on, 380
fried, 383-384, 487
   and bacon and fried tomatoes, 487
grading, 379
hard-cooked, in the shell, 381
   filling, 528
   sauce, 125
   Scandinavian, 134
   to peel, 381
   to prevent cracking, 381
   to store, 381
how to freeze, 160
how to store properly, 380
in ice cream, 438
landaise in electric frypan, 489
molded, see EGGS IN COCOTTES, 382
oeufs mollets, 381
oeufs sur le plat, see SHIRRED EGGS, 382
omelets, omelettes, 384-396; see also DESSERT OMELETS
   basic techniques, 385
   Bercy, 387
   berry, 396
   bonne femme, 387
   cheese, 488
   chicken-liver, 388
   classic or French, 385
   cooked-potato, 388
   fines herbes, 386
   folding, 385
   fresh chives, 386
   fresh mushroom, 388
   German, 390
   how to fill, 385
   Italian (frittata), 391
   leftovers (for fillings), 385
   Matignon, 393
   moissonneur, 387
   mousseline, 389
   niçoise, 393
   pan, 384-385
   paysan method to fill, 385
   potato, 387
   sauces for, 396
   seasoning a new pan, 384
   sour-cream, 395
   Spanish (tortilla), 391
   tomato, 386
   walnut, 389
pipérade, 392
poached, 382
à la française, see EGGS IN COCOTTES, 382
protein substitute for meat, 40
scrambled, 383
   double-boiler method, 383
   finnan farmhouse scramble, 264
   squaw corn, 338
shell, 380
shirred, 382
soft-cooked, in the shell, 380-381
   coddled, 380
   cold-water method, 380
   French method, 381
   hot-water method, 381
   oeufs mollets, 381
in soufflés, 397
uncooked (to freeze whole), 160
vitamin content, 380
white(s), 380
   beating at room temperature, 406
   beating for meringue, 406
   folding into heavier mixtures, 72
   fruit sugar with, 79
   separating at refrigerator temperature, 397, 406
   in soufflés, 398
   uncooked, to freeze, 160
   wire whisk for, 72
yolk(s), 380
   color, 380
   as sauce thickener, 122
   in soufflés, 397
   uncooked, to freeze, 160

Eggplant, 338-339
broiled, 339
French fried, 301
mashed, 338
ratatouille niçoise, 341
slices, baked, 339
whole, baked, 338

Electric and gas stoves compared, 75

Electric hot tray, 63

Elegant Victorian picnic, 516-520

Emulsified sauces, 128-133

Endives, braised, 330

Engagement party, tea-time, 525-527

English bread sauce, 133

English cheese, 454

English cold beef and kidney pie, 518

English dressing, 138

English gravy (beef) with horseradish, 201

English liver and bacon sandwich, 491

English Midland soup, 490

English mustard, 101

INDEX

English poached salmon, 260

English plum pudding, 533
decorating, 534
flaming, 535

Épluchette de blé d'Inde (corn-husking bee), 524

Espagnole sauce, 127

European flan pastry, 427

Extracts and flavorings
necessary supplies, 66

Fahrenheit temperatures for sugar boiling, 68

Fats, 14
for deep-frying, 361-362
necessary supplies, 66
for pie pastry, 417
salt with, 79
sources, 14
unsaturated, 14
used, clarifying, 362
  storing, 362

Fennel, 100
as vegetable, 334

Fiddleheads, 330

Filberts, 461

Fillings for cakes and desserts, see ICING and FILLING

Fillings for sandwiches, see Sandwiches

Finnan haddie, 263-264
farmhouse scramble, 264
savory, 263
savory pudding, 264

Finnish chilled tomato soup, 343

Finnish cucumber salad, 339

Fish, 251-265; see also names of fish; SHELLFISH; names of shellfish
amount to serve, 19, 252
aspic, 356
baked en papillote, 254
baking, 252
  times for, 253
  chart, 253
barbecuing, 281; see also SEAFOOD SAKANA, 292
basting, 253
batter-fried, 365
bread-crumb topping, 252
broiling, 254
cakes, frozen, 164
Cornell Method for baking fillets, 253
court bouillon, 257
croquettes, 364
deep-frying, 256
fillets, fresh and frozen, broiling, 255-256
flour topping, 252
frozen, 251-252
  thawing and cooking, 165
how much should you buy, 41
how to buy, 41
how to freeze, 164-165
  brine method, 164
  glazing method, 164
  ice-block method, 164
marinade for, 114
panfrying, 256
poaching, 257
salt with, 79
sautéing, 256
servings per pound, 41
Spencer Method for baking, 253
split, broiling, 255
  timetable, 255
steaks, broiling, 254
  timetable, 254
steaming, 257
stock, 117
to determine freshness, 251
to test for flakiness, 256
whole, broiling, 255
  timetable, 255
whole, charcoal-baked, 290

Fisherman's potato cakes, 304

Flambéed dishes, Flambéing, Flaming
dessert omelet, 395
English plum pudding, 535
foods, 477

Flan (custard), chocolate, 503

Flan pastry, 427

Flour
coating for sautéing and panfrying, 224
necessary supplies, 65
for pie pastry, 417
sifter, 62
topping (for fish), 252

Folding, 72

Food beater, portable, 63

Food budget, 32

Food costs, 25-26

Food grinder, 62

Food mill, 62

Food plans
liberal budgets, 35
low-cost budgets, 33
moderate budgets, 34

Foods
buying guide, chart, 44-47
effect of heat on, 75
storage life on pantry shelves, chart, 67
to serve at room temperature, 76

Fork, 61

Frangipane cream, 413

Frank's hot or cold artichoke dressing, 333

Frappé, 446

Freezer, 143-144
amount to freeze at one time, 144
arrangement of foods, 144
how to defrost, 168
size to buy, 63-64
to buy, 63-64

Freezing, 143-168
apples, baked, 151
  sliced, 150-151
  whole, uncooked, 150
applesauce, 151
  pink, 151
apricot purée, 154
apricots, 152
ascorbic acid for fruits, 149
banana purée, 154
basic information, 147-148
bread
  for poultry dressing, 165
  for toast, 165
butter, 166
cakes with frostings and fillings, 166
carrots, golden glazed, 156
casseroles, ready-cooked, 167
cheese, grated, 166
cherries, sweet or sour, 152
  sweet, stewed, see STEWED PRUNE PLUMS, 153
chickens, 143, 146
coffee in beans or ground, 167
containers, 147-148
corn, whole kernel, 157
cranberries, raw, 152
cranberry relish, 152
cream, 166
croûtons, buttered, 165
crumb topping for fruit pies, 168
cucumber purée, 157
dairy products, 166
doughnuts, 165
drugstore wrap, 148
eggs, 160
  cooked, 160
  uncooked, 160
fish, 164-165
  brine method, 164
  cakes, frozen, 164
  glazing method, 164
  ice-block method, 164
fruitcakes, 166
fruit peels, mixed, 166
fruit pie fillings, 155
fruits, 144, 146, 149-156
  basic steps, 149
  candied and glazed, storage, 144
  commercially frozen, storing, 143-144
  glazed, 166
  packages per year, chart, 146
  packing and sealing, 149
  packing with sugar or syrup, 150
  storage of, 156
  syrup for, 150
fruit sauces, 154
gingerroots, fresh, 167
grape favorite, 152
gravy, leftover, 167
green peppers, 159
ground meats, 161
hamburger mixture, 162
herbs, fresh, 158
ice cream, storage, 144, 148
labels, 148
leek base for vichyssoise, 158
leeks, 157
leftovers, storage, 144
lemon rinds, 166
marshmallows, 166
meat(s), 161-163
  cured, 145
  general procedures, 161
  packages per year, 146
  wholesale cuts, storing, 143
miscellaneous foods, 146
mushrooms, 158
nutmeats and whole nuts, 166
  storage, 144
onions, 158
orange rinds, 166
pancakes, 165
parsley, 158
peaches, 152
  purée, 154
pies, 168
planning season's food supply, 145-146
potatoes, baked, 159
  French fried, 159
poultry, 163
prune plums, stewed or raw, 153
rhubarb, 153
rice, 329
sandwich fillings, emergency, 167
sealing freezer packages, 147, 149
seasoning foods to be frozen, 147
shellfish, 165
  storage, 165
soufflé, 399
storage time for foods, chart, 148
storage time for frozen meats, 162
syrup from canned or stewed fruits, 167
tea, 167
vegetables, 157-160
  commercially frozen, storage, 143-144
  packages per year, chart, 146
what not to freeze, 145
wrapping and packaging for, 147

French cheese, 454-455

French colonial fruitcake, 540

French cream, 510

French crêpe meringue, 413

French dressing, 136
American-style, 137
herb, 514

French frying or deep-frying (vegetables), 300-301; for more information see DEEP-FRYING

French gravy (beef) without flour, 201

French mustard (Dijon), 101

French poached lamb shank, 230

French roasted chicken, 242

French toast, 489

French vanilla ice cream, 439

French velouté d'oignon, 491

Fricasseeing, meats, 231
poultry, 248
veal, 232

Frittata, Italian omelet, 391

Fritters, fruit, basic method, 365

Frostings, see ICING AND FILLING

Frozen desserts
frappé, 446
fresh lemon granité, 515
frozen punch, 446
ice cream, 437-445
  banana, 440
  chemical reaction of ice and salt, 437
  chocolate, 441, 444
  chocolate-butterscotch, 443
  coffee, 441, 443
  cream for, 438
  double-coffee, 443
  double-raspberry, 443
  Dutch chocolate, 442
  eggs in, 438
  equipment for making, 437
  fruits for, preparing, 438
  gelatine in, 439
  maple walnut, 442
  milk or evaporated milk for, 438-439
  mixtures, 438-439
  packing the freezer, 438
  raspberry, 443
  refrigerator, 443-445
  strawberry, fresh berries, 445
  frozen berries, 440
  sugar in, 439
  toffee, 445
  vanilla, 439-440
  refrigerator, 444
  variations, 442
maple-syrup sundae, 495
milk ice, 446
mousse, see Mousse
sherbet, 446-449
  cranberry, 447
  lemon ice, 447
  lime milk, 449
  rhubarb, 449
  stabilizers, 446
  stirring and beating during freezing, 446
  strawberry milk, 448
water ice, 446

Fruit(s); see also names of fruits
acid with, 77
amount to serve daily, 17, 19
ascorbic acid for freezing, 149
canned or stewed, syrup from (to freeze), 167
dried, citrus juice with, 77
  necessary supplies, 66
  to cut, 73
fresh-fruit pie, glazed, 434
fresh, how to buy, 42-43
  seasonal guide, chart, 48-49
fritters, basic method, 365
frozen packages per year, chart, 146
frozen, storage of, 156
  thawing and serving from freezer, 156
glacé (to freeze), 166
how to freeze, 149-156
  basic steps, 149
  packing and sealing, 149
  syrup for, 150
for ice cream, 438
juicer, 62
lemon juice to prevent discoloration, 77
marinade for, 115
oatmeal cookies, 498
à la pâte d'amande, 543
peels, mixed (to freeze), 166
pie fillings, frozen, 155
pies, crumb topping for, 168
rich in Vitamin C, 15, 17, 42
salads, honey dressing for, 138
  poppy-seed dressing for, 139
sauces, frozen, 154
testing for ripeness, 43
unripe, 43

Fruitcake, see Cake

Frying, electric pan, 63

Fumet, 125

Funnel, 62

Galantine de porc, 537

Game, marinade for, 115

Game birds, 247

Garbage-disposal unit, 63

Garlic, 100, 314
marinade, 283
mashing, 73
salt or powder, 100
uses for, 100

Garnishes
amandine (for snap beans), 320
chiffonade vegetables, for consommé, 73
julienne vegetables, for soup, 73
parsley, 86
pickled mushrooms, 348
sugared borage flowers, 92-93
vegetable curls, 74
Véronique, see CARROTS VÉRONIQUE, 306

Gas and electric stoves compared, 75

Geese, 247

Gelatin in ice cream, 439

German cheese, 457

German mustard, 101

German omelet, 390

Gin, 473, 478

Ginger, 105
gingerroots, fresh, preserved, 105
  as a seasoning, 82
  to freeze, 167
  to store, 105
ground, uses for, 105
sauce, 105
sugar, 105

Glaze for ham or other meats
American favorite, 213
buffet-style, 213
chef's favorite, 213
delicatessen special, 213
Finnish, 213
German, 213
Scotch, 213
simple, 213
Western Canadian favorite, 213

Glossary of spirits, 478-479

Graham-cracker crust, 425

Grand-maman's Christmas dinner, 535-543

Grape and cantaloupe (to freeze), 152

Grapes, Concord, whip, 356

Grater, 61

Gravy; see also SAUCE, ENTRÉE and HORS D'OEUVRE
brown (beef), with flour, 201
English (beef), with horseradish, 201
French (beef), without flour, 201
leftover (to freeze), 167
for panfried foods, to make, 224
for roast pork, see ROAST LOIN OF PORK GOURMET, 211
turkey, 537

Greek cheese, 458

Green mayonnaise, 132

Green onions, 312

Green snap beans, see BEANS

Green peppers, see PEPPER(S), CAPSICUM

Greens, 329-331

Grinding, 73

Haddock
finnan farmhouse scramble, 264
finnan savory, 263
  pudding, 264

Halibut steaks, grilled, 291

Ham, cured; for fresh ham, see PORK, FRESH
baked, glazing, 213
baking, timetable, 199
boiled, 231
cook-before-eating, 189
country-style, to buy, 188-189
croque-monsieur, 491
cuts for roasting, 199
filling, 528
fully cooked, 189, 199
glazed barbecued, 289
glazes, 213
mushroom-ham casserole, 524
picnic, to buy, 188
shoulder roll, or butt, to buy, 188-189
slices, to buy, 188
steak, barbecued, 289
  braised, 223
  broiled, 216
  timetable, 216
whole, to buy, 188

Hamburger, see BEEF

Happy peaches (to freeze), 153

Hard sauce, 534

Hawaiian teriyaki, 217

Hazelnuts, 461

Hearts, basic preparation and cooking, 233
to freeze, 161

Heat
effect on food, 75
gas and electric stoves compared, 75
how to apply, 75-76
microwave heat, 75-76
room temperature, 76
trapped heat in ovens, 75

Herb(s), 85 and ff; see also names of herbs
amount to use, 85
basic three, 86-87
best-known five, 86-88
best-known ten, 86-91
bouquet, 87
bouquet garni, 87
butter, 274, 286
essential oils in whole form, 85
fines herbes, with chives, 93
  omelet, 386
  sauce, 125
flavored vegetable soup, 90

INDEX

French dressing, 514
fresh (to freeze), 158
garden ten, 86, 92-97
gourmet's two, 86, 97-98
necessary supplies, 66
potpourri with verbena, 95
rolls, hot, 523
storage, 85
to grow, 92
with wine in cooking, 476

Herring, fresh, marinated, 266

Hollandaise sauce, 128-131
blender, 130
Bordeaux, 130
chef's, 129
hot-water, 130
reheating, 129
separation to correct, 129
special chef's secrets, 131
storing in refrigerator or freezer, 129
variations, 130-131
wire whisk, 129

Holland cheese, 458

Honey, 80
B.C. basting sauce, 284
dressing for fruit salads, 138
mint marinade for lamb, 282
spread with sage, 88
substituting for sugar, 80

Honeyed Sally Lunn, 498

Hors d'oeuvre
caper crackers, 499
caraway cheese, 99
celeriac, marinated, 311
cheese straws, 436-437
chicken-liver pâté, 499
chicken livers, chopped, 511
deviled almonds and walnuts, 499
deviled appetizers, 436
green-pepper appetizer, 342
jellied canapés, 355
marinated mushroom canapés, 529
marinated mushrooms, 346
marinated Swiss cheese, 501
melon Alcantara, 508
moules marinière, 270
pickled mushrooms, 348
picnic hors d'oeuvre, 516
rumaki, 350
tapenade de Nice, 507
teriyaki, world-famous Hawaiian, 217

Horseradish, 100-101
English gravy (beef) with, 201
mayonnaise, 132
mustard, 101

Husband's preference, sandwich filling (to freeze), 167

Ice cream, see FROZEN DESSERTS

Icing and Filling, dessert;
see also MERINGUE(S); SAUCE, DESSERT
chocolate frosting, 501
cinnamon walnut topping, 497
cream filling, 529
frangipane cream, 413
lemon filling, 414
meringue buttercream, 411
praline, 509
topping for bee's kiss torte, 529
topping for fruitcake, 540

Incorporating, 72

Indian barbecued salmon, 291

Internal meats, see VARIETY MEATS; see also names of specific kinds

Iodine, 16

Irish colcannon, elegant, 307

"Irish stew Honest", our Nanny's, 229

Iron, 16

Italian buttered rice, 328

Italian cheese, 458

Italian marinade, 283

Italian meringue, 411

Italian omelet (frittata), 391

Ivy smoked salmon celery (The), 335

J

Jardinière de légumes, 509

Jellied desserts
apricot delight, 527
charlotte russe, de luxe, 530
chiffon, 353
   to chill, 354
Concord grape whip, 356
molds for, 57, 353
mousse, 353; see also MOUSSE
orange and lemon snow aspic, 358
pineapple with gelatin, see SWEET ASPIC FOR DESSERT, 358
snow, 353
   to chill, 354
sugar proportions, see SWEET ASPIC FOR DESSERT, 358
sweet aspic for dessert, 358
to unmold, 354
whips, to chill, 354
wine and cherry aspic, 358

Jerusalem artichoke, 312

Julienne, 73

Juniper berries, 101

K

Kale, 318, 329

Kidney and beef pie, English, cold, 518

Kidneys, basic preparation and cooking, 233
to freeze, 161

Kitchen
equipment, 54
essential tools, 54-62
knives, 59-60
luxuries, 62-63
microwave oven utensils, 58
organizing for efficient use, 53
oven and broiler utensils, 57
pots and pans, 54-57
   substituting sizes, 58
small appliances, 62
storage space, 53
top-of-stove utensils, 56

Knives, 59-60
bread, 60
carving, 60
chef's, 60, 73
sharpening, 60
slicer, 60
slicing and scraping, 60
starter set, 60
utility, 60

Kohlrabi, 318

Lamb
braising, timetable, 220
butterfly leg of (barbecued), 286
chops (barbecued), 287
cuts, 196
   for barbecueing, 281
   for broiling, 215
   for roasting, 196
dill sauce for, 89
Hawaiian teriyaki, 217
hearts, basic preparation and cooking, 233
"Honest Irish stew", 229
honey mint marinade for, 282
kidneys, basic preparation and cooking, 233
lambburger, 218
   barbecued, 286
leg of, glazed roasted, 205
   à la grecque, 206
   roast, Italienne, 205
liver, basic preparation and cooking, 233
mint sauce for, 86, 134
Persian kebab, 287
rack of, roasted, à la française, 206
shank, poached, 230
roasting, timetable, 196
shoulder, à la grecque, 206
   rolled, braised, à la française, see BRAISED VEAL SHOULDER, 222
   rolled, Oriental, 208
   rolled, Texan style, 207
steak (barbecued), 286
tongue, basic preparation and cooking, 234

Langoustines, 271

Lard pastry, 425

Leavening, necessary supplies, 65

Leek(s), 313-314
base for vichyssoise (to freeze), 158
pie, Welsh, 314
to freeze, 157

Legumes, dried, 323-325
necessary supplies, 66

Legumes, fresh, 320-323

Lemon
basting sauce, 283
and bread stuffing, 243
butter sauce, 284
filling, 414
fresh lemon granité, 515
fresh, as a seasoning, 82
ice, 446
-juice pastry, 426
mint lemonade, 86
meringue pie, classic, 434
mousse, 506
and orange snow aspic, 358
pie, luscious, 435
poundcake, 500
rind (to freeze), 166
snow eggs, 531
and thyme dressing, 87
to use on fish, 76

Lemon balm, 93-94
iced tea, 94

Lemon thyme, 94

Lemon verbena, 94
applesauce with, 96-97
herb potpourri with, 95
tea, 94

Lentil(s), 323-324
creamed, 324
soup, 324

Lima beans, 322

Lime
citrus chiffon pie, 436
fresh, used as a seasoning, 82
milk sherbet, 449

Liqueurs, 474
for flaming foods, 477
glasses, 475; illus., 475
soufflé, 404

Liquor in a soufflé, 405

Littleneck clams, 269

553

Liver(s)
and bacon sandwich, 491
basic preparation and cooking, 233
calf's, for barbecue, 281
  brochettes, 286
chicken, chopped, 511
  omelet, 388
  pâté, 499
  soufflé, 402
comparison of varieties, 233
storage, 190
to freeze, 161
whole, braised, 235

Lobster, 273-276
baked, 274
boiled live, 274
broiled, 274
cooked, how to eat, 275
coral or roe, 273
crawfish, 273-274
grilled, see SEAFOOD SAKANA, 292
marinated, grilled, see SEAFOOD SAKANA, 292
meat (to freeze), 165
  storage, 165
Newburg, 276
puffs, baby, 497
rock or spiny, 273-274
seafood ramekins, 273
spring sauce for, 276
steamed, 274
stew, creamy, 275
tomalley, 273

Louisiana little loaves, 268

Lovage, 94
cordial, 95

Lunchtime food, 490-495

Macadamia nuts, 461

Macaroon omelet, 396

Mace, 105-106

Madeira, 473
glasses, 475; illus, 475
sauce, 127

Madère, sauce, 127

Maltaise sauce, 131

Maple-sugar shortcake, 495

Maple syrup
pie, 542
soufflé, 405
sundae, 495
walnut ice cream, 442

Margarine, amount to serve daily, 18
nutrient value, 31

Marigold, 95
in a salad, 96

Marinades, 113-115
for barbecue, 282-283
basic, 113, 282

for chicken, 114
for duck and game, 115
for fish, 114
for fruits, 115
garlic, 283
Hawaiian, for teriyaki, 217
honey mint, for lamb, 282
Italian, 283
Oriental, 114
sesame-seed, for teriyaki, 218
sherry, for teriyaki, 218
simple, for steak, 284
soy-ginger, 292
variations on the basic marinades, 115
for vegetables, 115
wine, for meat, 114

Marjoram, 90
tomato salad with, 91

Marmalade omelet, 396

Marshmallows, to cut, 73
to freeze, 166

Marzipan fruits, 543

Mashing, 73

Mayonnaise, 131-133
cressonière, 132-133
dijonnaise, 133
green, 132
horseradish, 132
indienne, 133
niçoise, 133
Russian, 132
for sandwiches (to freeze), 145
separation, to correct, 131
storage, 131
Swedish, 132
tartar sauce, 132
with tart flavor, 131
variations, 132-133
wire whisk for, 72, 131

Measures and Measuring, 67-68
cups and spoons, 60-61
grams and ounces, 68
equivalent measures, 67-68
guide to common container sizes, 68
liquid measures, 68
measurement conversion, 68
oven temperatures, 68
some difficult fractions, 68
wines and spirits, 475

Meats, 187-236; see also names of meats
acid with, 77
aspic, 356
bone chart, 189
bones, cracked, for stock, 116
bone stock, 116
braised roasts, seasoning, 220-221
braising, 219-221
broiling, 214-216
buying, 187-188
coatings for sautéing and panfrying, 224
cooking, basic techniques, 192 and ff
chart, 192
croquettes, 364

cured, storage, 190
cuts, for barbecueing, 281
  for broiling, 215
  for roasting, 195
  tenderness of, 189-190
freezing, general procedures, 161
fricasseeing, 231
frozen, broiling, 215
  cooking, 162-163
  packages per year, 146
  storage time, 162
ground, frozen, 161
hammer, 63
how much to buy, 39
how to buy, 39-40
how to freeze, 161-163
how to save money on purchases, 39-40
internal, 233-236; see also names of specific kinds to buy, 39
leftover cooked, storage, 191
marinating, 192
microwave, 192
mixed with other ingredients, 40
panbroiling, 218-219
  with a Swedish iron skillet, 219
panfrying, 223-224
poached, to serve cold, 226
  to serve hot, 226
poaching, timetable, 227
pot-roasting, 219-221
roasting, 192-193
roast or steak, to cook frozen, 163
salt (pan) broiling, 219
salt with, 79
sautéing, 223-224
servings per pound, 39
sliced, 40
stewing, 225
  timetable, 227
storage of, 190-191
thermometer, 194
  for frozen meats, 163
to recognize spoilage, 190
uncooked, washing, 191
wine marinade for, 114

Mei jiung (MSG), 81

Melon(s)
Alcantara, 508
best temperature for serving, 76
unripe, to ripen, 43

Mennonite green beans, 321

Menu(s)
after-football snack, 523-524
afternoon tea for VIPs, 499-501
autumn wild duck dinner, 504-506
Canadian autumn lunch, 494
casserole buffet supper, 511-515
Christmas dinner, my grand-maman's, 535-543

Corn-husking bee (épluchette de blé d'Inde), 524
dessert and coffee for an afternoon committee meeting, 530-531
elegant Victorian picnic, 516-520
grand dîner, 507-510
lazy breakfast, 488
party tea, 496-498
perfect little dinner, 501-503
picnic in the car, 521-523
plum pudding, coffee and brandy party, 532-534
romantic picnic for two, 520-521
shower for baby, 528-530
soup and sandwich fun, 490-493
teatime engagement party, 525-527
traditional breakfast, 487

Menu pattern
for meal planning, 30-31
for normal diet, 24
for overweight, 24
for underweight, 24
pointers in planning, 31

Meringue(s),
basic, 407-409
bowl for beating, 55, 61, 406
buttercream, 411
cold-water, 409
egg whites, beating, 406
electric mixer, 409
French crêpe, 413
hard, 407
  shell, to shape, 407
  small to medium, to shape, 407
Italian, 411
lemon pie, classic, 434
lemon snow eggs, 531
pie, 414
(for) pie, American, 412
pie shell, 414
soft, 408
  for pie topping, hot-oven baking, 408
strawberry, Swiss, 412
Swiss broyage, 410
to prevent weeping, 420
wire whisk for, 72

Microwave oven
heat, 75
standing time, 76
thermometer, 62
utensils, 58-59
  browning dish and grill, 59
  cooking bags, 59
  frozen dinner trays, 59
  glass, ceramic and china utensils, 58-59
  meat, 192
  paper, 59
  plastic wrap, 59
  straw and wicker, 59

Milk
acid with, 78
amount to serve daily, 17, 19

INDEX

evaporated, for ice cream, 438
    to whip, 140
ice, 446
(for) ice cream, 438
skim-milk powder
    nutritional value, 31
    reconstituted, 31
    to whip, 140
    to sour, 78

Minerals, 16
calcium, best sources, 16
iodine, best sources, 16
iron, best sources, 16
phosphorus, best sources, 16

Mincing, 74

Mint, 86-87
lemonade, 86
sauce, 86, 134

Mixer, electric, 62

Mixing, 72
bowls, 55, 61, 406

Mocha chocolate sauce, 140

Molasses (treacle), 80
lemon sauce, 489

Monosodium glutamate (MSG), 81

Mornay sauce, 124

Moules marinière, 270

Mousse, dessert, 353
applesauce, 542
lemon, 506

Mousse, entrée, 353
chicken aspic, 357

Mousseline omelet, 389

Mousseline sauce, 130
light, 131

MSG, 81

Muscovite sauce, 131

Mushroom(s), 345-348
canapés, marinated, 529
consommé, 347
creamed, 347
fresh, omelet, 388
    soufflé, 401
-ham casserole, 524
marinated, 346
pickled, 348
rolls, 496
sauce, 125
sautéed, 346
soup, cream of, see MUSHROOM CONSOMMÉ, 347
stems and peelings, uses for, 346
to freeze, 158
to store, 345
to wash, 346
Verona, 348
wild, dried, 345

Mussels, 269-270
cleaning, 269
fried, see FRIED SHRIMPS, 272
moules marinière, 270
steaming, 269

Mustard, 101
Bahamian, 101
cream sauce, 134
Dutch, 101
English, 101
French (Dijon), 101
German, 101
horseradish, 101
mayonnaise dijonnaise, 133
mild yellow, 101
sauce, 125

Nasturtium, 96
blossoms fried in batter, 96
butter, 96
flavoring for fresh green-bean salad, 96
seeds, pickled, 96

Normandy tarragon liqueur, 92

Norwegian cheese, 456

Nourishment value of foods, 13-16

Nuns' chicken pie, 538

Nut(s), 460-462; see also names of nuts
blanching, 462
bread, buttered, 526
necessary supplies, 66
praline, 509
shelling, 462
storing, 462
to freeze, 166

Nutmeg, 106

Nutrition
fitting requirements into budget, 32
weekly food plans, 33-35

Oatmeal fruit cookies, 498

Oeufs mollets, 381

Oeufs sur le plat, see SHIRRED EGGS, 382

Oldfashioned poundcake ring, 541

Omelet, 384-396; for recipe names, see EGG(S)

Omelet dessert; see DESSERT OMELETS

Onion(s), 312-313
Bermuda, 312
green, or scallions, 312
red, 312
rings, French fried, 301
sauce soubise, 124
Spanish, 312
and their relatives, 312-314
to freeze, 158
velouté d'oignon, 491
white, 312
yellow, 312

Ontario mild Cheddar soup, 494

Orange(s)
citrus dressing for stuffed roast pork, 212
and lemon snow aspic, 358
maltaise sauce, 131
rinds (to freeze), 166

Oriental chicken salad, 350

Oriental marinade, 114

Our Nanny's "Honest Irish stew", 229

Oven temperatures, chart, 68

Oysters, 267-268
fried, 267
hot on the half shell, 267
Louisiana little loaves, 268
raw as appetizers, 267
to freeze, 165
    storage, 165

Oyster plant (salsify), 308

Oxford sausages, 517

Oxtail soup, Calgary, 492

Panbroiling
meats, 218-219
salt broiling, 219
with a Swedish iron skillet, 219

Pancake(s); see also CRÊPES
buttermilk, old-fashioned, 488
to freeze, 165
turner, 61

Pan-cooking vegetables, 299

Panfrying, fish, 256
meat, 223-224

Pantry, 65-67
how long to keep foods, charts, 67
to stock, 65-66

Paprika, 107
in broiling meat, 215
Hungarian, 107
in sautéing fish, 256
Spanish, 107
in stewing, 225

Parmesan broiled tomatoes, 344

Parsley, 86
sauce, see FINNAN FARMHOUSE SCRAMBLE, 264
to freeze, 158

Parsnip(s), 308
French fried, 301
steam-baked, 300
to prevent discoloration, 308

Parties, 483-543; see also MENU(S)
afternoon tea, 496-501
buffet supper, 511-516
    setting the buffet table, 486-487; illus, 487
decorating the table for engagement party, 525
dinner parties, 501-510
formal dinner, 484-485
household requirements, checklist, 483
informal dinner, 485
joyous picnic time, 516-523
outdoor parties, 515
place settings, illus, 485
planning, 483-484
plum pudding, coffee and brandy party, 532-535
special occasions, 523-543
supper, 511-515
table-setting checklist, 484

Pasta
salt with, 79
Verona spaghetti sauce, 136

Pastry, 417-431
adding liquid to flour, 418
all-purpose shortening pastry, 421
baking-powder pastry, 425
basic pastries, 421-431
bits and pieces of dough, 436
brush, 62
chocolate piecrust, 426
cornflake crust, 424
cream-cheese pastry, Viennese, 426
electric-mixer pastry, 45-second, 422
fat for, 417
fitting piecrust into pie plate, 419
flan crust, 428
flan pastry, 427
    for baked pastry rounds, 427
    for baked pastry shells, for tarts, 427
flour for, 417
fluting piecrust, 420
graham-cracker crust, 425
ingredients, 417-418
how to prevent soggy bottom, 419
lard pastry, 425
lattice top for pies and tarts, 421
lemon-juice pastry, 426
liquids for, 418
make-your-own mix, 431
mixing piecrust, 418
no-roll pastry, 424
puff pastry, 428-430
    patty shells, 429
    uses, 429
    vol-au-vent, 430
rolling and filling dough for pies and tarts, 422
rolling piecrust, 419
rolling pin, 62
single crust, to prevent puffiness and bumpiness, 420

top crust, professional finish, 421
to prevent crust shrinking, 420
to prevent hard crust, 420
vegetable-oil pastry, 423

Pastry dishes
cinnamon rolls, 437
beef tenderloin Wellington, 203
cheese straws, economy, 436-437
deviled appetizers, 436
lobster puffs, baby, 497

Pâte feuilletée, see PUFF PASTRY, 428-430

Pâté, chicken-liver, 499

Peach(es)
best temperature for serving, 76
in frozen pies, to prevent darkening, 168
happy (to freeze), 153
pêches dijonnaise, 509
purée (to freeze), 154
to freeze, 152

Peanut(s), 461
husband's preference (sandwich filling), 167
peanut butter favorite (sandwich filling), 167

Peas, dried
brose, 325
pease pudding, 325
split, 325

Peas, fresh, 323
green, crown of turnip with, 539
à l'étuvée, 503
snow or sugar peas, 323

Pecan(s), 461

Pêches dijonnaise, 509

Pepper(s), Capsicum, 107, 340
cayenne peppers, 107
chili peppers, 107
green pepper(s), 340
appetizer, 342
pipérade, 392
rings, French fried, 301
stuffed, 342
to freeze, 159
paprika, 107
pimientos, 107, 340
Tabasco peppers, 107

Pepper, Piper nigrum, 106
black, 106
peppercorns, 106
places of origin, 106
white, 106

Perry cup, 519

Persian kebab, 287

Philadelphia vanilla ice cream, 440

Phosphorus, 16

Pickles
damson plums, pickled, 518
mushrooms, pickled, 348
nasturtium seeds, pickled, 96

Picnic
elegant Victorian, 516-520
hors d'oeuvre, 516
in the car, 521-523
romantic, for two, 520-521
time, joyous, 515-523

Piecrust, see Pastry

Pies and tarts, dessert, 432-436
apple pie, country, 433
Scandinavian, 432
upside-down, Balcom, 432
chiffon pies, to freeze, 168
citrus chiffon pie, 436
fresh-fruit pie, glazed, 434
frozen pies, 168
fruit pie, fillings, frozen, 155
crumb topping for, 168
lemon meringue pie, 434
lemon pie filling, to prevent runniness, 420
lemon pie, luscious, 435
maple-syrup pie, 542
meringue pie, 414
shell, 414
pans, 55, 57
pie meringue, American, 412
pies, baked (to freeze), 168
unbaked, (to freeze), 168
pumpkin pie, creamy, 541
strawberry pie, glazed, 434
tarte au sirop d'érable, 542
tarte mousse à la citrouille, 541
to prevent juices running, 420

Pies and Tarts, entrée and hors d'oeuvre
beef and kidney pie, 518
chicken pie, 538
frozen pies, 168
leek pie, 314
pork pies, 495, 537
tourtières, 495, 537

Pignolas, 461

Pilaf, barley, 326
with chicken, 326

Pimientos, 107, 340
mayonnaise niçoise, 133

Pineapple, to use in gelatine mixtures, see SWEET ASPIC FOR DESSERT, 358

Pine nuts, 461

Pipérade basque and family, 392

Piquante sauce, 128

Pistachios, 461

Plums
damson, pickled, 518
prune plums, stewed or raw (to freeze), 153

Poaching
fish, 257
liquids for, 226
meats, 226-227
vegetables for, 226

Pommes de terre grêlées, 159

Poppy seed(s), 101-102
dressing for fruit salads, 139
uses for, 102

Pork, cured; see also BACON; HAM; SAUSAGE
cook-before-eating, 189
cuts, 188-189
for roasting, 199
shoulder, to buy, 188-189

Pork, fresh
chops, barbecued, 288
citrus dressing for, 212
cuts
for barbecuing, 281
for broiling, 215
for roasting, 198
gravy, see ROAST LOIN OF PORK GOURMET, 211
hearts, basic preparation and cooking, 233
in jelly, 537
kidneys, basic preparation and cooking, 233
leg of, roast, 211
liver, basic preparation and cooking, 233
loin of, roast, gourmet, 211
pies, 495, 537
Québec tourtières, small, 495
roast, rolled, crisp-crusted (barbecued), 287
spareribs, barbecued, 288
tenderloin, roast stuffed, 212
tongue, basic preparation and cooking, 234
tourtières, 495, 537

Port, 472-473
glasses, 475; illus. 475

Potato(es), 302-305; see also SWEET POTATOES
baked (with dry heat), 300
baked (to freeze), 159
boiled, 302
to keep warm, 302
cakes, fisherman's, 304
with celeriac, 311
Duchess, 303
French fried, 301
to freeze, 159
Irish colcannon, 307
mashed, my favorite, 304
mashed-potato puffs, fried, 303
masher, 61
new, in chive butter, 520
new and old, how to cook, 302
omelets, 387
cooked potato, 388
moissonneur, 387
pan-browned, 202
scalloped, 302
steam-baked, 300
stuffing, 536
to cook, 297, 302
to prepare, 302

Pot-roasting meats, 219-221

Pots and Pans
aluminium, 54
cast iron, 54-55
to season a new pan, 55
copper, 55
earthenware, 55
enamelware, 54
porcelain enamelware, 54
Pyrex, 55
Pyroceram, 55
stainless steel, 54
Teflon, 55

Poulette sauce, 126

Poultry, 239-248, see also names of poultry
acid with, 77
barbecueing, 281
cooked (to freeze), 163
dressed, 240
frozen, to thaw, 163
how to buy, 40-41
how to freeze, 163
months when in greatest supply, 41
salt with, 79
to cut up, 240-241
to stuff, 240
types, 40
uncooked (to freeze), 163

Poundcake, see Cake

Praline, 509

Prawns, 271

Preserves, spiced prunes, 534

Protein, 13
foods, amount to serve daily, 18
sources, 13-14

Prune plums, see PLUMS

Prunes, spiced, 534

Pudding, dessert
burnt-sugar rice, 531
plum, English, 533
decorating, 534
flaming, 535

Pudding, entrée
finnan savory, 264
pease, 325
Yorkshire, 200

Puff pastry, 428-430

Pumpkin
baked, 300
French fried, 301
frozen, to cook, 160
pie, creamy, 541
soup, Brittany, 493

Quadrillage (in broiling), 215, 219

Quahogs, 269

Québec cream of cabbage soup, 492

INDEX

Québec roasted turkey with potato stuffing, 536

Québec tourtières, small, 495

R

Radishes, 312

Raita, 310

Raspberry
ice cream, 443
pie, see GLAZED STRAWBERRY PIE, 434

Ratatouille niçoise, 341

Refrigerator; see also FREEZER
efficient use, 64-65
to buy, 63-64
types, 64

Rhubarb
sherbet, 449
to freeze, 153

Riboflavin, see VITAMIN B2, 15

Rice, 326-329
baked, 327
brown, 326
  pungent, 505
  slow-cooking, 327
buttered, Italian, 328
converted, 326
  slow-cooking, 327
double-broiler, 329
freezing, 329
fried, Chinese, 328
long-grain, baked, 514
pudding, burnt-sugar, 531
ring, savory, 329
saffron, curried eggs with, 97
salad dressing for, 137
salt with, 79
steamed, 327
to reheat, 327
white, 326
  slow-cooking, flaky, 327

Roasting, meats, 192-193
pan, 57

Robert sauce, 128

Rock lobster (spiny lobster or crawfish), 273-274
tails, 273

Roquefort dressing, 138

Rose-geranium poundcake, 519

Rosemary, 98

Roux, 121-122

Rum, 473, 479

Rumaki, 350

Russian mayonnaise, 132

Rutabaga, 308; see also TURNIP(S)

S

Saffron, 97
rice, curried eggs with, 97

Sage, 88
cheese spread, 88
honey spread, 88
hot bread, 494
tea, 88

Salad
beef, cold, 204
beet, 310
  new, 311
calf's-brain, 236
celeriac, 311
chicken, Oriental, 350
chicken-salad puffs, 527
chopped, 522
cucumber, Finnish, 339
  and tomato, 345
  and yogurt, 340
fruit, honey dressing for, 138
  poppy-seed dressing for, 139
green-bean, 514
  nasturtium flavouring, 96
green-pepper appetizer, 342
greens, 329-331
marigold in a salad, 96
marinated mushrooms, 346
salade de cresson, 509
salmon, Vancouver, 494
  and vegetable, 262
salt with, 79
shredding vegetables for, 73-74
snap-bean, 322
spinach and cucumber, 331
tomato with marjoram, 91

Salad dressing, 136-139
American, 138
Danish, 137
English, 138
French, 136
  American-style, 137
  chiffonade, 137
  herb, 514
honey, for fruit salads, 138
marinated mushrooms, 346
mayonnaise, 131-133
poppy-seed, for fruit salads, 139
Roquefort, 138
thyme and lemon, 87
vinaigrette, 136

Sally Lunn, honeyed, 498

Salmon
B.C. special (sandwich filling), 167
baked stuffed, 258
Canadian, 258
Indian barbecued, 291
marinated, 262
molded, 261
poached, 260
  à la française, 260
  my best, 259
salad, Vancouver, 494
smoked salmon celery, 335
superb, cold, 521
and vegetable salad, 262

Salsify (oyster plant), 308

Salt, 78-79
with fats, 79
with fish, 79
for freezing ice cream, 437
with meats, 79
in meringue, 406
with pasta, 79
with poultry, 79
with rice, 79
with salads, 79
with sugar, 78
"to taste" 78
types of, 78
use of, general rules for, 79
with vegetables, 79, 296

Salt (pan) broiling, 219

Sandwich(es)
B.C. special, 167
Calgary's own, 492
cream-cheese filling, 528
croque-monsieur, 491
egg filling, 528
emergency fillings (to freeze), 167
ham filling, 528
husband's preference, 167
in a circle, 528
liver and bacon, 491
mushroom rools, 496
old French favorite, 493
peanut butter favorite, 167
sardine, 167, 493
shooters' loaf, 517

Sardine
Brittany (sandwich filling), 167
treat (sandwich), 493

Sauces, dessert, 139-140
caramel, 534
custard, 139
with dessert omelets, 396
with dessert soufflés, 405
Dijon syrup, 510
fruit, frozen, 154
ginger, 105
hard, 534
mocha chocolate, 140
molasses lemon, 489
strawberry, 515
to replace chocolate in, 140
vanilla brandy, 139
whipped cream in, 140

Sauce, entrée and hors d'oeuvre, 121-139; see also BUTTERS; BASTING SAUCES; GRAVY
acids with, 77
amount to prepare, 121
artichoke dressing, 333
Aurore, 124
for basting barbecued foods, see BASTING SAUCES; MARINADES
béarnaise, 130
béchamel, 123-124
  variations, 124-125
Bercy, 126
beurre manié, 122
bread, English, 133
bread crumbs as thickener, 123
bretonne, 126
brown, 127
  large quantities for freezing or refrigerator storage, 127
  variations, 127-128
butter as thickener, 122
buttering, 123
caper, 125
chaud-froid, 353
cheese as thickener, 123
Choron, 131
for corn on the cob, 524
cream, for finishing, 123
  as thickener, 122
curry, 125
diable, 128
dill, 125
  for lamb, 89
diplomate, 126
dipping, for steamed clams, 269
egg, 125
  Scandinavian, 134
  yolks as thickener, 122
emulsified, 128-133
  cold, 131-133
  hot, 128-131
  reheating, 129
  separated, to correct, 129
with entrée omelets, 396
with entrée soufflés, 405
espagnole, 127
fines herbes, 125
finishing with butter, 123
finishing with cream, 123
flour with cold liquid as thickener, 122
fresh tomato, 135
green mayonnaise, 132
hollandaise, 128-129
  blender, 130
  Bordeaux, 130
  chef's, 129
  hot-water, 130
  special chef's secrets, 131
  variations, 130-131
horseradish mayonnaise, 132
how to thicken, 121-123
lemon butter, 284
Madère or Madeira, 127
maltaise, 131
mayonnaise, 131-133
mint, 86, 134
Mornay, 124
mousseline, 130
  light, 131
muscovite, 131
mushroom, 125
mustard, 125,
mustard cream, 134
parsley, see FINNAN FARMHOUSE SCRAMBLE, 264
piquante, 128
poulette, 126
purées as thickener, 123
reducing, 121
Robert, 128
roux, 121-122
soubise, 124
sour-cream cucumber, 259
(for) spaghetti, Verona, 136
spring, for lobster, 276
starch as thickener, 122
suprême, 125
tapenade de Nice, 50'

tartar, 132
thickening, 121-123
   uses for, 121
velouté, 125-126
   Chantilly, 126
   variations, 126
verte, 261
vinaigrette, 136
white (for croquette mixture), 364
white-wine, 125

Sausage
Bercy omelet, 387
eggs landaise in electric frypan, 489
-meat stuffing, 243
Oxford, 517

Sautéing, fish, 256
meats, 223-224

Sauteuse, 56

Sautoir, 223

Savory, 90

Scales, 62, 195

Scallions or green onions, 312

Scallops, 270
bay, 270
coral, 270
sautéed, 270
to freeze, 165
storage, 165

Scampi, 271

Scandinavian apple pie, 432

Scandinavian broiled chicken, 245

Scandinavian egg sauce, 134

Scandinavian flan crust, 428

Scandinavian wax beans, 321

Scissors, 61, 73

Scotch brose, 325

Scotch pease pudding, 325

Scottish molded salmon, 261

Scottish sole paupiettes, 508-509

Scraper, 61

Seafood; see also FISH; names of fish; SHELLFISH; names of shellfish
acid with, 77
ramekins, 273
sakana, 292
soufflé, 402

Seasonal guide for fresh fruits and vegetables, 48-49

Seasonal treasures (vegetables), 336-350

Seasoning, 81-82
foods to be frozen, 147
my favorite, 82
necessary supplies, 66

Sesame, 107-108
oil, 107-108
-seed marinade for teriyaki, 218
seeds, toasted, 108

Shallots, 313

Shandygaff, 524

Shears, 61, 73

Shellfish, 267-276; see also names of shellfish
frozen, thawing and cooking, 165
how much to buy, 41
servings per pound, 41
to freeze, 165
storage, 165

Sherbet, 446-449; see also FROZEN DESSERTS

Sherry, 472
glasses, 475; illus, 475
marinade for teriyaki, 218

Shooters' loaf, 517

Shopping
buying guide, 43-47
record keeping, 38
shopping list, 37
suggestions to help you, 36-38
where to shop, 36

Shortening for pie pastry, 417

Shower for baby, 528-530

Shredding, 73-74

Shrimp(s), 271-272
barbecued, see SEAFOOD SAKANA, 292
curry, 513
fried, 272
frozen, in shells, 271
   without shells, 271
langoustines, 271
prawns, 271
scampi, 271
to cook, 271
to freeze, 165
   storage, 165
to shell, 513

Simmering meats, 226-231

Skewered dishes
calf's-liver brochettes, 286
Persian kebab, 287
rumaki, 350
wieners (barbecued), 286

Slicing, 73

Sliver, 74

Snack, after-football, 523-524

Snap beans, see BEANS

Snow, 353
orange and lemon snow aspic, 358

Snow peas, see PEAS, FRESH

Soubise, sauce, 124

Soufflé, dessert, 403-405; see also basic information under SOUFFLÉ, ENTRÉE AND HORS D'OEUVRE
brandy or liquor in, 405
chocolate, 404
coffee, 403
liqueur, 404
maple syrup, 405
sauces with, 405

Soufflé, entrée and hors d'oeuvre, 397-403
baking, 399
base, 397
cheese, 400
   to freeze ingredients, 160
chicken, 401
chicken liver, 402
dish, 398
   how to make a collar on, 398
eggs in, 397-398
errors in making, 399
folding (egg whites), 398
freezing, 399
fresh mushroom, 401
how to make a hat on, 398
sauces with, 405
seafood, 402
serving, 399
turkey, see CHICKEN SOUFFLÉ, 401

Soup; see also STEW
cabbage, cream of, 492
celery clam chowder, 522
cheese, 494
chicken, see POACHED CHICKEN, MY WAY, 246
consommé, 347, 504
creamy lobster stew, 275
English Midland, 490
lentil, 324
mild Cheddar, 494
mushroom consommé, 347
mushroom, cream of, see MUSHROOM CONSOMMÉ, 347
onion, 491
oxtail, 492
pumpkin, 493
tomato, 343
   chilled, 343
vegetable, broth, 117
   herb-flavored, 90
velouté d'oignon, French, 491
vichyssoise, 158
wine consommé, Carco, 504

Sour cream
cucumber sauce, 259
omelet, 395
to make, 78

Soy-ginger marinade, 292

Spanish cucumbers, 339

Spanish omelet (tortilla), 391

Spareribs, barbecued, 288

Spatula, 61, 63, 72

Spearmint, 96
applesauce with, 96

Special occasions, 523-543
after-football snack, 523-524
Corn-husking bee (épluchette de blé d'Inde), 524
dessert and coffee for an afternoon committee meeting, 530-531
grand-maman's Christmas dinner, 535-543
plum pudding, coffee and brandy party, 532-534
shower for baby, 528-530
teatime engagement party, 525-527

Spencer, Evelene, 253

Spencer Method for baking fish, 253

Spices, 102 and ff; see also names of spices
amount to use, 85
grinding, 102-103
necessary supplies, 66

Spinach, 330-331
creamed, 331
and cucumber salad, 331
frozen, to cook, 160
in mushrooms Verona, 348
in new-beet salad, 311
to use in a soufflé, 331

Spiny lobster, see Rock lobster

Spirits, 473-474
aquavit, 474
brandy, 473, 478
   glasses, 475; illus, 475
cordials, 474
   glasses, 475; illus, 475
gin, 473, 478
glossary, 478-479
liqueurs, 474
   glasses, 475; illus, 475
measures, chart, 476
rum, 473, 479
vodka, 474, 479
whiskey, whisky, 473, 479

Spoons, 60-61

Squab, 239, 247

Squash, baking, 300
French fried, 301

Stalks, crunchy, 333-335

Steak, see BEEF

Steam-baking vegetables, 300

Steaming, fish, 257
vegetables, 298-299

Stew; see also SOUP
Belgian beef carbonade, 228
boeuf bourguignon, 502
fricassee of chicken, 248
fricassee of veal, 232
Irish, 229
lobster, creamy, 275

Stewing, meats, 225
timetable, 227
vegetables for, 225

INDEX 559

Stir-frying vegetables, 299-300

Stock, 116-118
chicken, see FRICASSEE OF CHICKEN, 248
clarifying, for aspics, 118
fish, 117
fumet, 125
meat bone, my own, 116
mushroom consommé, 347
uses for, 116
veal, 232
vegetable broth, 117

Strainer, 62

Strawberry
brandied almond-strawberry jam, 498
fresh-fruit pie, glazed, 434
ice cream, fresh berries, 445
  frozen berries, 440
meringue, Swiss, 412
milk sherbet, 449
sauce, 515
trifle, jiffy, 530

Stuffing
bread and lemon (poultry), 243
chestnut, see SAUSAGE-MEAT STUFFING, 243
citrus dressing (roast pork), 212
potato (turkey), 536
sausage-meat (poultry), 243

Succotash, 322

Sucre rose, 541

Sugar, 79-80
boiling temperatures for, chart, 68
brown (Demerara), 79-80
fruit sugar, 79
ginger sugar, 105
granulated, 79
honey, 80
in ice cream, 439
icing (confectioners') 80
in meringue, 406
molasses (treacle), 80
necessary supplies, 65
red, 541
with salt, 78
types of, 79-80
vanilla sugar, 109
with vegetables, 296
very fine granulated (fruit sugar), 79

Sugar peas, see PEAS, FRESH

Supper, 511-515
casserole buffet, 511-515

Suprême, sauce, 125

Swedish cheese, 456

Swedish mayonnaise, 132

Swedish salmon and vegetable salad, 262

Sweetbreads
basic preparation and cooking, 234
storage, 190
to freeze, 161

Sweet potatoes, 304-305; see also POTATO(ES)
baked, 304
California, 304
whipped, 305

Swiss broyage, 410

Swiss chicken casserole, 512

Swiss strawberry meringue, 412

Switzerland cheese, 457

Syrup(s)
from canned or stewed fruits (to freeze), 167
Dijon, 510
for freezing fruits, 150

T

Tabasco peppers, 107

Tapenade de Nice, 507

Tarragon, 91
butter, 91
liqueur, Normandy, 92
vinegar, 91

Tartar sauce, 132

Tarte au sirop d'érable, 542

Tasting and taste buds, 81

Tea
Arabian, 496
herb (aniseed tisane), 98
lemon-balm, iced, 94
lemon-verbena, 94
sage, 88
tea kettle, teapot, 56
to freeze, 167

Tea parties
afternoon, 496-501
party tea, 496-498
teatime engagement party, 525-527
for VIPs, 499-501

Temperatures for sugar boiling, 68

Tempura batter (deep-frying), 363

Teriyaki, Hawaiian, 217

Texan style barbecue sauce, 207

Thermometer
candy, or frying, 62
for frozen meats, 163
meat, 62, 194
microwave, 62

Thiamine, see VITAMIN B1, 15

Thistles, edible, 332-333

Thyme, 87-88
and lemon dressing, 87

Toast, French, my mother's, 489

Toffee ice cream, 445

Tokyo beef roulade, 522

Tomato(es), 341-345
baked, 344
  with mushrooms and basil, 89
broiled, 344
and cucumber salad, 345
fresh tomato sauce, 135
fried (with) bacon and eggs, 487
with honey and chives, 80
omelet, 386
Parmesan broiled, 344
salad dressing for, 137
salad with marjoram, 91
slices, basil broiled, see PARMESAN BROILED TOMATOES, 344
soup, Aunt Amélia's, 343
to peel, 341-342
to prepare, 341-342
to remove acidity, 342
unripe, to ripen, 43
vegetable aspic, 356

Tongue, basic preparation and cooking, 234

Tourtières, 495, 537

Tortilla, Spanish omelet, 391

Treacle, see MOLASSES, 80

Triffle, jiffy strawberry, 530

Tripe, basic preparation and cooking, 234
to freeze, 161

Trout, fresh barbecued, 291-292
oven poached, with clam dressing, 266

Tuna fish, (in broccoli), divan à la moderne, 319

Turkey, 247
gravy, 537
roasted, with potato stuffing, 536
roasting, timetable, 247
soufflé, see CHICKEN SOUFFLÉ, 401

Turmeric, 108

Turnip(s), 308-309
crown of, with peas, 539
gratiné, 309
greens, 329
mashed, 309
rutabaga, 308

V

Vancouver salmon salad, 494

Vanilla, 109
bean, as a seasoning, 82
brandy sauce, 139
extract, 109
ice cream, 439-442
split bean, uses, 109
sugar, 109
whole bean, uses, 109

Variety meats (internal meats); see also names of specific kinds
basic preparation and cooking, 233-234
storage, 190
to freeze, 161

Veal
calf's brains, basic preparation and cooking, 234
  salad, 236
  to freeze, 161
calf's liver, 233
  brochettes, 286
cushion shoulder of, roasted stuffed, 210
cuts, see CHART OF BEEF CUTS, 189
  for broiling, 215
  for roasting, 199
fricassee of, 232
hearts, basic preparation and cooking, 233
kidneys, basic preparation and cooking, 233
leg of, Italiano, 210
  rolled, anglaise, 209
loin of, roast, 208
rib of, roast, 209
roasting timetable, 197-198
rognonnade, 208
shoulder, braised, 222
stock, 232
sweetbreads, basic preparation and cooking, 234
  to freeze, 161
tongue, basic preparation and cooking, 234

Vegetables, 295-350; see also names of vegetables
acid with, 77
amount to serve, 17, 19
baking with dry heat, 300
basic cooking methods, 298-301
bias or diagonal cutting, 74
blanching and refreshing, professional method, 298
for braised roasts, 220
broiled with meats, 215
broth, 117
buying, 295
cabbage family, 315-319
calorie chart, 21
chiffonade, 73
Chinese stir-frying, 299-300
crunchy stalks, 333-335
cutting in various ways, 73-74
dicing, 74
edible thistles, 332-333
French frying or deep-frying, 300-301
fresh, how to buy, 42-43
  seasonal guide for, chart, 48-49
frozen, cooking, 159-160
  packages per year, chart, 146
golden rule for cooking, 295
green, 297

greens, 329-331
herbs with, 296
how to freeze, 157-160
how to hold when cutting, 73
jardinière de légumes, 509
julienne, 73
kinds, 296-297
leafy, green and yellow, 17, 19
legumes, dried, 323-326
    fresh, 320-323
marinade for, 115
mincing, 74
onions and their relatives, 312-314
pan-cooking, 299
peeler, 61
perishables, 297
for poaching with meats, 226
preserving nutritive value and flavor, 295-296
ratatouille niçoise, 341
rich in vitamin A and C, 17
root, 296, 302-312
salad, chopped, 522
salad dressing for, 137
and salmon salad, Swedish, 262
salt with, 79, 296
seasonal treasures, 336-345
semi-perishables, 297
shredding, 73-74
slicing, 73
slivering, 74
soup, herb-flavored, 90
staples, 297
steam-baking, 300
steaming, 298-299
for stewing with meats, 225
sugar with, 296
testing for ripeness, 43
to curl, 74
to determine freshness, 295
tomato vegetable aspic, 356
unripe, 43

Velouté sauce, 125-126
Chantilly, 126
variations, 126

Verona spaghetti sauce, 136

Verte, sauce, 261

Vichyssoise, 158

Victorian picnic, elegant, 516-520

Viennese cream-cheese pastry, 426

Vinegar, necessary supplies, 66
tarragon, 91

Vin rouge chaud aux épices, 543

Vin du pays, 469

Vins ordinaires, 469

Vitamins, 14-15
A, best sources, 14-15, 17, 21
B1, best sources, 15
B2, best sources, 15
C, best sources, 15, 17, 19, 21, 43
D, best sources, 15
Other vitamins, 15

Vodka, 474, 479

Vol-au-vent, 430

Walnut(s), 461
and almonds, deviled, 499
-cinnamon topping, 497
maple walnut ice cream, 442
omelet, 389
to toast, 524

Water chestnuts, 350
chicken salad Oriental, 350
rumaki, 350

Watercress
mayonnaise cressonière, 132-133
salade de cresson, 509

Wax beans, see BEANS

Welsh leek pie, 314

Whiskey, Whisky, 473, 479

Whisking, 72

White sauce (for croquette mixture), 364

White-wine, cup, 520
fizz, 521
sauce, 125

Wieners (barbecued), 286

Wife-helpers for lazy breakfasts, 488

Wine, 465-477
after-dinner wines, when to serve, 467
apéritif wines, 473, 477
appellation contrôlée, 466
Bordeaux, red, 468
    white, 470
Burgundy, red, 468
    sparkling, 472
    white, 469
Canadian red wines, 469
Champagne, 471-472
    Blanc de Blancs, 472
    glasses, 475; illus, 475
    terminology for sweetness, 472
    when to serve, 467
and cherry aspic, 358
consommé, Carco, 504
cooking with, 476-477
demi-sec, 465
dessert wines, when to serve, 467
doux, 465
fortified wines, 472-473
German white wines, 470
with herbs in cooking, 476
Italian wines, red, 468-469
    white, 470
Loire Valley wines, 470
Madeira, 473
    glasses, 475; illus, 475
marinade for meat, 114
measures, chart,
port, 472-473
    glasses, 475; illus, 475
red, 468-469
    spiced hot, 543
    when to serve, 467
rosé, 471
    when to serve, 467
rules for serving, 475-476
sec, 465
Sekt, 472
sherry, 472-473
    glasses, 475; illus, 475
sparkling, 471-472
Spumante, 472
still table wines, 468-471
storage, 467
Swiss white wines, 471
temperatures for serving, 474
to serve with food, 467
vins du pays, 469
vins ordinaires, 469
vintage, 466
where wine is produced, 465
white, 469-471
    when to serve, 467
white-wine, cup, 520
    fizz, 521
    sauce, 125
wineglasses, 474-475; illus, 475

Wire whisk, 61
for beating meringues, 72, 406
for incorporating, 72
for omelets, 385
for sauces, 129
for soufflés, 397, 398

Yogurt
and beet relish (raita), 310
and cucumber salad, 340
green-pepper appetizer, 342

Yorkshire pudding, 200